THE
Book
Ninja

THE
Book
Ninja

ALI BERG &
MICHELLE KALUS

SIMON &
SCHUSTER

London · New York · Sydney · Toronto · New Delhi

A CBS COMPANY

First published in Australia by Simon & Schuster Australia Pty Limited, 2018
First published in Great Britain by Simon & Schuster UK Ltd, 2018
A CBS COMPANY

1 3 5 7 9 10 8 6 4 2

Simon & Schuster UK Ltd
1st Floor
222 Gray's Inn Road
London WC1X 8HB

Simon & Schuster Australia, Sydney
Simon & Schuster India, New Delhi

www.simonandschuster.co.uk
www.simonandschuster.com.au
www.simonandschuster.co.in

A CIP catalogue record for this book is available from the British Library

Paperback ISBN: 978-1-4711-7716-3
eBook ISBN: 978-1-4711-7715-6

This book is a work of fiction. Names, characters, places and incidents are either a
product of the authors' imagination or are used fictitiously. Any resemblance to actual
people living or dead, events or locales is entirely coincidental.

Printed and bound by CPI Group (UK) Ltd, Croydon, CR0 4YY

Simon & Schuster UK Ltd are committed to sourcing paper that is made from wood
grown in sustainable forests and support the Forest Stewardship Council, the leading
international forest certification organisation. Our books displaying the FSC logo are
printed on FSC certified paper.

To our Book Ninjas.
For dropping books on public transport –
rain, hail or peak rush hour

PART ONE

*'The person, be it gentleman or lady, who has not pleasure
in a good novel, must be intolerably stupid.'*

Northanger Abbey, Jane Austen

If Frankie's life were a book, she would title it *Disappointment*, named aptly after the disaster that was her career, her family and, of course, her love life.

Frankie's alarm blared accusingly, declaring that she was already twenty minutes late to get out of bed. She sighed, rolled over, and buried her face in her shabby copy of *Emma*, which she had shoved under her pillow the night before. Then she bit her lip, thinking she would never be remarkable enough to have a book named simply after her first name.

But Frankie never judged a book by its title. Nor by its cover. She liked to judge a novel purely by its opening sentence, which she and her best friend Cat dubbed a 'book birth'. In *Emma*'s birth, Austen described Miss Woodhouse as 'handsome, clever, and rich, with a comfortable home and happy disposition'. By contrast, the opening sentence of Frankie's birth was her mother proclaiming, 'She's bald and has her father's big nose.'

Frankie pulled her blanket over her head and drank up the words on the page in front of her. She knew she was approaching the proposal scene, and closed her eyes tight. Just like a good chocolate bar, she wasn't sure whether she should indulge in its goodness right now, or savour it later. And just like that, the jarring ring of her phone solved the dilemma for her. Frankie picked it up and saw her mother's name flashing on the screen. She rolled her eyes, clicked 'ignore' and slowly dragged herself out of bed.

Searching for an outfit that was easy to put together, she picked up a loose cotton dress from her floor and flung it on. Scooting through her bedroom door, she walked towards her pride and joy – her precisely colour-coded bookshelf. Filled with 172 of her all-time favourites, the bookshelf lined a full wall of her living room. Beginning with reds on top, the wall shaded into oranges, yellows, pinks, purples, greens, blues, greys and, finally, blacks. A rainbow of books. Her happy place. She dragged her fingers absently across the cloth-bound Austens, along the hardcover Fowlers, over the Brontës and then stopped haltingly at the muted green book with 'Frankie Rose' embossed on the spine. She picked it up cautiously, as if it were a snake about to bite, and peeled open the first page.

To Mum, Dad, Cat, Ads and, most importantly, pizza.
For all the love, support and cheesy goodness.

Frankie slammed the book shut and threw it to the other side of the room. She grabbed her handbag, which lay beside the couch, slipped on a pair of red sneakers and ran out the door of her too-small Richmond apartment.

After digging for the keys in the bottom of her bag, Frankie let herself into The Little Brunswick Street Bookshop; her home away from home for the last year and a half, right about the time her dreams shattered and her life fell apart. Working at the bookstore had saved her, in so many ways. It reminded her of the three months she had spent working at the famous Parisian bookstore, Shakespeare and Company, before she returned to start her Masters of English Lit at the University of Melbourne.

Free of responsibility, Frankie had relished this time spent lost between bookshelves, writing, and eating almond croissants. That same carefree feeling washed over her every time she entered The Little Brunswick Street Bookshop. She loved watching people from the inside out, like a backwards kaleidoscope of literature lovers gazing into their beautiful front windows from vibrant Brunswick Street. She loved being surrounded by powerful women such as Angelou, Atwood and Adichie. And most of all, she loved working with Cat. Cat's husband Claud had inherited The Little Brunswick Street Bookshop from his grandparents, and when he – an accountant at a small city law firm who maintained long hours and an intense knitting hobby – was unsure how he would juggle a second job, Cat had the genius idea of selling the books in the front, while he, occasionally, managed the books from the back. And when Cat offered Frankie a job, it didn't take long for her to say yes, yes, *yes*!

Since the days spent penning love letters to Mr Darcy instead of practising algebra in Year 8 maths, their bond had endured even though Cat, pregnant with her first child, now spent Saturday nights watching reruns of *The National Knitting Evening* on Netflix with Claud, and Frankie, pregnant with last night's pizza, spent hers on awful first dates. And now, with their days spent surrounded by, discussing and reading books (and of course appraising everyone else based on their book choices), Cat and Frankie were closer than Horatio and Hamlet.

Frankie wound her way through the shelves and unceremoniously flung her bag beneath the front counter. She cranked on the air conditioning, sank into the seat behind the register, placed her feet up on the counter and returned to her worn copy of *Emma*. She had just turned the page when the front door chimed open and Cat marched into the store. Her red frizzy hair was everywhere, sweat dripped down her face and she wore a hot pink knitted top, black lycra pants and bright orange sneakers.

'Catherine,' Frankie nodded from behind her book.

'Frankston,' Cat nodded back. She joined Frankie behind the counter, grabbed her copy of *Jasper Jones* and propped her feet up next to Frankie's.

'What's with the sweat?' Frankie asked.

'I had another K-Pop dance class this morning – which was amazing, by the way – but their showers are broken and I couldn't be bothered walking home to change and then coming all the way back here, so I thought if I just stood outside for a while I would dry. But I forgot that it's going to be thirty-two freaking degrees today! Plus, these knits Claud keeps making me do nothing for sweat absorption. Look at me dripping, I'm like an ice cream!' Cat grabbed Frankie and tried to pull her head into her sweaty chest.

If Frankie was the queen of dating, Cat was the queen of exercise classes. From barre to one very confronting summer of pole dancing, Cat became obsessed and then unobsessed with every sort of exercise and health kick imaginable, before dropping it like Marius drops Eponine. It all started a few summers ago and, at first, Frankie thought the fixation on fitness was simply Cat wanting to be healthier and more toned, but lately she had wondered whether it tapped into a deeper insecurity. Cat used to relish watching heads turn at her overly attractive husband, but was she starting to feel overlooked?

'What are you up to?' Cat asked, glancing at Frankie's battered book.

'Almost at the proposal,' Frankie gushed.

'Aren't you sick of reading the same books over and over?'

'You're reading *Jasper Jones* for the fourth time,' Frankie countered.

Cat spread her arms as if to say *touché*.

'So, something pretty weird happened at K-Pop today.'

'Oh?' Frankie asked.

The front door opened, halting their conversation. Frankie and Cat shut their books, dropped their feet to the floor and looked up, alert. A stout, slightly balding man walked in.

'Sci-fi!' hissed Cat.

'War biography!' spat Frankie.

The man, red in the face, smiled at Frankie and Cat. They smiled back sweetly and asked if he needed any assistance. He shook his head and then proceeded to walk excruciatingly slowly around the bookstore, scratching his head, not touching anything. The women stared at him, examining his every step.

'Just make your move,' Cat whispered at him.

'He's about to pounce!' hissed Frankie.

After what seemed an age, the man stopped in the science fiction section and grabbed two Stephen King novels, placing one swiftly under each armpit.

'Damn it! Shirt but no tie. Dead giveaway,' Frankie said, disappointed.

'Pay up, Frankston.' Cat held her hand out in front of Frankie's nose, wiggling her fingers in anticipation. Frankie slowly dragged a five-dollar note out of her wallet and slammed it into Cat's hand.

'Just these two wonderful *sci-fi* books, then?' Cat said to her customer while smiling devilishly at Frankie.

'Yes, I love a good Stephen King,' said the man, dropping the books on the counter for Cat to scan. 'I was actually going to try my hand at that war biog, *The Crossroad*, by Mark someone-or-other. You know the one I mean? But then I thought, why stop at a good thing? And King – well, he's a very good thing!' he chuckled.

Frankie stared, and Cat held back a laugh as she slid the two Kings into a paper bag.

'Have a lovely day. I'm so glad you decided to go with King over a *war biography*. King really is such a *good* thing,' chirped Cat.

'He really is! Well, toodaloo!' the man trumpeted as he walked out the door, the bell ringing behind him.

'Go you good thing!' Cat shouted after him, pumping her fist triumphantly.

'He was going to buy a war biog! Give me my five dollars back!' Frankie grabbed at the note, but Cat pulled away.

'He was going to. But alas, he didn't! The fiver is all mine,' said Cat smugly.

Frankie sighed. 'You don't have to sound so pleased about it.'

'I don't know what you're talking about!' Cat said, smiling, and sounding even more delighted with herself.

Frankie frowned. Balancing their legs back on the counter, they reclined in their chairs. The growing heat of the day pressed its way under the gap beneath the front door, only to be stunted by the harsh air conditioning in the store. Beads of cool sweat trickled down Frankie's neck and into her cleavage.

'Sorry, I'm in a silly mood,' Cat said.

Silence. '"Silly things do cease to be silly if they are done by sensible people in an impudent way,"' Frankie quoted the Austen she was reading, to a tee.

Cat smiled as Frankie gave a little bow of her head.

'So, why the silly mood, Kitty Cat? What happened at K-Pop? Are you moving to Korea?' Frankie joked.

'Oh, it was nothing. I'll go get the coffees.' Cat jumped up just a little too quickly and grabbed her bag.

'Cat! Seriously? What happened at K-Pop?' It was unlike Cat to be so evasive. Frankie usually got the lowdown from her about everything, from what she had for breakfast to the romance between the two buskers who sat opposite the bookstore.

'Nothing. Nothing.' Cat's face bloomed even redder, and her eyes darted towards the door.

'Catherine Adeline Cooper. Tell. Me. Now.' Frankie squinted suspiciously at Cat.

Cat stared back just as intently, and for a minute – a record for them – they had an ice-cold stare-off.

'Oh, all right, *fine!*' Cat threw her arms in the air, defeated.

'Yes?'

'Well, at K-Pop … there's this really cute dancer. A guy. Called Jin Soo.'

'Jin Soo?'

'Yes, Jin Soo.'

'And?'

'And … Jin Soo.'

'What about Jin Soo?'

'Well, I sort of, accidentally, slept with him a few weeks back,' Cat covered her mouth with her hand and bolted for the door.

'WHAT! Cat? Cat, come back!' Frankie shouted, refusing to believe what she had just heard.

Cat, cheating on Claud? No; Frankie knew it was impossible. Cat would never cheat on him. Cat and Claud's marriage wasn't perfect, but whose was? Cat loved Claud. In his stupidly good-looking, knitting-obsessed entirety. *And* she was four months' pregnant with his child, for God's sake.

Frankie jumped up from her seat and raced after her sweaty, recently adulterous friend. As she pulled open the front door she stopped. Instead of Cat, before her stood a man. Possibly the best looking man she had ever laid eyes on. He was tall; he was burly. He was, to her mind, the perfect mix of John Knightley, Mr Darcy and Edmund Bertram all rolled into one.

—2—

Perched safely back behind the counter with her nose buried in her book, Frankie studied the beautiful man as he strolled through the store. Broad, yet unimposing in a casual white T-shirt and blue jeans, he moved with a quiet confidence, his shoulders rotating as he squeezed through the shelves. Reaching down to the bowl of M&Ms stashed next to the computer, Frankie popped one in her mouth with a smile. *Let the games begin!*

He approached the classics. *A promising start. Yes, caress those antique dust jackets. No, hold on. Movement on the horizon!*

He pressed on, making his way towards the travel section. He paused, looking around as he gathered his bearings. Her breath caught as she spied him eyeing off the non-fiction section. *A well-read historian? An economist?* This, she could work with. But alas, he powered past the biographies and essays. Picking up his pace, the chestnut-haired man walked with decisive strides as Frankie, barely concealed by her paperback, devoured M&M after M&M and gawked at the stranger as he made his way to the back of the store.

No. No. No! Anything but that shelf. The Young Adult section? He must be disoriented. Frankie dropped her book, deciding enough was enough; this customer was obviously confused. Just as she was about to leave the safety of the counter, the man pulled out a hot-orange-spined book without a hint of hesitation.

'This has to be some kind of sick joke,' Frankie muttered under her breath. 'He's got to be at least thirty years old! Far too mature – and good-looking – to be reading—' Now Frankie really was confused. 'Is that *Twilight* he just picked up? Ach. I mean—'

The man looked up from his book and peered curiously at Frankie.

'Shit.' Frankie quickly turned her back to the shelves, leaning up against the front counter. *I knew he was too good to be true*, she said to herself – silently this time – and picked up her phone to dial Cat's number.

'Why isn't she picking up?' Frankie tapped her foot impatiently.

'Ahem.'

At the sound of this low, rhythmic grumble, Frankie swivelled around, almost taking out what remained of the precariously placed bowl of M&Ms.

'Sorry about that. How can I help?' Composure regained, she brushed a stray hair from her face.

'Just this one today, please,' the man said with a smile, two dimples creasing his cheeks.

Frankie assessed the book before her, squinting with dissatisfaction at the garish movie tie-in edition. She checked his left hand discreetly. No ring.

'Would you like it wrapped? This must be for your niece? Nephew? Child?' she asked hopefully.

'No, no. This one's all mine. I've been itching to know what happens next!'

'Mmm, sure.' She forced a thin smile.

Frankie scanned the book and placed it into a bag. Looking up from her work, she found the man looking almost longingly back at her. There was an unmistakable warmth about him. His blue eyes seemed to say, *There's simply no other person in this world I'd rather be gazing at right now.* As Frankie tumbled into his eyes, he appeared to move closer. Was that his hand she saw moving towards her? *He couldn't be! Is he—* The man's head was now a complete blur as he leaned over the counter, closing the distance between them. Without thinking, Frankie mirrored his movements and quickly edged towards him. Barely inches away, Frankie was overcome by the earthy scent of his cologne. *Surely that isn't his hand softly grazing my face?* She leaned in and so did he, her eyes drifting shut. They were now just centimetres apart. Reflexively, she pursed her lips. And kissed him. Smack-bang on the nose. *The nose!* As she hung there before him, lips still pressed together, she felt his fingers lightly pinch her left cheek. They both pulled back abruptly.

'Sorry, you had a bit of chocolate on your cheek.' He held up the offending morsel apologetically.

'Oh God. I'm so sorry, that was totally inappropriate. I just kissed you. On the nose!' she spluttered. 'I don't know what got into me. I just received terrible news and my head's not screwed on right.' Frankie stumbled over her words. 'That will be twenty dollars, thanks.'

With her eyes averted, she finalised the transaction and shoved the bag towards him. She shuffled out from behind the counter, placed an arm behind the man's back and quickly ushered him to the door. He seemed to be trying to say something, but Frankie mumbled her gratitude and apologies over the top of him, and within an instant he was pushed out onto the street, the door closing tightly behind him. Taking a deep breath, Frankie leaned up against the door, letting the heat of the glass seep through her dress, superficially soothing her. *When did I get so goddamn ridiculous?*

💬 Frankie: Cat, please tell me where you are. Let's talk this through. PS I just molested a customer. I need back-up. Stat.

After staring at the screen for a minute, willing Cat to reply, Frankie exited Messages and, in an attempt to distract herself, began to scroll through Instagram.

Cute puppy.

Flat lay.

Engagement announcement.

Smashed avocado.

Perfectly posed photographs flashed before her eyes. Then, flicking to Facebook, a particular image caught her attention. She smiled.

👍 **Cat Cooper: Thank you God for this heavenly creation! Lune Croissanterie, marry me.**

#cruffin #foodporn 📍 at Lune Croissanterie

There was Cat, revealed to the world, devouring what could only be described as pastry paradise. Frankie placed the 'Back in 10! Buying painkillers for book hangover' sign on the front door and locked up behind her. She zoomed down the footpath, mentally kicking herself. How could she have allowed herself to get so rattled by a couple of medium-sized biceps and a dazzling smile? And besides, his taste in books really ought to have sobered her up. No adult man who reads books featuring lovesick werewolves and angsty teenagers could be that much of a catch. But why was she surprised that a man had left her feeling disappointed? Underwhelmed?

Frankie flashed through her recent dating history.

Exhibit A – her last Tinder experience:

💬 **Michael: Hi there, Frankie. Whereabouts do you live in Melbourne?**

14

🗨 Frankie: Richmond. You?

🗨 Michael: I just got out of prison and my ex changed the locks. I could really use a place to stay?

Exhibit B – her last blind date: 'It's real silverware, touch it!' he said as he stashed the fancy restaurant cutlery in his pockets.

Exhibit C – her last random hook-up: 'Frankie, your vagina is like a velvet taco.'

And then there was Adam. It had been eighteen months since Ads had broken up with her after two and a half years together. Their relationship had been hot and heavy, until it wasn't. They'd fallen hard and fast, but external stresses weighed heavily on their young, blinded-by-love shoulders.

When reviews for Frankie's second book slammed everything from her characters to her use of semi-colons – 'Hilary' rated *Something About Jane* 0 stars, stating she would 'rather have severe, week-long diarrhoea than have to read this book again' – an intense bout of writer's block settled over her.

Ads got promoted to junior partner at his top-tier law firm and was too preoccupied to notice Frankie's devastation over her career falling apart.

🗨 Ads: Hey Franks. It seems like you're in a bit of a transition phase, and I don't think I can help you with what you're looking for. I think it would be better for both of us if we were just friends. See you around. Ads x

🗨 Frankie: I hope you fucking die.

🗨 Frankie: Sorry, I didn't mean that.

💬 Frankie: I love you.

💬 Frankie: Fuck you.

💬 Frankie: I miss you …

💬 Frankie: I'm deleting your number.

After surviving a tumultuous grieving period, Frankie was at an all time low. She lost not only all confidence in her ability to write, but also her part-time role as a primary school library assistant following a breakdown complete with expletives during Year 1 book club after discovering, via Facebook, that Ads had a new girlfriend. Months of Ben & Jerry's ice cream and *The Notebook* viewing sessions later, Frankie braved the dating world again, only to be assailed by failed date after failed ego-bruising date. Had these sexless and waking-up-spoonless months finally led her to lose her mind? Not to mention made her so self-absorbed that she no longer knew what was going on with her best friend?

Arriving at Lune Croissanterie, Frankie inched her way through the waiting crowd, scanning the tables. There, hidden in the back corner, she spotted Cat. In front of her lay an assortment of partially eaten croissants. With a final shudder, Frankie pushed aside the visual of the bookstore nose kiss, and slid into the chair next to her best friend. Startled, Cat looked up, and Frankie's heart broke at the sight of her friend's teary, croissant-crumbed face. She pulled Cat towards her, rubbing her back and consoling her with soothing whispers.

'How did this happen, Catty?'

'It's these baby hormones! They've invaded my body and have me doing all kinds of crazy things,' blubbered Cat, dabbing her eyes with a crumpled serviette. 'And the worst part is, I've literally never felt hornier. And Claud insists on being super cautious in the bedroom. He's worried he's going to dent the baby or something! But all I want to do is have loud, inappropriate, break-the-bed-in-three-places sex!'

'Well, it's certainly no pickles-and-peanut-butter at 3am,' Frankie said. 'So, you're high on hormones and, what, you just fell on his penis after class?'

Cat smiled guiltily, blushing. 'It just sort of happened. I was all pent up after the K-Pop session. He was just so dreamy. It was almost magnetic,' Cat gushed. 'After the class, he came over to help me stretch. You know that stretch when you lie on the floor and you have somebody push against your hip bone and leg? He was practically straddling me and, I don't know, I was just overcome with desire. I've never felt such a pull like that before! And the next thing I know, we're doing it in the bathroom squashed between the toilet and a Dyson Airblade.'

She sighed and buried her face in her sticky hands. 'Oh Frank, I've been racked with guilt ever since. Especially because Claud's been extra attentive since we found out about the baby. He tries so hard to make sure I'm comfortable and happy. And then there's you, Frankie! We just don't keep secrets from each other.'

Frankie squeezed Cat's leg. 'Does he have any idea?' Frankie asked as evenly as she could manage.

'God no!' she hissed, looking up. 'You know how he'd get. He'd be completely devastated.'

Frankie had always known that Claud adored Cat, but he was sensitive and, at times, unforgiving. It wasn't unusual for Frankie to arrive at The Little Brunswick Street Bookshop and find the two of them still simmering over the previous night's argument. They were two strong-minded individuals who lived together and worked together three days a week. They were bound by love and bookkeeping, and after many intertwining years their relationship had become less passionate and more practical. But still, Frankie was having a hard time believing what she was hearing. 'Do you still love Claud? You want to be with him, right?'

At that, Cat's whole body seemed to cave in on itself. She hesitated for a moment, then said, 'Yes, of course. We're having a baby.'

Frankie sighed again, now at a complete loss for words. She wanted to protect her friend and keep her calm; Cat had precarious blood-sugar levels at the best of times. And was she really expected to throw away a twelve-year relationship after a moment of hormone-induced insanity? Even though they didn't always see eye-to-eye exactly, Frankie felt a sense of loyalty to Claud, and wanted to protect him from this newly discovered infidelity. Cat had always been a little addicted to life, moving from one infatuation to the next. *This has to be another one of her fads*, Frankie told herself, *a momentary lapse in judgement.*

'And it's over with this guy?' she gently prodded.

Cat's bottom lip quivered. 'It's over with this guy.'

'Have you read Esther Perel's new book? *The State of Affairs*?'

Cat shook her head. 'But with an accent like hers, I'd believe just about anything she said.'

'She wrote about how sometimes people stray not because they don't love their partner, or because they are looking for somebody better, but because they are searching for another part of themselves, a part which has become lost in the folds of a safe and comfortable relationship.' Frankie rubbed Cat's arm and picked up a half-eaten *pain au chocolat*. 'Sweet Jesus, this is heaven in my mouth!'

And there they sat, arms resting against each other, quickly sampling the treats before them. Cat checked her watch, deciding they could spare another few minutes, then turned the interrogation around. 'So, you sexually assaulted a customer?'

It was Frankie's turn to bury her face in her hands, cringing and laughing in equal measure as she recounted the incident in all its excruciating glory, periodically blurting out, 'On the nose, Cat! On the *fucking nose!*' Cat was beside herself with laughter, regularly spraying the table with crumbs and bits of custard.

'And I thought *I* had problems,' Cat said between gasps for air.

'It was hands down the most embarrassing moment of my life.'

'Was he at least easy on the eyes? Or nose?' Cat winked at Frankie, who rolled her eyes in return.

'You have no idea.' They both broke into a fit of giggles. 'Oh, but you won't believe which book he bought.'

'*High Fidelity*? *Wuthering Heights*? *Rosemary's Baby*?' Cat inquired.

'Worse.'

'*Fifty Shades of Grey*?'

Frankie raised her eyebrows, egging Cat on.

'*Fifty Shades Darker*?'

'*New Moon!*' Frankie guffawed.

'No! I mean, don't get me wrong, I'm partial to hot vampires seeking to avenge death and the odd sexy werewolf, but *New Moon*? Are you sure this was an adult-sized man whose nose you pashed?'

'I know. Why are all the good-looking ones such terrible readers?' Frankie despaired as she attempted to make I'll-have-a-strong-cappuccino eyes at the nearest waiter.

'So, what are we going to do about it?' Cat said to the back of Frankie's head.

'Do about what?'

'This horrible man-drought that's doing weird things to your fine-motor reflexes.'

'Nothing. I'm not fit to date!'

A young waitress in distressed jeans and a black tank top finally approached their table, and they ordered a cappuccino and peppermint tea to go.

'Frank, did you ever consider that you need to be more open-minded? We've talked about your "gap",' Cat said. 'Even with Ads, you kept him at arm's length. Maybe you're not being open enough, not willing to let anyone in. You know, romance isn't all Mr Bingley and Atticus Finch!'

'Well, at least they were well-read.'

Back on the street, Cat clung dramatically to Frankie. 'I'm too exhausted to walk!' She fluttered her eyelashes. 'Can we catch the next tram back? *Please?*' Frankie couldn't help but laugh as they meandered over to the nearest tram stop and collapsed on the bench.

'You know, Frankenstein,' Cat said as Frankie bent forward, peering down the street in search of an approaching tram, 'we're brought up being told not to judge a book by its cover. Maybe you should start applying the same logic to men.'

'That's rich coming from you, Cat Cooper. You just about deck anyone who comes into the store asking for Nicholas Sparks.'

'Mr Sparks needs to diversify!' Cat retorted. 'Fine, you have a point.'

'See, you can tell a lot from what a person reads.'

At the familiar clang of the approaching tram, the two friends rose from the bench and began their furious hunt for their travel cards. As they tapped on to the packed vehicle, Cat took one look at the teenagers lounging across the priority seat and powered towards them. She stood directly in front of them, legs apart, hands on hips and coughed unsubtly. Looking terrified, they skittered away and Cat sat down with a satisfied grin. Even though she wasn't showing yet, pregnancy had given Cat a whole new appreciation for the concept of power posing. Frankie sheepishly followed and hung onto the rail next to her smug friend.

'So,' Cat said, suddenly sitting up straighter, as if an idea had been beamed into her, 'use books to find a man!'

'Excuse me?'

'Boooooks!' Cat cooed, as if it were obvious.

'What are you on about, woman?'

'Seriously, Frank. If you think you can tell so much from a person's bookshelf, why not put it to the test? Get your mates John Willoughby and Jo March to veto your men.'

Frankie scoffed. 'So, I should force my way into men's homes and peruse their bedside tables to decide whether they're marriage material? If I've learned one thing today, it's to not invade people's personal space.'

'I didn't say anything about a break-and-enter. Frankie, think about it. Literature is your life. You've been trawling Tinder looking for well-read intellectuals, but it's not working. Let's shake things up! Just use your favourite books to find a man.'

'Just use your favourite books to find a man? You're losing your mind.' Frankie stared absently out the window, allowing her eyes to relax and move back and forth with the tram's movement.

'Yes, start a book club. You can put a sign on the front door saying, "Hot men with a grasp of classic and contemporary fiction wanted!" You can lead it, write notes, test them on their analytical skills … At least it would get you writing again.'

Frankie rolled her eyes, but then, as the rhythm of the tram lulled her into a gentle daze, an idea flashed before them.

—3—

A Train of Thought

I was standing in a train carriage, clinging to a (I hope that's not human residue) moist handrail and a worn copy of *Persuasion*. There was a man sitting opposite me playing a ukulele, wearing only a pair of green briefs and a top hat (to keep it classy). I could hear a distant banging in the background. *Bang. Bang. Bang.* You've. Hit. Rock. Bottom. It seemed to taunt.

What am I doing here, in this vast, open, new-to-me world of the blog, you'd like to know? After accidentally kissing – ahem, molesting – a stranger's nose at my place of work, I have been forced to seek alternative methods of finding a mate. So, I hopped aboard the 5.42pm to Alamein, armed with a good book and just a shred less self-respect. My plan? Use my deeply judgemental bookish self (because let's be honest, we do actually judge books by their covers) to sift through the bad boys, the bad-in-beds and the bad readers. Using the heroic and hopelessly romantic words of some of my favourite novels, I am determined to find a half-decent-looking man who makes me laugh and is capable of sitting through an entire dinner party without using phrases like 'ROFLMAO' and 'That's what she said'. Surely I'm not asking too much?

So, after surreptitiously raiding the shelves at the bookstore at which I work (#kleptomaniac #shelfie #bestbossever) and taking just a few from my personal collection, I flipped to the seventh-last page of each one and scribbled the following:

You have great taste in books. Fancy a date?
Email me, Scarlett O' x hello@thebookninja.com

Over the next few weeks I will stealthily ninja said books (everything from Atkinson to Zafón) on various train and tram services travelling in and out of the city. My hope? For a man to find one, read it, and be so deeply and irrevocably moved by the words (because he has superb taste in books, is obviously intelligent and has his shit together) that he is compelled to contact me. We shall then hit it off. Date for a few months. Move in together. Get married. And before you can say Fitzwilliam Darcy, live happily ever after with three kids, two Dalmatians and an American walnut veneer bookshelf, of course.

Now, I know what you're thinking ... Does this woman not have a shred of dignity? What about feminism? Her concern for privacy and security? Does she realise that her life's worth is not measured by the man in it?

I'll admit it: I'm lonely. I haven't had sex in too many months to count, and the last time another human being held me, really held me, was when I tripped entering a 7-Eleven at 11.40pm to collect a second bucket of Ben & Jerry's. Don't get me wrong, it's okay to want more than the warmth of a stranger late at night. But in actual fact, I'm willing to open myself up to you (whoever and wherever you are) because I need to find a way to bridge 'the gap' (as my best friend so eloquently terms it) that I put between myself and other people, and just take a punt at life, and love. I need to get over my desperate fear of failure and put pen to paper again, and maybe along the way I can find the man of my (fictional) dreams.

Oh, and the other thing you must be wondering is: HOW COULD YOU PART WITH YOUR BOOKS?! For that, I have nothing. It's the single flaw in the plan.

It's been four days since I released *Persuasion* to the rails. Tomorrow I'll put *The Goldfinch* out there, and the day after that, *Catch-22*. And all the while I will obsessively refresh my browser until something either expected or (I hope) unexpected comes of this strange social experiment. All notable correspondence and dates will be documented here.

To protect my identity, and by that I mean to prevent my mother from tracking this down, over the next few months you'll come to know me as Scarlett O' – the woman whose sanity has *Gone with the Wind*.

Until next time, my dears.

After all, tomorrow is another date.

Scarlett O' xx

Leave a comment (3)

Cat in the Hat > I'd date you. Now get over here already so we can watch *Outlander*.

No offence but ... > Going to all this effort to find a man? As an independent woman, this *does* strike me as slightly anti-feminist.

> **Stephen Prince** > @Nooffencebut ... I think you need to Google the definition of feminism. Scarlett O', you're my queen.

—4—

Lost and Found by Brooke Davis
City Loop train to Parliament Station

Frankie had never been surrounded by so much lycra in her life. She watched on in amazement as striped glittery leggings and sweaty lime-green crop tops danced around the room.

'I cannot *believe* I let you drag me into this,' she shouted over the loud Korean pop music that thundered throughout the warehouse.

Cat slid down to the ground and put her leg out at a ninety-degree angle, tapping it ferociously. She rubbed her belly, pulsating to the beat. Frankie crouched next to her and stuck out her leg, trying awkwardly to keep up.

'I don't think you understand how bad you are at this,' Cat said, laughing.

'I don't think you understand how much I hate you right now,' Frankie said between a hip grind and a hair toss.

The purple-haired dance instructor, wearing a white track-suit and orange sneakers, cranked up the music. 'Now stand up and Arrogant Dance! One-two. One-two. One-two.'

All eighteen dancing Koreans stood up at once. They shimmied effortlessly into position, legs apart, hips swaying, followed by the very non-Korean Frankie and Cat, who were dancing inelegantly at the back.

'That's it! Arrogant Dance! Arrogant Dance!' yelled the instructor with so much enthusiasm Frankie thought he might explode into a puff of glittery smoke.

Everyone crossed their arms and sashayed their bodies towards the front of the class. Everyone except Frankie, who was concentrating on not falling over.

'And now the Butt Dance. Quickly, Butt Dance! Butt Dance!' commanded the instructor seriously, as if he were teaching them how to perform CPR, not wiggle their behinds.

Everyone turned their back to the instructor, and as Frankie looked around at the lycra-clad, fluoro-haired, exceptionally coordinated dancers, along with her red-haired, red-faced, exceptionally uncoordinated pregnant friend, shaking their bums as if their lives depended on it, she suppressed a laugh.

'Okay, this may be the funniest thing I have ever done in my life,' Frankie called to a sweaty, derrière-wiggling Cat.

'Stop talking and wiggle that butt, Frankston! Wiggle, goddamn it!' Cat slapped Frankie's bum.

'Yes, sir!' Frankie laughed.

Moments later, while attempting the Fantastic Baby, a dance move requiring the simultaneous flicking of legs and arms, Frankie puffed, 'So, can you please tell me now which one is Jin Soo?'

'I told you already, I'm not telling you. It was a one-time thing and it's never happening again. I never want to think about it or talk about it. Ever!' Cat hissed, angrily moving her arms and legs all over the place like a psychotic octopus.

'And *I* told *you* that the only way in hell I was coming to this dance class was if you pointed out the second guy you have ever slept with!' Frankie wheezed while shimmying.

'Oh, all right, *fine*. But stop shimmying; that's not even a K-Pop move,' snapped Cat, looking around nervously. 'It's him,' she said, pointing vaguely towards the front of the room.

Frankie squinted and twisted her neck to get a better look. 'Who? The one in the silver mesh singlet?'

'No, *him*. At the front of the class.'

'Who? The instructor?'

Cat nodded sheepishly.

'You slept with *the instructor* of your K-Pop class? Cat!' gasped Frankie.

'Yes. And now you know, we are never talking about it again,' Cat said firmly.

Frankie shuddered. Cat's confession suddenly felt all too real. 'Okay, fine,' Frankie agreed reluctantly.

'And to finish up, let's move into the Ring Ding Dong! Do the Ring Ding Dong!' bellowed Jin Soo.

'Do you want to ring ding his dong, Cat?' Frankie smiled innocently.

'Stop it!' Cat punched Frankie's arm, hard.

Everyone started to grind towards the floor, sweat rolling down their foreheads. Suddenly, the music came to a halt and Frankie jerked to a stop, two beats behind everybody else. Jin Soo, in a surprisingly high-pitched voice, thanked the group for their attendance. As the dancers started to disperse and chat in small groups, he took off his shirt, revealing drool-worthy, sculpted abs. Frankie wolf-whistled in Cat's ear, but then stepped back and saw her friend staring uncomfortably at the floor.

'What's wrong?' Frankie said.

'Nothing. Nothing. I just want to get out of here,' Cat replied, leading the way quickly out of the K-Pop warehouse and onto bustling Swan Street.

'I still can't believe you slept with him, Cat. Are you really not going to tell Claud?'

They strolled past cafes, the rich scent of coffee and freshly baked bread wafting around them.

'I can't tell him, Frank. He would therapy-knit himself into a frenzy,' Cat said, stopping out the front of Feast of Merit, their favourite Richmond cafe.

'I think that's a good idea, Catty,' agreed Frankie as they joined the queue at the takeaway window. 'And remember, you promised me you would never do anything like this again, or off with your head!'

'Yeah, I know. I know,' Cat replied.

'A double-shot latte and one peppermint tea, please,' Frankie said to the barista, handing over a ten-dollar note.

'Coming right up. What's your name, please?' The barista scribbled down their order directly onto two takeaway cups.

'Jin Soo,' Frankie answered with a wry smile. Cat scowled.

They sat on two crates perched on the footpath, waiting for their name to be called.

'Oh God. I cannot wait to drink coffee again. Only five more months till this baby comes shooting out of me. Promise me that when you visit me at the hospital you'll bring coffee, sashimi, soft cheese and—'

'And a bottle of pinot. I know, I know. You've only reminded me every single day since the second you found out you were pregnant,' Frankie said.

'And I will continue to remind you every day until I see a sashimi-and-soft-cheese platter with a side of coffee and pinot laid before me.'

Frankie nodded, checking the time on her phone. It was already 8.45am. She was going to be so late to open the shop.

Frankie spied her reflection in the cafe window and snorted in disgust. Her hair was wild and frizzy and her I ♥ NY T-shirt clung to her, but there was no way she'd make it home in time to shower.

She forced her eyes away from herself and focused instead on Cat, who was explaining how Claud was stuck in Adelaide after progressing to the next round of the Fastest Needles in the South annual competition.

'He's devastated to be missing the next appointment with my obstetrician, but I said, "You've been training for months, honey! You'll be there for the next one."'

'Probably for the best; he doesn't need any more inspiration for baby clothes. How many woollen onesies are you up to now?' Frankie glanced over to the takeaway station, increasingly anxious to get a move on. If she was going to have to change in the backroom of the bookstore, she at least wanted enough time to run their emergency work straightener through her hair.

'Did you bring books to drop on the train on your way?' Cat asked.

'I sure did, they're right here.' Frankie patted her backpack.

'Any emails about them yet?'

'Not yet, but it's only been a week. It takes time to get to the end of the book,' Frankie said.

'Oh, hurry up already, dream man! Or crazy stalkers—' Cat suddenly went silent and ducked her head behind a stray menu, furiously poking Frankie.

'What are you doing? Ouch! Cat, that hurts.' Frankie swatted Cat's hand away.

'He's here,' Cat said.

'Who's here?'

'Jin Soo. He's in line to order a coffee. Shit. Don't make eye contact. Don't look.'

'Why do you still go to his classes if you want to avoid him?' Frankie hissed, crouching behind the slightly sad-looking fiddle-leaf fig sitting on the crate in front of them.

'Because you just don't get that kind of soundtrack anywhere else. And I never speak to him anymore. I'm just in and out. In and out. In and out!' said Cat, flushed.

'Okay, okay. Please stop saying "in and out"! Do you want to leave? I'll grab the drinks and meet you round the corner.'

Cat nodded furiously, slowly standing up.

'Jin Soo!' shouted the barista.

Frankie and Cat both froze.

'Jin Soo! Jin Soo!'

'That's us,' whispered Frankie to Cat.

Jin Soo looked up from his phone and immediately spotted Cat. He smiled at her, clearly confused.

'Jin Soo!' the barista called again.

'Run,' hissed Cat.

'What?'

'Run!' Cat repeated, and raced off, as fast as her little legs would carry her. Abandoning their drinks, Frankie sprinted after her, trying to suppress her laughter.

Once a safe two and a half blocks away, Frankie stopped. She curled over and put her hands on her knees, breathing heavily. 'Jesus you're fit,' she called after Cat. 'Oh God, now I'm even sweatier. And I haven't even had my coffee!' Frankie said, between breaths.

'Sorry, that was ridiculous of me.'

'That name thing was ridiculous of *me*,' Frankie countered with a grimace. She checked her watch and looked herself up and down. 'I should get going; I feel filthy and I have some book ninja-ing to take care of on the way. Are you going to be all right?' Frankie smiled.

Cat nodded. 'I'll see you in a couple of hours, Frankston.' Cat laughed, and walked the other way, leaving Frankie to hop on the train with books ready to plant.

🐢

Frankie walked through Richmond station and peered up at the train times on the electronic board. One minute till the City Loop train line; she dashed to platform three and skidded through the closing doors of the train just in time. Leaning against the door for a second, she closed her eyes and attempted to catch her breath. *God, I am so unfit; I really have to do more exercise. Maybe more K-Pop?* She opened her eyes, scouting out the carriage. Most seats were occupied by commuters on their phones, on their laptops, on their Kindles. Nobody flicked through real books.

'Typical,' Frankie muttered as she made her way to a spare seat. She sat down and slowly slid her copy of *Lost and Found* out of her backpack, balancing it surreptitiously on her lap while peering around to check if anyone was watching her. But everybody was too busy with their heads in their devices. Opening the book to the seventh-last page, she ran her fingers over the indentations left by her pen. Frankie closed the book, kissed it and put it down inconspicuously next to her.

Please let the man who finds this book be my soulmate.

'O.M.G. Are you Frankie Rose?' she heard a shrill voice say behind her.

Frankie turned around. 'Yes,' she replied sceptically.

'O.M.G! O.M.G! O.M.G!' the lanky teenage girl screeched, clambering out of her seat to perch, uninvited, next to Frankie, half-sitting on *Lost and Found*.

'Sorry, but have we met?' Frankie asked.

'I'm only your biggest fan. I've read *A Modern Austen* AND *Something about Jane*, like, a million times. They are seriously amazing. O.M.G. – I can't believe it's you. I recognised you from your headshot inside the cover. Although, you were a bit more done up there,' the girl said, taking in Frankie's dishevelled appearance.

Frankie smiled uncomfortably, shifting in her seat.

'So, are you going to release a number three? I *have* to know what happens to Charlotte and Alexander. I just have to!' The girl edged closer and closer, until Frankie could smell her salty breath.

'Oh, um, no. No more books, I'm afraid. I'm not writing anymore,' Frankie said, inching further away.

'What? Why? That is the worst thing I have ever heard in my whole entire life. Seriously, don't let those terrible reviews get you down, babe. I don't know what they were talking about. "The worst book to have ever been published"? Please, have they not read *Othello*? We had to read it for school and it was boring with a capital B.' The girl laughed, playfully nudging Frankie's shoulder.

Not this, not now, Frankie whined to herself. She had to get away from this Shakespeare-bashing fan. 'I … I, think I see my colleague,' said Frankie, suddenly flustered. She slung her backpack over her shoulder and skidded towards the train's internal doors.

'You forgot your book, babe!' the girl called after her.

Frankie slipped into the next carriage and flung herself onto a spare seat.

She put her head in her hands. 'What a fucking nightmare,' she said under her breath.

'Tough day?' said the man sitting opposite her.

She looked up and almost died. It was John-Knightley-Mr-Darcy-Edmund-Bertram from the bookstore. The man she had recently kissed, without invitation, smack-bang on the nose. And Frankie had just sworn under her breath at a teenage girl. And she looked … like *this*.

'You could say that.' Frankie attempted a smile but was certain it came off as a wince.

'Anything I can help with?' he said, his startling blue eyes twinkling everywhere. He looked even more perfect than during their horrific first encounter, this time wearing a checkered shirt and beige chinos.

Who is *this guy?* Frankie thought as she felt herself blush. The man, entirely composed, smiled warmly and returned to his book. *The Hunger Games.* Frankie couldn't stop staring, so she took out her copy of *Mansfield Park* and pretended to read.

He looked up from his book. 'What are you reading?'

'Uh, *Mansfield Park*. For the hundredth time.' She let out a low, forced chuckle.

'Oh, I've never heard of it. Any good?'

Never heard of *Mansfield Park*? Frankie choked back a gasp. *But look at those eyes*, she thought as she tried not to gape. *That bone structure. Maybe I could change his ways*, Pygmalion-*style*.

But before she could answer his question, the man took out his wallet, nodding to a group of inspectors flooding the train.

'Shit!' Frankie thought and said at the same time as she remembered her train card sitting in her bag at home.

'My travel pass, it's in my other bag. I just changed bags.' She knew she was babbling, but she couldn't stop. 'I was in such a rush for K-Pop and—'

'Ticket please?' the inspector said to the couple behind her.

'Don't worry. I've got this.' The gorgeous man half-smiled. *Oh, I could get lost in that smile,* Frankie thought, and then she snapped out of it and focused on the fact that she was about to be hit with a two-hundred-dollar fine.

The ticket inspectors approached, and just then, as Frankie was scrambling for an excuse that might sound reasonable, the man dropped his book and moved his face dangerously close to Frankie's. There was no doubt about his intentions this time. He grabbed her face, leaned in and kissed her. He pushed his hands through her hair, and a small moan escaped her lips. He kissed her with an ardent need unlike anything Frankie had experienced. If they had been characters in a book, everything around them would have slipped away, buttons would have flown, shoes fallen off. And then, just like that, he broke away.

'They're gone.' He smiled.

'Who?' Frankie replied in a trembled whisper.

'The ticket inspectors.'

'Oh, uh, thanks,' Frankie said huskily.

'No problem. Works every time.'

Every time? This guy is smooth. Frankie let out a breathy, awkward laugh, her cheeks burning and heart fluttering like a caffeinated butterfly.

'Well, that was better than our first kiss.' The handsome stranger winked, and then returned to *The Hunger Games* as if nothing had happened.

—5—

Romeo, Romeo, wherefore art thou Romeo?

Beginning a new book is much like dating.

First, there's trepidation. You ask yourself: What am I looking for in a book? What mood am I in? What are my friends reading? Work is picking up, do I really have the capacity to invest in the *War and Peace*s of this world, or should I be looking for something lighter, perhaps a little more *Vinegar Girl*?

Next comes the blinding hope. You've finally selected a book and you're feeling pretty damn good about yourself. You've brewed a cup of tea, you're sprawled out on your couch and the heater is on high. The book rests delicately on your lap and you're alight with the possibility of it all. You dream about the rich dialogue and the entrancing characters (you'll even love to hate the bad guys). You imagine being so enthralled by the twists and turns that you forget to eat that block of chocolate you really shouldn't have bought. Facebook will suddenly become obsolete, you'll consider selling your television and you won't need to worry about going to the gym ever again because the emotional journey you're about to embark on is the only exercise you'll ever need. Just about anything could happen.

During the next stage, you find yourself being incredibly open-minded. You're a few pages in and there's no denying that the plot has captured your attention. You're enjoying the fresh (yet understated) description of scenery, and you like the protagonist's vibe. You think to yourself, *Yeah, I could really like this book* and *Maybe excessive use of alliteration actually is my thing?* So, you read on.

Ooh, did that character really just say that? You've reached a bit of a stalemate. Dialogue is getting a bit repetitive and the main character just refuses to get the job done! But you loved all of the author's previous works and you really don't mind the underscoring themes of the book. You've come this far. Maybe things will get better in a few chapters?

The aggravation juncture: NOT ANOTHER SPLIT INFINI-TIVE! GREAT, ANOTHER HALF-ARSED LOVE TRIANGLE! YOU CALL THAT A RED HERRING?! BITCH, *PLEASE*!

Then you hit the refusing-to-accept-reality phase. You really hate how the author keeps using the same adjectives over and over again, but you find yourself LOLing every time the sister enters stage left. Plus, you hate leaving your business unfinished. But then again, maybe James Joyce was right when he said something about life being too short to read a bad book. You persevere, sentence by sentence, chapter by chapter. Then you find yourself putting off reading. You start making excuses. You've managed to do all of the ironing (rustic creased is so in right now, yeah?) and your eyebrows have never been so sculpted. You might only be getting through a couple of pages at a time, but at least you can tell yourself that you're giving it a good go.

It'll change. Things will turn around. If you just overlook the fluffy, We're Just Fucking Around To Up The Word Count And Increase Suspense chapters, it will actually be an interesting book. Maybe the author will consider feedback from Goodreads reviews and do a little nip-and-tuck on the extraneous plot lines in the sequel? Perhaps jazzing things up with a funky bookmark will improve things?

You're at your wit's end. You've tried. You've really given it your all, but you're just not feeling a connection. It's time to get real and work out how to end things.

Do you:

A. Let it peter out. Increase the burst between reading and slowly phase it out without anybody being any the wiser.
B. Start reading another book at the same time, because it's not like you're exclusive or anything.
C. Be more direct. (Note: a little white lie never hurt anybody.) Explain to the book that, 'It's not you, it's me.' You've really enjoyed your time together – wasn't it so funny when the main character walked in on his parents having sex? – but you don't think you really see it in 'that way'. Things are pretty hectic at the moment between your colleagues having babies and that new side project you're trying on for size. Would you mind if we left things for now? Can we just be friends?
D. Change your name, and your number, and get the hell out of town.

Until next time, my dears.
After all, tomorrow is another date.
Scarlett O' xx

Leave a comment (6)

Cat in the Hat > I love you.

No offence but ... > Be honest and open, like the mature adults we are. A–D seem a little juvenile to me.

> **Stephen Prince** > @Nooffencebut ... You are the definition of a buzzkill.

> **No offence but ...** > @StephenPrince, you are the definition of a rude human being. Mind your own business.

> **Cat in the Hat** > @StephenPrince & @Nooffencebut ... loving your banter.

Love sick > Love your work, Scarlett O'! It's like you've read my mind.

—6—

Mila 18 by Leon Uris
Belgrave train line towards Flinders Street

'Finally, somebody I can talk to!' Frankie pounced on the gangly boy who walked through the door.

'Cool your jets, Rose. Desperate much?' Seb tried to act coy, but the slight curl to his lip suggested that he was only too happy to be greeted with such enthusiasm. At the first sign of attention from Frankie, Seb's cheeks always turned beetroot red.

'Oh, Seb. Seb! Thank God you're here. You will *not believe* what just happened!' Frankie practically shrieked as she pulled Seb towards her, grasping him by the shoulders.

'Rose,' Seb said sternly, half-heartedly brushing Frankie away, 'new releases first. Then adult stuff.'

With bright red hair and a peppering of freckles, Seb was a regular at The Little Brunswick Street Bookshop. He would make sure to make an appearance most days after school, always dressed in a pale blue school uniform that was two sizes too big for his gangly body. Seb had somehow managed to rope his seventeen-year-old self into being one of Frankie's key confidants. In exchange for advance copies of new-release books (preferably in the realms of political satire), Seb humoured Frankie and dished up a surprising variety of helpful tips on How To Not Self-Sabotage. Frankie did occasionally feel embarrassed that her second-best friend had only recently hit puberty, but she accepted that finding somebody else who would listen to her rants and provide reassurance and advice for the measly price of heavily discounted books and occasional sugary bribes, was a distinct impossibility.

Frankie pulled Seb behind the counter and pushed him onto a chair. As he helped himself to what remained of the M&Ms, Frankie fished through the books stacked along the back wall.

'Holds, holds, holds,' Frankie narrated, as she flipped through the shelf. 'Ah-ha! Here you go, Seb. The very latest to hit Brunswick.' Frankie held the pile in front of her, bowing her head theatrically.

Seb took a moment to sift through the books, slowly, running his fingers down the blurbs and flicking through the first few pages. Without looking up, he stashed one in his school bag and the other two straight back into Frankie's open hands.

'Pop it on the tab, darl.' Seb grinned, crossing his legs. 'Now, what can I do for you?'

'First, we've talked about you calling me "darl". Second, pass the M&Ms.'

Seb handed her the chocolate and watched as she nervously popped two in her mouth. 'Out with it, Rose.'

'Okay, so I told you about the guy who came into the store the other day. Beautiful biceps, terrible taste in books?'

'Yeah, yeah, the handsome man-child. The nose pash. *New Moon*? What an amateur.'

'So, I was on the train just now and guess who I sat down opposite?'

Seb sniggered. 'Let me guess, he was eating a Happy Meal and playing with the latest-release Shopkin?'

'Focus, Sebastian!' Frankie said with a frown, clicking her fingers under Seb's nose. She pulled up a chair close to him and leaned in conspiratorially. 'Well, he was reading *The Hunger*

Games, but that's hardly the point. So, there I was, sitting *right* opposite him and suddenly ticket inspectors jump aboard. I'd left my ticket in my gym bag at home and was completely—'

'Woah, woah, woah,' Seb interrupted, 'hold it right there, Rose. You go to the gym?'

'Seb, I don't have all day. Some of us have work to do and rent to pay! Where was I? Train. Ticket inspector. Gym bag.' Frankie squeezed her eyes shut, tapping her forehead. 'Right! So, I didn't have my ticket on me, which Edward Cullen somehow cottoned on to. And before I know it, he's got me in a headlock and is kissing me! Kissing me in the middle of the carriage! I mean, strip me naked in public, who does that?'

At that, the front door chimed. Frankie and Seb swiftly turned their heads as an older lady, sporting a blossom-pink skirt suit and matching pillbox hat, ambled into the shop. 'Good day you two,' she said with a slight tilt of her head. 'How was the rest of Graeme Simsion's book reading the other week? I'm sorry I had to dash off. I had my granddaughter's play. She was the star you know? She played ... now what's the name ...'

'She played Yente in *Fiddler on the Roof.* You told us last time, Rosa.' Frankie smiled, wanting only to return to her conversation with Seb.

'Oh yes, yes my dear. Now, where might I find the cooking section, love? You've rearranged the place again!' Frankie gently pointed her in the right direction, and Rosa, ever so slowly, made her way through the store.

'Kissed you? In the carriage? Why?' Seb whispered.

'I don't know. Distract the inspectors? Make them feel too uncomfortable to ask for our tickets? Penchant for getting it on in public? Oh and he was so smooth. It was just like another day at the office for him! But I, on the other hand, am not used to such dalliances. I was so dumbstruck I barely said goodbye, let alone got his number before getting off the train.'

'So, what's the problem, Frankie? It's about time you got a little nookie. We all know this drought of yours can't last forever. You're wound up tighter than Nick Carraway's mantelpiece clock!' Seb said with bravado, to cover the smirk that had appeared as soon as Frankie said she never got his number.

Frankie placed her palms on her cheeks in exasperation and felt them redden as she let her mind wander back to the moment on the train. His lips had been so warm, so inviting, his touch surprisingly gentle. She couldn't remember the last time a man had made her insides flutter and heart beat just a little bit quicker.

'Snap out of it, Rose! Don't tell me you actually *fancy* him,' Seb said, prodding Frankie awkwardly with his index finger.

'Huh! Fancy *him*? He's hardly boyfriend material. I mean, what a flirt! Not to mention his total lack of maturity; he doesn't even bother with age-appropriate reading material. Not that I even care, I'll probably never see him again anyway.' Sometimes Frankie hated it when Seb pointed out the obvious; it made her even more determined to stick to her narrative. She would simply opt for casual nonchalance and denial of feelings.

Rosa shuffled towards the counter and pushed a thick recipe book towards Frankie. 'Just this one today, deary.'

'Wonderful! You've got yourself a good one here,' Frankie said as she scanned, swiped and bagged the book.

'You know dear,' Rosa bent forward, 'it does sound awfully romantic!'

'Excuse me?' Frankie said, startled.

'The kiss! On a train! I mean, you kids these days, so spontaneous. And ...' She paused, smiling wickedly, '... sexy! What I would give to have a fine gentleman sweep me off my feet with a little over-the-shirt action.' She winked, collected her package and scuffled out the door. Frankie and Seb looked at each other and burst out laughing.

'Well, well, well, what do we have here?' As if out of nowhere, Cat appeared, holding a cup of an unidentifiable green substance and a hard-boiled egg. Cat looked from Frankie to Seb and back again, narrowing her eyes. Cat, always a little possessive of Frankie, did not appreciate anybody moving in on her best-friend territory.

Staring Seb down, Cat took a long, dramatic sip of her drink. 'Don't you have a spelling bee to attend, Sebastian?'

Needing no more hints, Seb grabbed his bag and slung it over his shoulder. 'Rose, it's been a pleasure.' He nodded in Frankie's direction. 'And try not to read too much into it. He sounds like he could be the spicy Shura to your Tatiana.' He casually strolled to the door. 'Later, preggo,' he called back with a dismissive wave of his hand.

'Frankie, what on earth is Puberty Blues talking about?'

With a sigh, Frankie filled Cat in on The Train Kiss, sparing no detail. The two were huddled together, letting out the occasional whoop and 'He did *what*?', when the door to the back office creaked open.

'Cat, are you here?' Claud strode through the store and unceremoniously dropped a big bouquet of knitted red roses on the table. He had just come from his job at the law firm and was now going to sneak in some invoicing for the bookstore in the afternoon.

'Who are these for?' Cat stood up, pieces of eggshell falling to the floor.

'For you, silly.' Claud pecked her cheek. 'Happy anniversary.'

'Oh, of course. Happy anniversary!' Cat stretched across the counter and gave her husband another rushed kiss.

Claud's beautifully chiselled face contorted, as if he had just been shot. 'You forgot, didn't you?'

'Of course not, honey.' Cat grinned, obviously lying. She held back an eye-roll at her husband's overreaction.

Frankie eyed off Cat and Claud, trying to tap into her best-friend intuition. She knew that Claud was sensitive, but was he overreacting because he suspected something about Jin Soo? Seeing her staring at him, Claud gave Frankie one of his signature 'fingers up' (the two always put up their index fingers to signify everything is great, ever since their heated discussion about how thumbs are overrated). She smiled, satisfied that Claud was being his usual self, and slipped quietly away as Cat and Claud pored over paperwork. She grabbed a stack of review cards written by herself and Cat and meandered over to the Bestsellers section at the front of the store. As she married up the reviews with the books, she found her mind wandering to the place it went most often: Ads.

They were on their way to Tasmania for a friend's uber-bohemian winery wedding. They'd been together for about eight months; that time in a relationship where they were no longer crippled by the unease of the unknown and were heading straight for honeymoon cove. They were in love and even the most mundane task, like consuming plane food while crammed next to a man with surprisingly pungent body odour, was an exotic adventure.

'We'll have two cups of your finest red, please!' Ads exclaimed, planting a kiss on Frankie's cheek.

They huddled together, munching on their cheese and crackers and downing the acidic wine. Frankie adored this side of Ads: spontaneous, affectionate and utterly uninhibited. There was no cafe too cool or plane too cramped to prevent Ads from being Ads.

'You know I love you, Frankie Rose.' Holding her face tenderly, he kissed her. Even with cheese breath, he was so damn sexy.

'Frankie, Frankie, Frankie! Anybody there?' Cat shook her best friend until she jumped out of her daydream. Cat smiled, gave Frankie a pat on the back and went to plop herself down on the plush armchair in the kids' corner, returning to *Lily and the Octopus.*

Frankie left her friend to be soothed by the words of Steven Rowley and returned to her post at the front of the store. As she went to respond to the day's emails, Frankie felt the familiar vibration of her phone in her back pocket. Without hesitating, she whipped it out and saw a fresh email waiting for her. A wave of excitement rushed over her.

My first response!

—7—

From: Ashley Woodhouse
To: Scarlett O'
Subject: I found your book, Miss O'

Wow. I always thought that my favourite romance would be between Gatsby and Daisy, but something about Anne Elliot and Captain Wentworth's reunion after years apart – well, it just swept me off my feet. Thank you for introducing me to *Persuasion*, Scarlett. It appears that we share a love of great books.

I must admit, I was almost not going to send this email. For all I know, you could be an axe murderer. But then I thought, an axe murderer who loves Jane Austen? Well, that seems all right. So, here I am, emailing a stranger for a date after finding their book on a train.

I should probably tell you a few things about myself. I moved here from Oxford, UK, three weeks ago to start a new job. I have no friends in Australia (yet) except for a Scottish Terrier named Beatrice who spent two weeks in quarantine to move here. She's not adjusting well. She misses the cold and my mother – both things I'm happier keeping my distance from. If you'd like to be my first human friend in Melbourne, you'd better get in quick. I've signed up to start volunteering at Lifeline next week, and I was given the guarantee to 'make friends for life', on the form.

So, if I haven't scared you off, what do you say to a drink this Friday night? Say 6pm at 1806? (I just googled 'cool cocktail bars in Melbourne'. Such a tourist!)

Yours,
Ashley Woodhouse
Principal Architect
JFC Architects

PS: I don't mind if you're an axe murderer. But if you're not a dog person I might have to cancel.

From: Scarlett O'
To: Ashley Woodhouse
Subject: Re: I found your book, Miss O'

Dear Ashley Woodhouse, Principal Architect of JFC Architects,

I'm so glad I could introduce you to the magic that is *Persuasion*. I'd love to go for a drink with you Friday evening at 1806. Google has good taste.

I must tell you that my name is actually Frankie Rose. Scarlett O' is a pseudonym from *Gone with the Wind*, to protect my identity from said axe murderers. (Just for the record, I'm not one of those either.)

Beatrice sounds lovely. I grew up with three dachshunds called Sausage, Bratwurst and Frankfurt, and I am very much a dog person.

See you on Friday.
Frankie x

From: Ashley Woodhouse
To: Scarlett O'
Subject: Re: Re: I found your book, Miss O'

See you then, Frankie x
   PS: Sausage, Bratwurst and Frankfurt. That's hilarious.

From: Scarlett O'
To: Catherine Cooper
Subject: FWD: Re: Re: I found your book, Miss O'

I HAVE A DATE WITH AN ARCHITECT/VOLUNTEER/DOG LOVER/AUSTEN AFICIONADO WITH A BRITISH ACCENT!!!

— 8 —

The Scarlet Letter by Nathaniel Hawthorne
Route 86 tram to Bundoora RMIT via Smith Street

S he couldn't push The Train Kiss from her mind. The more
Frankie thought about her romantic run-in on the train,
the madder she felt at herself for not getting Edward Cullen's
number. For not even getting his name.

The front door jingled, and Cat and Frankie mechanically
looked up to see Seb beaming as he strutted towards them. His
flaming red hair swayed and his green eyes gleamed at Frankie
as if to say, *Please forget our eleven-year age gap, the fact that I still
have pimples and can't grow a beard … and be mine!*

'Proletarian literature!' Frankie and Cat both shouted,
Frankie beating Cat by a mere second.

Cat groaned. 'Sebastian, you ruin everything,' she muttered
grumpily, aggressively tearing open her wallet and handing a
five-dollar note to Frankie.

Seb approached the front counter and bared his metal
braces. 'What's cooking, good looking?' he said, wiggling his
eyebrows at Frankie.

'Seb! What are you doing here? Aren't you meant to be
at school?' Frankie leaned over the front counter to pinch his
cheeks.

'I'm skipping,' he shrugged, playing cool.

Frankie and Cat rolled their eyes.

'Plus, I heard Putu was coming in today.' Seb grinned.
Putu, Frankie's mother, had what Frankie thought was a very

inappropriate relationship with Seb. What had started with an innocent *Words with Friends* game was now a full-blown texting relationship. Frankie was biased, though. After all, she blamed her mother – and her father – for being so hopeless at love. They epitomised everything that shouldn't work in a marriage. Her mother, Putu, was outrageously loud and inappropriate. Her father, Rudolph, was reserved, deeply thoughtful and completely overshadowed by his wife. And then there was her conception story, which her mother loved to tell anyone who would listen.

'It was thirty years ago, back when I was still called Elizabeth. Before I changed my name to Putu after visiting that Balinese ashram in '89,' Putu always started, jumping at any opportunity to mention her two-week life-altering *Eat, Pray, Love* experience.

'I was in search of an adventure. Wasn't I just mad back then, Rudolph?' Putu would gush, twirling her Navajo Ghost Bead necklace around her fingers. Rudolph would simply nod; he was a man of few words.

'So, there I was, standing in the middle of Flinders Street station and I decided – on a whim – that my adventure should be to make a baby with the first man I laid eyes on!' Putu would continue, bolstered by her audience's shocked expression. 'And then, boom! Who should I spot? Frankie's father pottering about at the ticket office! Wasn't that right, Rudy?' Without missing a beat, she would power on. 'We hopped aboard the first train to Frankston and, as soon as we zoomed through a tunnel, we conceived beautiful Frankie, right there and then! That's how we came up with her name: Frankston. I've always been a little before my time, you know. Beat that Posh Spice to the punch. Brooklyn Beckham, what kind of a name is that?' she would always end with a flourish.

Just like that, the bookstore door chimed again, and there, as if on cue, stood Putu, wearing a purple cape and carrying the aroma of incense with her.

'Hello, darlings!' She rushed over to the party of three, air-kissing Seb then Cat and finally Frankie.

'Mum, what are you doing here?' Frankie said coolly.

'Oh, darling, can't a mother pop in to visit her favourite child?' she cooed, as she straightened the sign on the 'Book of the Month' display.

'Plus, she needed to bring me a vial of Damiana.' Seb put out his hand expectantly. Putu reached into her hemp bag and retrieved a test tube full of bright yellow liquid. Seb bared his braces-clad teeth, took the tube and stashed it in the front pocket of his shirt.

'Do I even want to know?' Frankie grumbled.

'It's a special herb for my love potion. I'm going to make myself irresistible to the girl of my dreams.'

'Who, Frankie?' Cat laughed.

Frankie glared at Cat, subtly shaking her head.

'No, Celeste Fitness. She's in my English Lit class,' Seb bit back.

'Fitness? Surely that's a fake name,' Cat retorted.

'It is not and she is not and, with the help of Frankie's lovely mother, she is going to fall head over heels for me,' Seb replied, defiant.

Putu pulled Seb towards her so that they were embracing, shoulder to shoulder. 'Exactly! Seb just needs to add these herbs to his little potion and then rub it gently behind her ears without her knowing.' Putu smiled.

'Without her knowing? Mum, that's terrible advice! If Seb starts rubbing oil behind somebody's ears, all he'll get is a restraining order,' Frankie snapped.

'Oh Frankie, you're always such a Debbie Downer. I'll show you how to rub oil discreetly behind the ear, Sebastian. Just look at this.' Putu leant over the counter and gently dabbed her finger behind Frankie's ear.

Frankie rolled her eyes. 'That was hardly discreet.'

Without warning, Cat pressed her finger behind Frankie's ear too, making her giggle.

'Cat!'

'Sorry, I wanted to see if I could do it,' Cat said dismissively.

All of a sudden, Seb pressed his fingers behind Putu's ear, who squealed with delight. It wasn't long before all four of them were touching their fingers behind each other's ears, laughing hysterically.

'Er, hello?' a man uttered, suddenly appearing right beside the pandemonium that was Cat, Frankie, Seb and Putu.

Frankie jumped back as each of them quickly dropped their hands to their sides. She looked quickly at Cat and screamed silently at her: *It's him! Edward Cullen!*

'Sorry, have I come at a bad time?' he asked.

'No, no, not at all. Everyone was just leaving,' Frankie said, flustered. Seb, Cat and Putu merely stared at the two of them, giving no indication of moving.

'You must be Train Boy. I'm Cat, Frankie's best friend of all time,' Cat interjected, holding out her hand.

He smiled. 'You heard about that, hey? I'm Sunny, with a U. Nice to meet you.' He shook Cat's hand as Frankie tried not to stare at his luminous face, his sparkling eyes.

Sunny turned expectantly towards Frankie, eyebrows raised. 'And you are?'

'Frankie,' Cat said, nudging the gawking Frankie forward.

'Ah, yes,' she managed. 'So, have you come in for *City of Bones*? *Divergent*, perhaps?' she asked, regaining her senses.

'*Please*, I've already read both series. Twice. They were robbed of Man Bookers, if you ask me.'

'You disgust me,' Seb gasped.

'Seb!' Frankie glared at her young friend, then managed to turn back to Sunny. 'Don't mind him. He detests anyone who picks up a book that doesn't revolve solely around government dissent and civil liberties. And as I just said, he's also leaving right now.' Frankie looked expectantly at Seb, who again remained stationary.

'Sooo,' murmured Putu, flinging her arm around Sunny, 'tell me, how does a handsome man like you know my beautiful daughter, Sunny-with-a-U?'

Sunny laughed. 'I really am meeting the whole crew today. First, your best friend and now your mother.'

'Yes, but they all really should be going,' Frankie repeated with growing urgency. 'Cat has a bookstore to manage, and Mum has … Mum?'

'Nonsense dear, I don't have anywhere to be.' Putu edged her face closer to Sunny's, her arm still wrapped around his waist.

'I helped her out of a train fine.' Sunny grinned.

'If by "helped" you mean "snogged"!' Seb blurted out.

'Sebastian, get out!' Cat snapped.

'He kissed Frankie?' Putu released Sunny, stepping forward to prod her mortified daughter.

Frankie groaned and flung her head in her hands.

'Frankston Rose! Why didn't you tell me you kissed such a good-looking man? Does he want children?'

Frankie glowered at her mother.

'Well, does he?' Putu smiled cheekily.

Cat stifled a laugh as Seb nervously patted the vial just visible in his pocket.

'I'm so sorry about this, Sunny. Everyone is in a bit of a weird mood today,' Frankie said, turning to face him again. But Sunny was nowhere to be found. 'Where'd he go?'

'I didn't see.' Cat shrugged apologetically.

'He ran out at the mention of a nuclear family. What a loser, Frank. He thinks Veronica Roth should've won a Man Booker? You're better off without him,' Seb sniggered.

Frankie inhaled deeply, then turned to her mother and best friends. 'Out! Everybody out! I've had enough. Why can't any of you just be normal for one bloody minute?' Frankie yelled. Seb, Putu and Cat stared back at her in stunned silence.

'But—' Putu protested.

'Putu, Seb, let's go.' Cat grabbed them both by the arm and they scuttled out of the bookstore, the bell of the front door calling out after them.

Frankie sighed. The bookstore was empty. All she could hear was the gentle purr of the air conditioner. She tilted her head, gazing at the beautifully coloured books lining the shelves in front of her, and exhaled. Fitzwilliam Darcy, Mark Antony, George Emerson, Edmond Dantès, Prince Charming. She was surrounded by these poetic heartthrobs every single day. Maybe that should be enough for her? Maybe she was only destined to be in love with literary leads? Frankie picked up *Northanger Abbey*, which she had left lying next to the Eftpos machine, ready to return to cheeky, yet adorable, Henry Tilney, when something fell out of the book and fluttered to the floor. Frankie picked it up. It was a bookmark, and in fine blue scribble it read:

Frankie, let's book in a more private date.
0455 718 281 – Sunny

Frankie couldn't hide her smile as she held the bookmark to her chest.

Frankie: Hey, it's Frankie :)

Sunny: Hey, it's Sunny :)

Frankie: Sorry about before … My friends and family are nuts. Completely, utterly bonkers.

Sunny: I love bonkers. Much better than boring.

Frankie: Ha. So, about that date …

Sunny: Yes, let's get down to business. Are you free Saturday night at 8? I'll pick you up.

Frankie: I am indeed. 8/12 Bell Street, Richmond. Where are we going?

Sunny: 'Time will explain …'

Frankie: A Jane Austen quote?!

Sunny: Yep, I googled it. Still never read a thing by the so-called author.

Frankie: All in good time. See you Saturday, Mr Sunny.

Frankie: PS Katniss Everdeen is a Thomas Hardy tribute, did you know? (I googled that one for you.)

Sunny: LOVE *The Hunger Games.*

An hour later the front door to the bookstore was flung open and Cat tiptoed in, her red hair a crazy mess on top of her head. She stood behind Frankie's chair, wrapping her arms around Frankie's shoulders in a tender embrace.

'I'm sorry, Frank,' she said. 'Sorry we scared Sunny away. But you were right. He *is* John Knightley, Mr Darcy and Edmund Bertram all blended into one.'

'You didn't scare him away.' Frankie smiled, sliding her phone towards her.

'Oh my God,' breathed Cat as she skimmed the messages. 'You're going on a date with that handsome man? You're going on a date! You're going on a date! You're going on a date!' she chanted, jumping up and down.

Frankie leapt up from her seat and took Cat's hands. 'I'm going on a date! I'm going on a date! I'm going on a date!' she joined in, bouncing up and down with her friend.

'And don't you have a date with that yummy-sounding Brit tomorrow night?'

'I sure do. Just call me Madame Bovary,' Frankie gushed.

'You're on fire, girlfriend! You know what you should do now?' Cat said, breathlessly.

Frankie looked at Cat, wide-eyed.

'Write! Something more than your blog. A new novel. You're always waiting for that spark. And look at you, you're glowing.' Cat grabbed Frankie's cheeks between her hands, squeezing them affectionately.

'No, I can't,' Frankie said, nudging Cat's hands away.

'Do it, Frank. You're a brilliant writer, and we all know it. Don't worry about the reviews, don't worry about any of it.

Just get back into it and show them what you're made of. There's no harm in trying.'

'Should I?' Frankie asked tentatively.

'Yes! The bookstore is literally a graveyard right now. Grab this, go out to Stagger Lee's and start bloody writing,' Cat demanded, unzipping Frankie's bag and taking out her laptop.

'Okay. Okay!' Frankie laughed as Cat thrust the computer against her chest. 'Yes, I'm going! I'm going!' she added excitedly.

'So long, Madame Bovary!' Cat called after her.

'Thanks, Cat. For everything. I love you.' Frankie blew a kiss as she skipped out of the bookstore.

Okay, writing, writing, writing, Frankie thought, staring at the blinking cursor on the blank computer screen. She was sitting in a corner of her favourite Brunswick Street cafe. She loved it because the baristas were lovely, the coffee was bloody excellent and it was relatively quiet. Though recently, like the fate of any good cafe on Brunswick Street, it had begun swarming with hipsters in tight jeans and scraggly beards. Frankie took a bite of her avocado toast, dropping crumbs on her white jeans.

'Another coffee?' a shaved-headed waiter asked, his lip piercing twinkling in the light.

'No, thank you. This was my fourth today. I think I've just about overdosed,' Frankie said.

'Have you tried our beetroot latte? It's delicious and caffeine-free.'

'Caffeine-free? What's the point?' Frankie laughed.

'Trust me, you'll love it.' The waiter winked.

'You know what? Why not! One beetroot latte, please.'

'Coming right up!'

Okay, Frank, she schooled herself, *back to it. If you can write some piffle in a blog, surely you can get through a chapter of a book.*

'Here you go!' The waiter reappeared, cheerily placing a steaming cup of red frothy liquid in front of her.

'Wow. That's bright.'

He smiled, waiting for her to sample his offering.

Frankie took a small, hesitant sip. 'That *is* delicious,' she said, savouring the refreshingly sweet liquid. 'I can practically taste the antioxidants.'

'What did I tell you!' The waiter sashayed off to hand a man a long black and fruit toast.

Okay, back to writing. Back to writing. Frank, you can do this. She closed her eyes and inhaled, waiting for creativity to strike, but mostly the thoughts that came were reminders of why she had let her writing go. Just a couple of years ago she was living her dream: a published writer in a long-term relationship with the love of her life. Then it all fell apart, piece by piece. She hadn't written since her second book received the worst possible reviews of all time and her editor, Marie, had stopped returning her calls. She loved working at the bookstore with Cat, but sometimes she feared that it was all there would ever be to her life. Her mind floated back to what it had felt like to first be offered a book contract with Simon & Schuster. Pure, unadultered joy. She wanted that feeling back. More than anything.

Which is why now, for the first time, she was trying to open up; to give life, love and writing another shot. It was true, she was afraid to start writing again. She was scared that she was a terrible writer, just like the reviews had said. But today was all about starting fresh, about turning a new page.

Frankie placed her hands delicately on the keyboard, wiggling her fingers over the letters. *Okay, just start, Frankie. What would Jane do?* She typed: *Today was the first day that Evie had really lived.* Frankie smiled. It was no 'It is a truth universally acknowledged,' but it was a good start. *I can work with this.* She placed her hands back on the keyboard, ready to continue, but somehow found herself opening Facebook. Just for a moment. Just to see what everyone else was up to.

Baby photo.

Dog photo.

Bride and groom photo.

Political rant.

Dog photo.

'What's your flow? A five-minute quiz to find out what sort of period you have.'

Ooh, thought Frankie as she clicked into the quiz. *It only takes five minutes! What's the harm in that?* The cursor hovered over the link. *But back to the book*, she told herself, *straight after this.* She took another sip of her pungent beetroot latte and cupped the hot drink in her hand, using the other to click through a series of menstruation-related questions.

'Three tampons a day,' muttered Frankie, flicking through the questions briskly, one by one.

'Fetal position.'

'Cramps.'

'Maxi pad.'

Frankie clicked submit on the quiz, waiting for her period type to promptly pop up. *Oh, the wonders of technology!* A flashing answer appeared in the middle of the screen.

'Heavy period? Heavy period my arse!' Frankie said a little too loudly, leaping up and spilling her bright red latte all over her white jeans. Frankie yelped, feeling the burn of the hot liquid seep through her pants. She grabbed a serviette and tried to dab her jeans, but this only spread the bright red liquid more. A snigger from across the room dragged her attention away and she noticed two schoolgirls, covering their mouths and laughing, tears streaming down their faces. They both held phones in Frankie's direction.

'Hey! *Hey!*' Frankie shouted. 'Are you filming me?' The girls continued to laugh, phones unmoving.

'Stop it!' Frankie shouted. The girls kept chuckling, not reacting to her in the slightest. Frankie groaned. She grabbed her laptop and bag and stormed out of the cafe, forgetting to pay for the stupid beetroot latte.

—9—

Senselessness and Insensitivity

Once again, it was one of those dates that just read oh so well on paper.

Architect. Tick!

Volunteers in spare time. Tick!

Loves dogs. Tick!

Promise of an accent. Tick! Tick!

Having recently relocated from Oxford (A British accent? All hail the Queen!) this date had 'exotically debonair' written all over it. Could it be that a seemingly mature, ethically minded and pooch-loving bachelor had stumbled across one of my literary train-trotters? Thank the Lord, George Wickham, maybe there was a dating god after all!

So, optimistic, but totally-not-invested, I braved the date armed with an effortlessly cool 'no make-up' make-up and just a dash of Jane Austen swagger. I arrived at the bar a few minutes early and, as arranged, placed my well-loved copy of *Sense and Sensibility* on the table.

After a few non-Ashleys sauntered past my post, I was kept occupied by a couple of flirtatious nods from a Roger-Federer-circa-2014-cum-Jamie-Fraser lookalike (talk about a Grand Slam) sitting across the room. Man, was I feeling good.

Until this happened.

A petite-framed woman draped in purple velvet and chunky resin beads slithered into the seat opposite me. And it went a little like this:

'You must be Frankie,' she purred with an unmistakable British lilt.

'Sorry, you must have the wrong person. I'm actually waiting for a friend,' I replied, a little too defensively.

'Ashley? Sorry I'm late.'

I was all, *This cannot be happening!*

It turns out Ashley *is* an architect, volunteer, dog-lover, dyed-in-the-wool Austen tragic from Oxford. It also turns out that Ashley is a lesbian.

I spent the next hour and a half sidestepping the elephant in the room. How was I going to break it to her that, as much as I might have once tried to become a lesbian in 2009 after swearing off men post a particularly traumatic second date with a frisky barista, I would never be hot under the collar for this lithe English rose?

In a bid to distract her from my feminine allure, I steered the conversation towards neutral, totally non-romantic topics. During our time together we covered:

The gas crisis of 1998.

Michael Jackson's death.

Bookmarks versus The Dog-ear.

The royal wedding.

Moby Dick.

Man buns.

Not even recounting the story about how I once didn't shower for two whole weeks seemed to repulse her. I could feel her feet slowly encroaching towards my side of the dusty floorboards. (Have I mentioned my foot phobia?) 'Do you think Michael Jackson really was a paedophile?' Her hand delicately grazed my knee. 'And how about that Kate, doing her own make-up!' I felt her squeeze my thigh. Damn it, I was utterly beguiling! Where had this newfound allure come from? While Ashley was lovely and engaging and oh-so-well-read, she was unfortunately not my type and I decided it wouldn't be fair to lead her on any more.

So, with a subtle daintiness, I found myself suddenly and uncontrollably blurting out, 'I LOVE DICK!'

So, one humiliating drink in the face later, it's back to the tracks for me. Stay tuned for another bumpy edition of 'How I managed to derail my love life and alienate perfectly good people' soon.

Until next time, my dears.

After all, tomorrow is another date.

Scarlett O' xx

Leave a comment (8)

Cat in the Hat > Can't. Stop. Laughing.

No offence but ... > (cough) homophobe (cough)

   Stephen Prince > (cough) buzzkill (cough)

   No offence but ... > @StephenPrince, you're a misogynistic clown. Stop writing to me via comments in this blog.

   Cat in the Hat > @Nooffencebut ... & @StephenPrince I could cut the sexual tension between you two with a knife.

Babbling Book > This was a hilarious read. Can't wait for the next date!

Paperback Boy > Been looking for one of your books everywhere!

Alex David > Just found this blog and I am actually obsessed – you are my queen.

The Rosie Project by Graeme Simsion
Route 78 tram to North Richmond

'Rose, you're going to send me into premature labour!' Cat was curled over her laptop, ripples of laughter raging through her. 'Your blog is priceless.'

'Oh God, stop laughing! I feel bad enough as it is.' Frankie was utterly mortified, not to mention dejected. 'Who am I kidding, this whole book-planting mission is a farce! An utter waste of energy.'

'Chin up, Frank. It was your first response. At least we know people are already loving your blog! You're getting more hits than Claud's knitting blog. And people are finding the books,' Cat reassured her. 'It's not like we thought it would be all romantic strolls on the beach and talking about your childhood by the fire. At least she wasn't a lunatic!'

'Yes, Cat, the silver lining of the day.' Frankie began to rearrange the counter displays, nervously tidying the gift cards. 'You're really not making me feel any better.'

'Frankie, my dear, I don't give a damn,' Cat deadpanned.

Frankie tossed one of the bookmarks she was holding at Cat, who swiftly dodged it, letting it fall against the framed *Knitting Championships Finalist* poster on the back wall. 'God, you're quick for a pregnant person.'

'Twerkshop. You really should join sometime.' Cat gyrated, bottom first, towards Frankie. 'Shake it off, Rose, you've got bigger fish to fry! Don't you have your date with Sunny tonight?' she purred.

Sunny. Frankie shuddered. For the first time in a long time, she felt nervous going into a date. Sunny was charming and mysterious but also unpredictable (especially when on moving vehicles). And what if the first man she'd been vaguely interested in *in so long* rejected her? Or worse yet, didn't live up to her expectations?

'Oh, my knitting needles!'

Cat and Frankie locked eyes as the muffled sound of Claud's cries thrummed from the back office.

'Oh Lord, what is it this time?' Cat rolled her eyes.

A moment later the back door flew open, the force of it sending a small tremor along the shelves in the rear of the shop. Two books toppled to the floor.

'You have got to see this.' Claud stifled laughter, jabbing a finger at Cat, a piece of wool wrapped around it. 'Look what my sister just forwarded me.'

'What?' Cat asked, curious.

Claud thrust his phone in Cat's direction, angling the screen towards her.

Over the next fifteen seconds, Cat's face told a miraculous story. From a look of barely concealed frustration, Cat's expression turned to one of confusion, to crazed bewilderment, then to shock, back to confusion, then finally to a look of deep-set and unmistakable joy. Frankie looked on in amusement, until she peered over Cat's shoulder, squinting at the screen. And then her jaw dropped.

'What is this?' She snatched the phone from Claud.

On the screen was what appeared to be a freeze-framed image of Frankie. The clip was paused on her mid-stance behind a cafe table with her face askew. Frankie looked up at Claud.

'It gets better,' Claud breathed. 'Press play.'

She felt herself getting hot as she hovered her finger over the phone and, with a final groan, pressed play. She watched herself on the screen as she shot up, her hands jutting towards her crotch, as a stream of, yep that was definitely beetroot latte, ran down her white pants. And there, branded in white bold letters, flashed *#PeriodGirl*.

Frankie's hand flew to her chest as she took a sharp intake of breath. 'Those little bitches!' she cried. 'I'm. A. Meme!'

'And a popular one at that, Rose. You've been shared ...' Cat reached for the phone, scrolling down, 'more than four thousand times. There's even a hashtag doing the rounds: #freetheflow. You're an internet sensation!'

Frankie covered her mouth with her hands and stood statue still, staring blankly.

'Look, she's finally cracked!' Cat waved her hand in front of Frankie's unblinking face.

Putting her arm around Frankie's shoulders, Cat guided her towards a chair. 'All right, time to snap out of it, Frank.' Cat quickly glanced at the door, checking for incoming customers, and, with nobody in sight, slapped Frankie across the face. Frankie yelped, grabbing her face.

'Jesus, Cat! Talk about tough love.'

'Welcome back, friend.' Cat brashly rubbed Frankie's cheek and crossed her arms. 'Better?'

'Oh God,' Frankie said, putting her face in her hands.

'Don't worry about it, Frankie. It'll be no time before you're replaced by some hyperactive baby or emotionally unstable feline,' Claud called over. 'Embrace your fifteen minutes while it lasts!' He threw his arms in the air in a gesture of excitement.

Frankie stayed slouched over in the chair. 'Be a doll, Cat, and cancel my date with Sunny, please?'

'Are you kidding?' Cat exclaimed. 'You are absolutely *not* getting out of this one, Period Girl!' She shoved both hands under Frankie's underarms and pulled upwards until Frankie was standing, mostly upright.

'Enough self-pity. It's time to get pumped!' Cat picked up her phone and began to tap away furiously. 'Okay, what do we feel like? Adele? No, too emotional. Some old-school Timberlake? Drake? Well, hello there, old friend!' Cat flashed a saucy grin at Frankie. 'Nelly.'

Frankie stood in front of her wardrobe, wrapped in a towel. She surveyed the options before her. *Polka-dot dress? Too matronly.* She squeezed her clothes along the rack. *Silk V-neck singlet? Too risqué.* She pulled out a white shift dress. *Ach, too white!*

She glanced at the clock on her wall. 'Shit,' she muttered. Sunny would be pulling up at her door in just over twenty minutes. Hastily, she grabbed a reliable pair of black jeans, threw on a delicately embroidered silk top and went to finish her hair. She opened her laptop on the bathroom bench and clicked on the YouTube clip waiting for her. Along with a dance-off, in which Frankie had begrudgingly allowed herself to be cajoled into participating, Cat had sent her an assortment of YouTube videos made by 'leading dating-advice gurus and trailblazers'.

'Haven't you heard? YouTube is the new shrink,' Cat had said. Frankie pressed play.

'Three ways to be irresistible to a man!' a squeaky voice declared. 'One! When complimenting him, think outside the box!' *God, this girl is chipper.* 'Hone in on unique parts of him that people wouldn't normally acknowledge! Say things like,

"You have such a warm smile!" or "I really appreciate the way you seem to value what others have to say!'"

'I really value you,' Frankie addressed the mirror, wrapping a strand of hair around her curling iron. 'I really like the way you give such novel dating advice.' She nodded gravely. No amount of YouTube self-help guides could get her through tonight's date.

As her buzzer sounded, Frankie ruffled her hair, loosening the curls so that they fell effortlessly across her shoulders, and skidded towards the intercom, swiping up her handbag on the way. 'I'll be right down,' she called. She put her hand on the doorknob, closed her eyes and took three deep breaths. *Be irresistible. Be confident. Embrace your femininity.* Frankie rolled her eyes at herself and made her way downstairs.

Frankie pushed her way through the front door of the building and caught herself from visibly swooning at the Greased Lightning moment that greeted her. There, leaning casually against his car, was Sunny, wearing a worn leather jacket and dark jeans. At the sound of her arrival, he turned his head towards her, almost in slow motion, and grinned broadly. 'Heya, Frankie,' he called, making his way towards her. 'Great digs.' He planted a warm kiss on her cheek. *Damn, he's smooth.*

'Is this your car?' Frankie asked, staring at the bright red Honda Civic.

'It sure is.' Sunny proudly patted the bonnet.

'S-N-N-Y D-Y? Sunny Day?' Frankie read the bold personalised number plate.

'That's my name,' Sunny beamed.

'Come on. Seriously? Your first name is Sunny and your last name is Day?' Frankie said.

'Yep. I know, parents can be so cruel,' Sunny quipped as Frankie burst out laughing.

'I'm sorry, I'm sorry. Don't worry. My name is horrendous as well,' Frankie said through fits of giggles.

'What's your last name?' Sunny asked.

'Rose.'

'Frankie Rose? There's nothing wrong with that. That's beautiful,' Sunny said and Frankie's heart fluttered. No need to confess that she was named after the train line on which she had been conceived. Not just yet, anyway.

In the car, Sunny leaned back deep in his seat, one hand on the wheel and the other resting against the open window.

'So, where are we going?' Frankie inquired as casually as possible. The nerves were hitting her in waves.

'You'll have to wait and see.' Sunny's lips curled into a half-smile. 'So, that crew of yours at the bookstore. Bit of a quirky bunch, eh?'

'My crew? I don't know what you're talking about. I've never seen them before in my life.'

'Yes, I regularly call strangers Mum, just to see how they react.'

'Calling strangers Mum, kissing them on public transport. What else do you like doing with unknown passers-by?'

Sunny chuckled. 'Oh you know, just the usual stuff. Hand out my email password and give them a detailed list of my allergies.'

Frankie smiled in return. 'If you are unable to digest pizza, this isn't going to work.'

Fifteen minutes later they parked and walked a couple of blocks before pulling up outside what appeared to be a standard office building.

'Where are we?' Frankie looked around.

'Right this way, my lady.' Sunny held out his arm and nodded for her to follow the direction of his outstretched hand. As they walked towards the building, Frankie felt a shiver of electricity as his arm grazed hers. *Did he mean to do that?* He pushed open the door and led her through a white, marble lobby and then down a set of winding stairs, at the bottom of which stood a lofty bookshelf crammed full of dusty books. Frankie ran her hand along their spines.

'Well, here we are,' Sunny said proudly.

'And where is here exactly?' The only entrance Frankie could spot was the one they had just come down.

Sunny gave Frankie a wink and approached the towering shelves. He started to pull books out at random. 'It's got to be here somewhere,' he said. 'Uh-huh!' He angled a faded blue hardcover book, and the shelf gave a click and creaked ajar.

Sunny looked back at Frankie with a smile. 'I thought you might like it here.' He placed both hands along the side of the bookshelf and heaved it open. Frankie stepped out from behind him and looked through this magical portal: there, revealed before her eyes, lay a dimly lit space bursting with plush antique armchairs, side tables stacked high with books and walls blanketed in lushly framed mirrors and eerie taxidermy. A bar stretched along one wall, and behind it stood a man in a crisp white shirt and suspenders, shining a whisky glass.

'How on earth did you find this place? And how can I have not known about it?'

Unmistakably chuffed with himself, Sunny took her hand and led her to a chaise tucked away in the back corner. 'Pretty great, hey?'

Frankie tried not to stare at Sunny. This gorgeous, effort-lessly cool man, who so far was nailing the date. *Play it cool,*

Frankie. Let's not get ahead of ourselves. She looked across the room at a woman standing at the bar, wearing an emerald gown with a low back, a peacock feather in her hair. A man dressed in a tuxedo crept up behind her, casually putting his hand on the small of her bare back. She turned and kissed him. A group of three women all dressed in brightly coloured skirts, huddled together conspiratorially, laughing heartily at a private joke shared. *Oh God, I am so underdressed.*

A waiter approached and handed them each a menu.

Frankie opened her menu and perused the list of cocktails. Gin and Twain, Bloody Jane, Grenadine Brooks, Lady Chatterley's Loves Aperol, Gone with the Whiskey, Or-well, Better Make it a Double. *This Young-Adult-reading man really pulled this one out of the woodwork.*

'Menu looks good, but there's no The Fault in our Spritz or The Maze Rummer.' Frankie looked up innocently. 'Maybe they have a kids' menu?'

'So, just a Tequila Smugrise for you, then?'

'Huh, there's nothing arrogant about reading the classics!' Frankie retorted. 'It's just common sense.'

'Okay, Mar*tini* bit haughty, what can I get you, then?' he asked with a cheeky grin.

'A Margarita, Dahl-ing, please.' She smiled sweetly.

'Coming right up.' Sunny walked off with their drink orders, Frankie's gaze trailing him. Even from behind he was perfect. Frankie sighed, taking in her surroundings. She peered underneath the table sitting in front of her and spotted a stack of books. *Okay, Frankie, so far so good.* She picked up a copy of *Animal Farm* and searched for her favourite part about four legs being good, two legs being bad.

Sunny returned holding two clouded martini glasses topped with sugary rims. He placed one in front of Frankie and sat back down on the couch. Without a word, he took a long, exaggerated sip of his drink.

They sat for a moment, appreciating their drinks. 'So, Sunny. When you're not busy reading the latest Patrick Ness, what do you do with yourself?'

'I work in advertising. But I'm sort of between jobs at the moment.'

'How so?' Frankie asked, immediately thinking, *Great, my date's unemployed.*

'I got a bit fed up with the culture at the last place,' he said, taking another gulp of his drink. 'Decided to pack it in and see if I could make it on my own.'

'On your own? Like, start your own business or live off the land?'

'The first one, I hope,' Sunny said, a little too quickly. 'What about you? What does Frankie Rose like to do when she's not working at the bookstore or being kissed by strangers on the train?'

'That about sums it up,' Frankie answered.

Sunny raised an eyebrow, obviously unimpressed with her answer, but what else was there to say? She wasn't exactly swimming in potential at the moment. He put his hand on top of hers, but she pulled away, trying to conceal her sudden feeling of rejection by picking up her drink.

'You know, come to think of it, I don't think I've ever met a Frankie before. How did your parents come up with it?' he tried again.

'It's a long story.'

'Good thing I'm in no rush, then.' He reclined and put a hand behind his head. 'Humour me, Frankie.'

She sighed, and decided to share a little something. 'Long story short, my mum had a moment of crazed impulsivity and decided to take advantage of an abandoned train carriage to do it.'

'It?'

'Yes, *it*.'

'And what's this got to do with your name?' Sunny's eyes began to crinkle.

God, she thought, *how does he manage to smile with his whole face?*

'They were riding the, Fr ...' Frankie took a long drink as she mumbled the word 'Frankston'.

'What was that?' He leaned towards her, thoroughly amused.

'The Frankston line,' she murmured.

'The what line?'

'The Frankston line. I'm named after the Frankston line!' she said a little too loudly, drawing the attention of a waitress holding a tray of full champagne flutes.

Sunny broke into peals of laughter, holding his stomach.

'Stop it, it's really not that funny.' Frankie lightly pinched his arm.

'I'm just relieved it wasn't the Craigieburn line. You don't strike me as much of a Craig,' Sunny said with a final laugh.

'We can't all have adorably seasonal names like you, *Sunny Day*.'

'You think I'm adorable?' he teased.

'Oh you'd like that, wouldn't you?'

'Yes, I would, Frankston.'

Frankie couldn't help but smile. But it was just too much trying to keep up with this sudden rollercoaster of a date. Did the playful remarks ooze friend-zone? Or a hint of flirtation? Frankie grabbed their empty glasses and shot up. 'Next round's on me.'

'I'll have The Girl on the Train please,' he called as she headed towards the bar.

It wasn't long before the waitress, wearing a sparkly flapper dress, bent down to slide their next round of drinks onto the table. She looked across at Frankie curiously. Feeling uncomfortable, Frankie averted her eyes.

'Have we met before?' the waitress asked. 'You weren't at Bobby Pentrith's thirtieth the other week?'

'Sorry, you must have me confused with somebody else.' Frankie picked up her drink and turned towards Sunny.

'No, I've definitely seen you somewhere,' she persisted. 'Do you live near the Streat cafe in Collingwood?'

'Nope, sorry.'

'Oh. My. God. I've got it!' the waitress squealed. 'My boss would kill me for asking this, but can we have a selfie together?'

'This is so embarrassing, Sunny,' she whispered. 'I wrote a couple of books a few years ago, but I didn't think anybody actually read them!'

'A book?' the waitress butted in. 'No, you're Period Girl!'

Frankie's heart stopped. She snatched up her drink, sloshed it down in three huge mouthfuls and grabbed Sunny. 'Sorry, we really should be leaving.' Frankie dragged Sunny towards the door and up the stairs, and it was only once they were on the street that she dared look him in the eyes.

'I don't even know where to begin,' she said, but stopped when she felt his hand squeeze her shoulder.

'Why not start at the part where you said you wrote a book?' Frankie peered up to see his soothing face staring back at her. 'And then finish with a kiss.' He smiled.

The Thing About Jane Spring by Sharon Krum
Alamein train line to Flinders Street

'I think it's a chest infection. And I also think I'm coming down with conjunctivitis. I feel very snotty, gooey and contagious.'

Frankie was curled up on her couch, flicking through a tattered copy of *And the Mountains Echoed*, her mobile phone balanced precariously between her shoulder and ear.

'Yeah, it sounds like you're coming down with a really bad case of hibernation, Period Girl. Come on, get your arse into work, Rose. It's been two days. We need to start prepping the store for the Zoë Foster Blake book signing. We've been waiting for this one forever!' Cat was breathing heavily down the other end of the phone. Frankie could just imagine her running down Brunswick Street, pushing past anyone who got in her way as she tried to make it on time to open the store at nine.

'Cat, you don't appreciate how humiliating this is for me!' Frankie threw her book down in frustration. 'I can't walk down the street without someone calling out "Free the flow!" I can't even go on a date without getting recognised as bloody Period Girl. No wonder I haven't heard a word from Sunny. I definitely scared him away.' She sighed.

'It's been two days, Frank. He's probably playing hard to get! Now, are you coming in today, or do I have to drag you in here myself?' Cat asked.

'One more day, Cat. Please. I'm really not feeling well.' Frankie coughed halfheartedly into the phone.

'You suck,' Cat said.

'Thank you, thank you, thank you. I owe you one.' Frankie grabbed a half-eaten Snickers bar she had left lying on the floor the night before, and took a bite. Through the phone, she heard the faint tinkle of the bookstore's front bell.

'Oh! Who is it? Let me guess. Seb? Millie? Mum?' Despite her proclaimed lethargy, Frankie jumped at the chance to be entertained. There was only so much time even she could spend living off old chocolate bars and binge watching Austen mini-series.

'Nope, nope and nope,' Cat whispered.

'Bryan the bubbly? That old woman who only buys erotic fiction? The hipster who's obsessed with Marian Keyes?' Frankie said through mouthfuls of chocolate.

'Guess again,' Cat purred.

'Oh! Is it Lizard Man?'

'Hi there, Cat. Frankie around?' Frankie heard a man's voice in the background, and she almost choked on the Snickers. *Oh God!*

'Cat! Is that Sunny? That's Sunny, isn't it! Tell him I'm sick. Tell him to call me. Actually, don't; that sounds desperate. Tell him I'm not in. Act cool. But not too cool.' Frankie shot up from the couch like a jack-in-the-box, her mind running a million miles a minute.

'Hello, Sunnnny,' she heard Cat say, her smirk audible from the other side of the city.

'Cat! Please don't say anything stupid,' she begged.

'So, you're looking for Period Girl?' Cat sang to Sunny. 'I'll just get off the phone to this annoying customer and then I'll see what I can do for you, handsome.'

The last thing Frankie heard before Cat hung up was her loud, full-bodied laugh. She threw down her phone and rolled her eyes, praying to God that Cat wouldn't say anything else embarrassing. *Who am I kidding?* she thought, sinking back down on the couch. *It's Cat. Of course she will.* Frankie pulled up her fluffy grey blanket all the way to her chin. This was a new low, even for her: hiding inside her apartment like a hermit. Her life was officially ridiculous. She couldn't help but wonder about Sunny, though. Had he swung by the bookstore to officially end things with her? They had only been on one date; a text would have sufficed.

Frankie's stomach rumbled as if in approbation of being fed only chocolate bars and milk for the past eighteen hours, so she opened up her Uber Eats app and mindlessly scrolled through photos of burgers, sandwiches, noodles, sushi and pho. Her stomach thundered in anticipation as she reached just what she was looking for: Jo's Pizza – open all day, every day, and ready and willing to deliver a Vegetarian Supreme, two garlic breads and a chocolate mousse direct to her door. Then she flicked on the TV, closed her eyes and dozed off to the soothing hums of static television.

Frankie woke to a loud, monotonous knocking at her door. The thought of pizza immediately made her jump up, toss on a baggy stained jumper and step into her ugg boots. She was tying her knotty hair into a bun on the top of her head as she reached her front door.

'Hello, my saviour!' she called as she swung open the door.

'Why, hello to you too.' Sunny smiled, giving her scruffy appearance a once-over.

Frankie jerked back in surprise, crossing her arms to cover her bra-less chest. 'Uh, what are you doing here? How did you get up here?'

'The front gate was unlocked. I heard you were sick, so I thought I'd drop something off to help you feel a little better.' He smiled as he held out a paper bag.

'Oh, uh ... oh. Thanks. How did you know my apartment number?' Frankie quickly retied her hair into a ponytail while slowly dying inside.

'Cat told me,' he said, resting his solid arm casually against her doorframe. He was wearing denim shorts and a bright yellow T-shirt which stretched firmly across his chest. He was, as always, droolworthy.

Damn you, Cat! Frankie thought, beginning to devise ways to murder her friend.

'So, aren't you going to invite me in?'

'Uh, I don't think that's a good idea. I'm very contagious.' Frankie coughed, picturing all the chocolate wrappers, empty mugs and dirty underwear littered across her home.

'Doesn't bother me,' Sunny replied brightly. 'I have the best immune system in Australia. I haven't been sick since seventh grade when Kimmy Swanton spat in my mouth when she had glandular fever.' Sunny tried to walk inside, but Frankie quickly blocked him.

'That's disgusting.'

'I know. So, can I come in?'

Frankie sighed. 'My apartment is a pigsty. Worse than a pigsty. Pigs would not be caught dead in my apartment right now.'

'Luckily, I'm not a pig,' laughed Sunny, pushing his way past Frankie and into her cramped, messy apartment.

Frankie followed nervously. 'Just sit here. And don't move.' She pushed him onto the couch she had just been lying on, and scuttled around, picking up wrappers and discarded lingerie.

'Seriously, you don't need to clean up for me. You should see my apartment.' Sunny kicked off his shoes and settled back onto the couch.

'Just give me one minute!' Frankie called back, carrying the pile of rubbish and laundry into her bedroom. She tore off her stained clothes and tossed on a pair of blue jeans and a floral tank. A liberal spray of perfume helped, but there was nothing she could do about the disaster that was her hair, so she rummaged around her top shelf, found a black baseball cap and flung it on.

'Okay,' Frankie said, emerging from her room.

'Okay.' Sunny smiled cheekily, sitting calmly on her couch.

'So, what are you doing here again?' Frankie sat down, leaving a safe gap between them.

'I told you, I brought you something to help you feel better.' Sunny held up the small, brown paper bag which had been folded over at the top.

'Oh, you really didn't have to do that.' She tentatively picked up the bag and looked at it curiously. 'What is it?'

'Guess.'

'Chocolate? Cake? A muffin? Please tell me it's a muffin,' Frankie said, practically salivating at the thought.

Sunny shook his head, his eyes alight as he watched her peel open the bag.

'I hope it's edible, I'm starving,' she cried as she pulled the lid off the Chinese takeaway container and held it up to her face.

'What?!' Frankie exclaimed as she saw the contents of the container and immediately pushed it away.

'It's a turtle. Look at the little guy.' Sunny picked up the tiny green animal by its shell, placing it gently onto his palm.

It wriggled slightly to the left, its tiny body only taking up a third of Sunny's outstretched hand.

'A turtle? You got me a *turtle*?'

'Yeah, isn't he adorable? Look at that face.' Sunny stroked its tiny shell with one finger, while Frankie looked on in disbelief. 'I went to Chao's last night. You know Chao's? The best sweet-and-sour chicken on the north side? I was picking up dinner when, what do I see out of the corner of my eye, but a tiny turtle, in a cage! With barely any water to swim in! Everybody knows you can't keep turtles in a cage. I don't know what Chao was thinking. I'm telling you, it was like a cruel, turtle-itarian regime in there. Anyway, I asked Chao, "How much for the turtle?" And he told me if I gave him another fiver, I could have it! So, there I was with sweet-and-sour chicken in one hand and a turtle in the other, and I thought, "You know who would love this turtle? Frankston Rose!"' Sunny rambled on, his face alight with excitement.

'But Sunny,' Frankie spluttered, trying not to laugh, 'you can't just get someone a turtle. What am I going to do with it?' *I can't look after a turtle*, she thought a little desperately. *I can barely look after myself.*

'They're a piece of cake to look after. I already googled it. It's a Murray River Short Neck Turtle, so it's semi-aquatic. I've bought the ultraviolet lighting, heating, filtration and tank. They're in my car, I'll go down and grab it all now. This little guy needs to go back in water every two hours or so. But we'll need to buy more food, and calcium supplements. We can go down and get them all from the pet store on Church Street.'

'Are you being serious right now? You seem strangely knowledgeable about turtles.'

'As serious as this little turtle right here,' he replied, tapping his shell.

'Calcium supplements? A tank? I never asked for a turtle, Sunny! I can't keep it!' Frankie blurted, just a touch too loudly.

Sunny said nothing, and neither did Frankie. The word 'turtle' pulsated in the air, mocking them as Frankie tried to figure out what on earth was going on, and who on earth this man was. The silence was beginning to stretch when it was broken – thankfully – by another knock at the door.

'Pizza for Frankie?' A short man stood in the hallway holding out the big paper bag that she *had* wanted.

'Thank you!' Frankie grabbed it from him as Sunny snuck out the front door. Confused and suddenly – and irrationally – annoyed, she slammed the door and laid the pizza, garlic bread and chocolate mousse on the coffee table. Then, after taking a moment and a deep breath, she tore open the pizza box and took a bite of the warm, cheesy slice. She closed her eyes and inhaled, but before she could take another heavenly bite, there was another knock on the door. Begrudgingly, she got up and peered through the peephole.

She groaned as she swung open the door and watched Sunny lug in large amounts of turtle paraphernalia, including a giant glass aquarium, complete with a mesh lid and lighting. He took one look at Frankie's bemused expression and, without a word, began to assemble the items in the corner of her living room.

Frankie sighed dramatically and resumed her post on the couch with her pizza.

Four slices later, she felt Sunny's gaze resting on her. He had finished building the aquarium and was holding up the turtle, who now wore a purple-crocheted knit over its shell. Frankie couldn't help but laugh.

'Pretty cute, hey?' Sunny smiled.

'Where did you get that?' Frankie was now openly laughing at the absurdity of a baby turtle wearing a knitted jacket in her living room.

'I bought it off Claud's Etsy store. That's why I popped by the bookstore today.'

'It's a turtle wearing a turtleneck! I can't. Okay, come here. I need to Instagram the shit out of this.'

'So, we can keep him?' Sunny moved towards her, waggling his eyebrows comically. *Oh, damn you, Sunny Day*, Frankie thought as her heart fluttered and her eyes rolled simultaneously at the use of 'we'. She was still annoyed at this unwanted gift, but how could she possibly say no to a turtle wearing a turtleneck?

'Fine, I guess he can stay,' Frankie surrendered, taking out her phone and happily snapping a photo of the turtle curled up in Sunny's hand.

While Frankie updated her Instagram, Sunny placed the turtle in the tank and sat down next to Frankie. 'So, this your usual 10am breakfast?' he said, looking at the greasy feast laid out before them.

'This isn't my usual anything.' Frankie grinned.

'What about Shellford?' Frankie suggested. She was folded up on the couch, staring at the turtle swimming in the giant tank, which easily took up a quarter of her living room. Sunny was sitting next to her, his head resting on her shoulder.

'Nah, too predictable. How about Emily?' he proposed.

'Emily? It's definitely a boy!'

'How do you know?'

'Mother's intuition.'

They had been brainstorming names for the last ten minutes, and were getting nowhere.

'So, do you buy all the new women in your life a pet turtle?' Frankie teased.

'I usually like to stick with something more traditional, like a budgerigar,' Sunny replied, almost too quickly.

'So …' Frankie said after a few moments of silence spent trying not to wonder what he meant, 'it must be a while since the little guy ate. I'd hate to be accused of neglect.'

'Shall we visit the pet store now?' Sunny shot up from the couch.

'Why not?' Frankie fought a sudden urge to back away now. *Surely this guy is too good to be true*? 'Let me just grab my shoes,' she said cautiously, her terrible case of hybernating-while-meme-disaster-blows-over-itis slowly lifting.

As she fossicked around in her wardrobe, she couldn't help but think of the man sitting in her living room. *He's … odd. Very odd. But a nice sort of odd. A stay-forever-young sort of odd. A devilishly handsome, take-me-right-now-in-my-living-room sort of odd. He's not necessarily someone I would settle down with, but …* But Cat was always saying she should have some fun while it lasted. *Perhaps I* should *go with the flow*, she decided as she slipped on a pair of leopard-print espadrilles and closed her bedroom door behind her.

'What are you doing?' Frankie asked nervously when she saw Sunny standing in front of her bookshelf, holding onto a green book. *Please let it be any book but the one I think it is!* She dared to tiptoe forward. Yep, the book had 'Frankie Rose' embossed along the spine. *Fantastic.*

'This is your book? The one you wrote?' Sunny looked at her in awe.

'Yes. Please put it down.' Frankie tried to grab it from Sunny's hands, but he held onto it tightly.

'Can I borrow it?' Sunny asked.

'No. You wouldn't like it. It's not Young Adult.' Frankie snatched at the book again. Sunny took a step back, the atmosphere shifting around them.

'I'm happy to venture out of the realms of dystopia and teen fiction for an author like you, Frankie,' he tried again.

Frankie pursed her lips and scanned her bookshelf, now desperate for a different book to distract him with. A much-loved tattered yellow cover caught her eye.

'Try this one! It's my all-time favourite book.' Frankie pushed a copy of AA Milne's *The Complete Poems of Winnie-the-Pooh* into Sunny's hands.

Sunny eyed the book, which now covered Frankie's.

'Yep, it's my favourite piece of literature. Has been since I was two,' Frankie shared.

'I know this whole book by heart,' Sunny said, suddenly serious. I slept with it under my pillow until I was seventeen.'

Oh.

'So, yeah. I already have a copy of *my* favourite book. But thanks. Should we go to the pet store?' To Frankie's great relief, Sunny returned her book to the shelf and put Frankie's hand in his.

🐢

'What on earth is this?' Frankie picked up the tiny chair balanced on a ledge in front of her.

'It's a Chihuahua high chair, so they can eat dinner with you. My sister has one,' Sunny said.

Sunny and Frankie were wandering the aisles of the giant

Pet Barn, past colourful toys and oversized bags of dog food. Fish swam elegantly in tanks stacked high at the back of the shop and the distinct smell of fresh puppies and kittens filled the air.

'Can I help you with something?' the pretty shop attendant asked. Her jet black hair fell gracefully to her shoulders and her dark skin glowed. Being surrounded by cute animals all day probably did that to a person.

'Yes, yes you can. My wife Darlene and I have just bought a delightful little turtle. Our daughter Stephanie has been begging for one and we finally caved. First a golden retriever, then a pony and now a turtle. She really does get everything she wants, that one,' Sunny finished with a coy smile.

Frankie threw him a surprised look before joining in. 'Ah yes, my dear husband Derek and I, we just can't say no to our Stephanie. And what's one more animal to us? Our mansion is so big it could fit Noah's ark!' she said in a terrible, faux-British accent. Sunny squeezed Frankie's hand, stifling laughter.

'Ah, okay. So, what do you need for your turtle?' the girl said, smacking her chewing gum as she spoke.

'Well, we'd like some food. Your cheapest – but finest – turtle food!' Sunny exclaimed.

'Yes, only the best for our precious turtle!' Frankie said, losing her fake accent.

The assistant looked the pair up and down, quickly turned on her heel and strutted down the aisle. 'Does he have a name?' the girl called over her shoulder.

'Winnie. Named after The Pooh,' Sunny replied without missing a beat. Frankie and Sunny locked eyes.

'Oh, that's nice,' the girl said in an unamused, monotone voice. She directed them to an aisle near the back of the store and left them to fossick through bags of dried crickets, cockroaches, mealworms, maggots, frozen fish foods, and commercially prepared turtle pellets.

'Winnie. I like it,' Frankie said. Sunny winked and tucked a piece of her hair behind her ear.

'How should we shell-ebrate?' Sunny leaned closer towards Frankie, his nose almost grazing hers.

'That's terrible.' Frankie sighed, taking a step forward.

Sunny tilted his head towards her, grazing his finger lightly along her jaw. And then, right there, pressed against the turtle tanks, he pulled her firmly towards him and kissed her. Slowly, passionately, truly. She slid her fingers through his hair, an intoxicating giddiness spinning her round and round.

After a couple of minutes, she pulled away. 'Where's Winnie?' she asked breathlessly.

From: Dean Masters
To: Frankie Rose
Subject: Period Girl?

Hey Frank,

Long time. I think the last time I saw you, we were making out on Becca Rudaizky's washing machine after our final school exams?

I thought I'd reach out because I just saw your meme! Very funny. You always were hilarious.

So, what else is happening with you? I'm still in a band with John, Allan and Nutto. We're almost about to make it big time. Our song 'Pumpkin Ketchup' ranked 97 on the Triple J Hottest 100 list in 2010.

I'm married to Rachel Wong. (Turns out you were right, I did always have a crush on her!) We have two beautiful kids and one more on the way.

Anyway, hope you're well. Congrats on the Period Girl stuff again.

Dean x

From: Frankie Rose
To: Catherine Cooper
Subject: FW: RE: Period Girl?

Kill me now.

Chocolat by Joanne Harris
Glen Waverley train line from the city

🐚 Sunny: Are you religious?

🐚 Frankie: Not in the slightest. Are you?

🐚 Sunny: Nope. But Winnie is.

🐚 Frankie: How do you know?

🐚 Sunny: I just know these things. So, I think it's only fair that we baptise him. You keen?

🐚 Frankie: A turtle baptism? What the shell! I'm in.

🐚 Sunny: Brilliant. Pick you and The Pooh up at 8pm. x

🐚 Frankie: See you then, crazy. x

'He's even more insane than you are.'

Cat stared at the photo of Winnie in his knitted purple jacket. It was now Frankie's screensaver.

'I know.' Frankie sighed. She had been senselessly placing price stickers on copies of new releases, her mind drifting towards Sunny and *that kiss*. After twenty minutes of running around the pet store, frantically looking for Winnie, they had finally found him perched on top of a fish tank, staring back at them as if to say, *What took you so long?* They had burst into fits of crazed laughter, before returning to their passionate, incredible kiss, which had made Frankie feel like she could face the world again.

'But I just don't understand. He just presented you with a turtle? On your second date? Out of nowhere?'

'Yep. He's ridiculous,' she said with a smile, her make-up-less face flushed a shade of rose.

Sure, Sunny was impractical, spontaneous and just a little bit foolhardy. They wouldn't last long – that much Frankie knew – but he was fun and exciting, and he made Frankie feel more fun and exciting. Plus, he was the best kisser she had ever experienced. Even better than that French drummer she had a fling with when she was working at Shakespeare and Company. And that was saying something. He was French, after all.

'Frankie. Frankie. Frankie. Frankie,' Cat called incessantly.

Startled, Frankie swivelled around to look at an annoyed Cat.

'I've been calling you for the past thirty seconds. Stop thinking about making out with Sunny. I need you to help me sticker these books.' Cat pulled at Frankie's mint green cotton shirt.

'Okay, okay, sorry. Let's change the topic. How's Claud?' Frankie asked, sidling up next to Cat. She placed a discount sticker on Jodi Picoult's latest novel.

'I don't want to talk about Claud! I want to talk about Sunny. Just with you responding to me, instead of closing your eyes and practically orgasming at the mere memory of his lips,' Cat snapped.

'Cat! All right, what do you want to know? Ask away.' Frankie leaned back in her chair and swapped her pricing gun for a bag of honey-roasted cashews from her bag in preparation for the inquisition.

'I don't want to know anything. I have an opinion to share.'

'And that opinion is?'

'I don't think it's going to work.' Cat grabbed the cashews from Frankie and put three in her mouth, haughtily.

'And why is that?' Frankie laughed.

'Let's take a moment to review the facts,' Cat said with a mouthful of nuts. 'He reads James Dashner. You have a Masters in English Lit. He buys you a turtle as a gift. You once drowned a goldfish. He's ridiculously good-looking. You—'

'Cat!' Frankie interrupted. 'You are in such a mood. What's got into you?'

'Nothing.'

'Tell me.'

Cat emptied the nutty dregs at the bottom of the bag into her mouth, crumbs catching in the rolled-up sleeves of her pink knitted top. 'I'm just feeling guilty, you know?' Cat said, hanging her head, pieces of red curly hair falling across her face.

'About Jin Soo?' Frankie tore open a bag of sugared almonds.

'Don't say his name in here!' Cat slammed her hand over Frankie's mouth and anxiously looked around the empty shop.

Just then, the front door chimed. Frankie and Cat shot up from their seats, glancing at the door.

'Kama sutra and political satire!' Cat shouted as Putu and Seb walked in.

Frankie took out Cat's winnings from her wallet and placed them before her.

'Why hello, child of my loins.' Putu, draped in an emerald dress and matching green jewellery, leaned over the counter to brush a stray piece of hair from Frankie's face.

'Why hello, Mother. What are you two doing together?'

'You know that Sebastian and I like to meet up once a month for a chai. I teach him about the world, and in exchange he teaches me about my one and only daughter, who refuses to tell me anything about her life.' Putu smiled sweetly.

'I *didn't* know that.' Frankie turned to face Seb. 'You're not bothered by what people must think? A fifty-eight-year-old woman taking a seventeen-year-old boy out of school to corrupt his young mind?' Frankie said.

'*Please*, Frankston. I'm already corrupted. Putu just helps me to explore my identity.' Seb winked at Putu. 'Plus, I don't have school today. The opening night of *Oliver* is tomorrow, in case you've forgotten. We have the day off to "mentally prepare".' He looked directly at Frankie. 'You are still coming, aren't you?'

'Of course! Cat and I will be there with bells on.'

'You better be! Last year you "forgot" to see me playing Bruce Bogtrotter.'

'We didn't forget!' snapped Cat. 'We were protesting. There's no way a skinny kid like you should have been playing Bruce Bogtrotter. It's an insult to Roald Dahl.'

'As I was saying,' Seb continued, ignoring Cat's outburst. 'This year I'm playing Mr Sowerberry.' He turned to Putu. 'He's the undertaker in *Oliver*. It's a big part for me. The school paper's already calling it a life-changing performance.' Seb beamed, chest puffed out.

'Oh, darling, I wish I could come. But you know I teach bead-making tomorrow night. But I'll be there the following night. I promise.' Putu ruffled Seb's flaming red hair.

'So, which of my secrets have you been telling my mum, my verbose friend?' Frankie asked Seb.

'Oh, just the important ones, my cagey friend,' Seb said, swiping an almond from the freshly opened packet and popping it into his mouth.

'Oh yes, including your reptilian gift from a certain man friend!' Putu sang.

'Yeah, so I got you something too.' Seb awkwardly took out a hot-pink knotted cord from his backpack. 'It's a turtle leash. Apparently it's very helpful when taking them out for walks.'

'A leash? Between last night and this morning, you went out and bought me a leash? That is so sweet of you.' Frankie leaned over and squeezed Seb's cheek, then turned away before she saw him blush crimson.

'Yeah, I bought it with my girlfriend, Celeste, last night.'

'Your girlfriend?' Frankie exclaimed.

'Yes, that's right dear, you'll be happy to know that my love potion helped Seb win the girl of his dreams,' Putu exclaimed proudly.

'A girlfriend? I'll believe it when I see it,' Cat muttered.

Frankie tore off her Aztec jumpsuit and tossed it on the floor, along with the eight other dresses she had tried and then discarded. She stared at her curvy body in the mirror, clad in nothing but a black bikini, which Sunny had insisted she wear. *What does one wear to a turtle baptism?* she thought, assessing the contents of her cupboard for the seventeenth time in search of the perfect outfit. *He'll be here in two minutes.* Sighing, she picked up a yellow dress from the floor and put it back on. She slipped on some strappy brown wedges and flung on a denim jacket just as the intercom buzzed.

'Coming!' she shouted to no-one in particular as she grabbed her handbag and dug around inside to find her strawberry lip gloss. After swiftly smearing it across her lips she popped a mint in her mouth, carefully transferred Winnie to his carrier case and ran out the door.

'Hi,' Frankie said to a smiling Sunny, who was leaning casually against his car again, like a rock star. He moved towards her, bending down to plant a warm kiss on her cheek.

'We're ready to be baptised!' Frankie exclaimed, holding up Winnie's case.

'We? I only promised a baptism for Winnie. But I'll see what I can do.' Sunny reached through the cage and patted the turtle's small head before opening the car door for Frankie.

'Sorry about the draft. My sunroof's broken.' Sunny pointed to the half-open roof, which was letting in a gust of wind.

'So, where to?' Frankie asked.

'You'll soon find out.' Sunny revved the engine.

'You're always so coy. Hmm … It must be somewhere with water. The beach? The St Kilda baths?' Frankie guessed, holding onto Winnie tightly, using her hands as a seatbelt.

Sunny shook his head, a hint of a smile creeping across his face.

'The Richmond public swimming pool? That fancy bathhouse in the city?' Frankie asked.

'The place where they give you banana smoothies on arrival? Definitely not. I hate bananas. With a passion,' Sunny said seriously.

'Hate? How could you hate bananas? That's ridiculous. They're the base of any good smoothie, cake or fruit salad.'

'They're disgusting,' he shuddered.

Frankie studied his white knuckles clutching the wheel and his tightened jaw. 'Oh my God. I've read about this. Bananaphobes. You're actually *afraid* of bananas. If I had a banana right here, right now, would you be scared?'

'Shut up, shut up,' Sunny said.

'Because I actually brought one as a snack in my handbag here.' Frankie rustled around in her bag. 'You jumped! You *are* afraid of bananas! I'm on a date with a banana-phobe!' Frankie exclaimed, enjoying this moment very much.

'I guess you are, Frankston. And I'm on a date with a very beautiful woman.' Sunny took her hand and held it.

Frankie inhaled deeply, and stopped talking about bananas.

Frankie, Sunny and Winnie arrived at a small, unmarked red door in the middle of a graffiti-splashed city alley. 'What is this place?'

'Let's find out.' Sunny smiled and slowly opened the door. Frankie followed him cautiously as they climbed five steep stairs before opening another door. Here they were greeted by a beautiful Japanese woman dressed in a long, flowing red and yellow kimono.

'Hello, and welcome to The Onsen Ma. Here in our bathhouse you may relax, unwind and feel Zen. Please take off your shoes before entering your private bath,' the Japanese woman said with a bow.

Frankie slid off her wedges and put them in a box. She stood, barefoot on the warm tiles, holding Winnie and looking quizzically at Sunny.

'Come this way,' the woman said, walking off briskly. Sunny took Frankie's hand, and the two followed their host down a short corridor. They entered a curtained-off change room that smelled strongly of incense. Sounds of birds chirping and harps playing echoed throughout. Two lockers stood in the corner of the room, and a big sink with two big bottles of water stood beside it.

'Please remove your clothing and place your items in the locker next to you,' the Japanese woman said firmly, holding eye contact. Frankie and Sunny looked at each other nervously and began to strip down to their swimwear, placing their clothing in the lockers, all the while aware of the woman's unyielding stare. Sunny gave Frankie's bikini-clad body a not-so-subtle once-over, and smiled warmly.

'What?' Frankie said.

'Nothing. Can I put my phone in your bag?' Sunny asked.

Frankie placed Winnie on the table next to her while she stored Sunny's phone in her bag and shoved it into her locker along with her dress.

'We do not allow swimwear. Please remove all clothing,' the woman said again.

'Excuse me?' Sunny and Frankie asked in unison.

The woman, clearly annoyed, pointed to a sign on the wall that stated, *Please remove your clothing and wash yourself before entering the onsen.* She then picked up her kimono so it wouldn't graze the ground, and said, 'Do not put turtle in the onsen. It is too hot,' and walked out, leaving Sunny and Frankie alone.

'I'm not getting naked,' Frankie said, crossing her arms over her chest.

'But the sign ...' Sunny winked.

'Was this your plan? Drag me to this so-called onsen to "baptise Winnie" and get me naked?' Frankie huffed.

'No, no, no. I promise, I had no idea. It's not like that. My friend Matt is always coming here with his girlfriend, and he said it would be a great place for a date. He never said anything about the no-clothes policy! I guess the joke's on me,' Sunny said anxiously, pushing his hair back with his hand. He was wearing nothing but red swimming shorts. *Oh my, that body. That beautiful, beautiful body*, Frankie thought, before snapping out of it.

'Winnie isn't even allowed in the onsen!' Frankie laughed.

'I know. Shit, I really stuffed this one up. Let's just go in the onsen *in our swimwear* and enjoy what's left of this failed date,' Sunny said, grabbing a towel from the bench next to him.

'Now, wait a second. You brought me here. And the sign does say no swimwear. I think it's only fair if one of us goes the full Monty.' Frankie smirked, now looking Sunny up and down, unsure where this newfound confidence had come from but deciding to run with it.

'Me? No way. We either both do it or neither of us does,' Sunny said.

'There's no way I'm taking off this bikini, Mister. I'm just an innocent bystander here. You're the one who's dragged us to a naked onsen.'

Sunny edged closer to Frankie, his nose almost grazing hers. 'You expect me to strip down to nothing, while you keep your bikini on?'

Frankie nodded smugly.

Sunny raised his eyebrows and, in one swift motion, dropped his shorts to his ankles.

Frankie, mouth agape, a hint of saliva pulling in the back of her throat, brazenly ogled the sight standing before her.

Sunny smiled casually. 'So, are we going into this onsen or not?' he called, stepping out of his shorts and strolling through the curtains.

Frankie grabbed Winnie, put him gently in the basket next to her and followed a now butt-naked Sunny through the door and into the steaming hot water.

🐢

'I think I'm cooking,' Sunny said. He was immersed in the steaming onsen water, which sat conveniently up to his belly button.

'I'm finding it very difficult to look at you right now,' Frankie said, sitting next to Sunny while averting her eyes from his nakedness.

'You asked for this.'

'I'm having second thoughts,' she blushed. 'You know, just because I asked you to get naked, that doesn't mean I'm sleeping with you,' Frankie added.

'You've only told me seven times.' Sunny grinned and uncrossed his legs, baring himself to the world.

'Jesus, Sunny!' Frankie laughed, shielding her eyes.

'So, did you know that if you were in Japan, you wouldn't be allowed in here?' Sunny said.

'Yes, yes I know. Because I'm not naked,' Frankie said, splashing Sunny.

'No, because of this.' Sunny moved closer to Frankie and touched the tiny, heart-shaped tattoo hidden behind her ear. Frankie shivered.

'My tattoo? I hate it. I was eighteen, living in Paris and trying to rebel. Typical cliché story. Biggest regret of my life,' Frankie said, nonchalantly.

'I like it.' Sunny moved closer. 'You haven't told me any stories like that from your past. Tell me more. What were you doing in Paris?' he asked.

'I was working at a bookstore, but mainly it was just a lot of *fromage*,' Frankie replied. 'So, what does Japan have against tattoos?' she asked, changing the subject briskly.

'Tattoos are banned at most onsens as a way to keep out the Yakuza, the organised crime syndicates in Japan,' Sunny said, still tracing Frankie's tattoo.

'How do you know that?' Frankie said, trying to keep her breathing to a normal rate.

'I studied Japanese culture and history for ten years.'

'Really?' Frankie said, surprised.

'No, I read it on Google about five minutes before I came to pick you up, to impress you.'

'And you didn't read the bit about us having to be naked?'

'I must have missed that part.' Sunny smiled.

'This is the strangest date I've ever been on.'

'Speaking of which, when are we baptising our turtle?' Sunny asked.

'Right after this.' Frankie bit her lip, and kissed him.

🐦 Frankie Rose: Winnie the turtle is officially baptised. Feeling very #zen.

🐢

'She *didn't*,' Sunny said, aghast. They had been sitting outside Frankie's apartment block in Sunny's car for the last hour talking about everything from horoscopes to horseradish.

'She did. When you were in the bathroom, that Japanese lady came up to me and said, "You're not Period Girl, are you?"' Frankie grumbled. Earlier, Sunny had admitted to having stumbled across her infamous video that night at Chao's. Frankie had two options: deny, deny, deny or offer a casual I'm-resilient-as-shit-self-deprecating attitude.

'Literally everyone knows you. I'm dating a celebrity.'

Frankie grinned. 'I better get going,' she said, a little hesitantly. *Do I ask him to come in?* said a voice in her head.

'Yeah, me too. See ya, Frankston. See ya, Winnie,' Sunny said, kissing both of them on the head, not giving her a chance to invite him. *Does he even want to come up?*

'Bye, Sunny,' Frankie replied, grabbing her bag and her turtle and hopping out of the car.

Frankie stopped in her tracks when she saw her front door slightly ajar. She was sure she had locked it before leaving that afternoon.

'Hello?' she shouted into her home. No answer.

She safely tucked Winnie into his carrier, and slid her keys between her knuckles, her mother's 'stranger danger' lectures replaying clearly in her mind; 'Punch them in the face and tear their eyes out' had been the general gist. She took a deep breath and cautiously entered, hands held out in front of her.

'Hello?' she called again in her deepest, most intimidating voice. Loud sobs responded, coming from the direction of her bedroom. She crept slowly towards the noise.

'Who's there?' she whispered, as the whimpers grew louder. She slowly pushed her bedroom door open and found Cat lying flat-faced on her pillow, in the dark. 'Jesus, Cat. You scared me half to death. I thought I told you not to use my spare key unless it was an emergency,' Frankie said, moving to lie next to Cat.

'It ... was ... an ... emergency,' Cat said between sobs.

Frankie stretched out on the bed. 'What happened, Cat? Talk to me.' She patted Cat's back, spooning her from behind.

'I'm a terrible person. I slept with Jin Soo while pregnant with Claud's baby. I'm worse than Henry Crawford, worse than

Wickham, worse than all of them!' Cat was crying so violently it was difficult to understand her.

'You are not, Cat. You are *not*. You're a wonderful, amazing, incredibly kind-hearted human being who made one cruddy mistake.' Frankie stroked Cat's hair.

'Chocolate.' Cat sniffed.

'What?'

'Chocolate. I need chocolate!'

'Yes, yes, of course. I've got some in my bag.' Frankie rifled through her handbag but stopped when she touched Sunny's phone.

'What is it?' Cat curled over on her side, watching Frankie pull the phone out. 'Is that what I think it is?'

'Cat, no.'

'This will cheer me up. Hand it over,' Cat said, wiping her nose on her sleeve.

Reluctantly, Frankie passed the phone to Cat and sidled down next to her, so they were both looking at the screen. 'But only because you are emotionally distraught. It's probably locked anyway,' Frankie said, as Cat clicked open the phone to reveal a harsh glow.

And it was locked. But on Sunny's screensaver – the man with whom she had just spent the night practically naked – was a photo of him and a very beautiful woman.

Kissing.

—14—

Just another Tom, Dick and Harry

The adage may be true, that there are plenty more fish in the sea, but if my dating history is anything to go by, it's more canned sardines than Koi.

There are the dates that feel like attempting to read *Ulysses* in one sitting (all 732 pages).

There are those that are so terrifyingly awful, they make *The Shining* look like a trip to Disneyland.

Then you have those dates that are more *Fifty Shades of Grey* and less *The Princess Bride*.

And finally, there are the men you meet who are just so *A Tale of Two Cities*. You know you should be falling head over heels, but you just don't feel 'the spark'.

Tom is one such fellow. A tall, conventionally good-looking, well-read lawyer, he is everything your mother dreamed of and your ex would despise.

He opens the door for you. Stands up when you leave the table. Asks interesting questions, like, 'What was the first book you ever remember reading?' and listens with attention. Thinks being 'funemployed' means really loving your job. Laughs at your jokes and dishes out a decent pun every now and then. And he's read every single Oscar Wilde novel.

After discovering my copy of *We Are All Completely Beside Ourselves* (he stumbled across my details while casually flipping through it on his way to place it in lost property #saint #isthisguyforreal?), he felt compelled to read it to find out more about the 'nifty girl' behind the note.

'So why *WAACBO*?' (I'll be using this acronym from here on out, because ain't nobody got time for that.)

Wine was on its way and we were getting straight to business.

'It holds a special place in my heart. It took me right out of my reading slump of 2013.'

'I'm not surprised. Animals, family love, witty characters, Karen Joy Fowler. What more could you ask for?'

'You like Karen Joy Fowler?'

'Are you kidding me? *The Jane Austen Book Club* is my life.'

The conversation flowed steadily for another two hours after that. We chatted about everything from *Sarah Canary* to *Sister Noon*, to whether Emily Blunt was a good Prudie in the film adaption. It felt good to talk to someone who appreciated literature as much as I did. Whose eyes lit up at Jane Austen's name, who laughed at the mention of Gavroche and knew immediately the source of the idea about never really understanding a person until you've considered things from their point of view. I can't explain it, except that it was like I was a tourist in another land, and I had just found the first person who could speak my language.

As the date came to an end, we walked out of the restaurant and finished our bookish banter with novel recommendations. I suggested Orwell's *1984* (who hasn't read *1984*?!) and he told me I just must read *A Little Life* by Hanya Yanagihara (which was already on my to-read list). And then came that make-or-break part of all first dates: to kiss or not to kiss. Tom had obviously decided on the former, because as soon as

I said goodbye, he swooped in. Literally. He grabbed me by the cheeks, and planted his lips firmly on mine. I desperately wanted this to be a Scarlett O'Hara and Rhett Butler 'I want to make you faint' kind of kiss. I really did. But alas, my dating life is not a romantic novel, but more a ridiculous satire. That's why my smooch with Tom, perfectly lovely Tom, was absolutely, exceptionally average. Just what you want from a first kiss.

Until next time, my dears.

After all, tomorrow is another date.

Scarlett O' xx

Leave a comment (23)

No offence but ... > Rhett Butler really knew the power of kissing someone often and doing it well!

Stephen Prince > @Nooffencebut ... That's the first thing I've heard you say that's remotely thought-provoking.

No offence but ... > @StephenPrince You're a horrible man.

Stephen Prince > @Nooffencebut ... That might be so. But I know how to kiss ... often.

Miranda Brissa > I hear ya sister! Still waiting for that great date that gives me the Jamie Fraser shakes!

Cat in the Hat > I'll give you a more-than-average smooch, my sexy thing ;)

Cindy-Emma > What about those dates that make you want to Agatha Christie the shit out of somebody?

15

Big Little Lies by Liane Moriarty
South Morang train line from the city

'Yes, it's a turtle,' Frankie nonchalantly addressed the girl behind the box office, as she collected her tickets. 'He suffers from extreme separation anxiety,' she whispered, tucking a muted Winnie under her arm.

'Don't worry,' Cat piped up, 'he's on a leash.' She swung the hot-pink knotted cord around in the air.

Cat and Frankie walked through the crowded foyer of Yarrawood High School. Fresh from a Beyoncé dance class (which was forty-five minutes of Cat shouting, 'Where the hell is my wind machine?'), they had arrived just in time to watch Seb play Mr Sowerberry. Yarrawood was a rare find. Hidden within a suburban mecca for all things hip and cool, it espoused staunchly traditional values. There would no doubt be a strict observance of every syllable and key in this play. *Look out 1948* Oliver Twist, thought Frankie, *you're about to get an even drabber makeover.*

'What am I doing here again?' Cat elbowed Frankie.

'Training for motherhood.' Frankie and Cat squeezed through the row of plastic seats and settled down between a family of four, all of whom were hooked up to their respective devices, and a pair of gushing grandparents. 'Oh, and to prevent me from doing something stupid with Sunny's phone.'

'How long has it been now?'

'Twenty-two hours and fifty-three minutes. Not that I'm counting,' Frankie muttered as she flicked through a roughly stapled program.

'I say leave him like Fermina left Florentino. What nut doesn't check his phone at least every five-point-two-three minutes? If that doesn't scream sociopath, I don't know what does.'

'Maybe he's just really into mindfulness at the moment?'

'Tell that to the Buzzfeed article about the top five Eurovision fails he'll probably never see.'

'I don't want to hear from him now, anyway. I mean, there's a very good possibility I'm the ...' Frankie lowered her voice to a mutter. 'The *other woman*.'

'I don't know why you're not trying harder to crack his passcode. It's like he's the first man you've ever stalked! You're an absolute rookie, Rose.'

'He's probably not calling because he knows I've seen the photo of him smooching another woman.' *I knew he couldn't seriously be interested in someone like me.* Frankie mentally kicked herself for daring to believe otherwise.

'Well, he's been caught in his own filthy web of lies now!' Cat said too loudly for the quiet auditorium, which swarmed with children.

Frankie nudged Cat and whispered, 'What an idiot for leaving his phone with me. What an idiot I am for trusting him. He probably wanted me to find out, you know? Tell me I'm the woman on the side without actually saying it. What a coward.'

'What a creep.'

'What a tool.'

'What a Nick Dunne.'

'What a Hester Prynne.'

'What a Moby Dick.'

The auditorium lights began to dim. Whispers hushed and phones were switched to silent. The orchestra rumbled as a chorus of dishevelled orphans marched onto the stage. Metal spoons clanked against bowls as the students belted out (mostly in tune) 'Food Glorious Food'. Frankie felt Cat's shoulders heave up and down moments before she leaned over and whispered in Frankie's ear, 'You and Ron Weasley owe me. Big time.'

Twenty-five excruciatingly long minutes later, Seb, draped in a heavy black cloak, slunk onto the stage. Frankie shook Cat awake and let out a whoop.

'The prices allowed by the board are very small,' he said in a mean Cockney accent.

'So are the coffins,' said a tiny boy dressed as Mr Bumble, in a thick Indian accent.

'It just doesn't add up,' Cat whispered. 'First, he jumps you on the train. Then he takes you to a book-themed bar because you love reading. Next, he buys you a turtle. I mean it's no diamond ring, but just look at that thing!' Cat peered down at Winnie. 'So beautiful. So pathetic.' They both took a moment to gaze lovingly at the unmoving shell. 'Oh, oh, oh and not to mention the romantic Japanese extravaganza!'

'But was it *really* romantic? He took me to one of the few places in Melbourne I was guaranteed to be naked.' Frankie stroked Winnie, who was curled up tightly in his shell.

'Well, in that case, surely he'd be all "Please sir, may I have some more?"' Cat, ignoring awkward hushes masquerading as coughs, pressed on. 'Give me his phone. I need to look at the photo again.'

Frankie reached into her bag and pulled out Sunny's phone. As Cat squinted at the screen, there, glowing in the dark room, was Sunny pressed up against that gorgeous woman. It hit Frankie all over again. The body language, the longing in his eyes: this was no regular kiss.

Cat shook her head. 'Well, she's definitely not his sister.'

The phone started to vibrate, causing them both to jump in their seats.

'Who is it?' Frankie hissed, grabbing at the phone. Cat, too quick for her, pulled away. 'Do not answer that phone, Catherine.'

Before the Artful Dodger could *pick-a-pocket or two,* Cat whispered, 'Hello, Catherine Cooper speaking, how may I help you?'

Heads spun awkwardly towards Cat. 'Sorry,' Cat covered the phone, 'I better take this.' She stood and shuffled to her left, stepping on toes and bumping her bag and belly against backs of heads. Frankie shrugged at the spectators around her. *This is not going to end well.* She crossed her legs back and forth, clutching Winnie firmly as she tried to direct her attention towards the stage.

Five agonising minutes of ear-piercing 'Consider Yourself' later, Cat finally returned. She fussed through the seats and sat down casually next to Frankie, not saying a word. Frankie nudged her expectantly.

Without averting her eyes from the stage, she replied, 'We're meeting him after the show.'

'Meeting who?' Frankie tried to keep her voice low as her anxiety rose.

'The adulterer.'

'Sunny? After the show? Look at me! I'm a mess.' Frankie thrust her hands towards her face. Even in the darkness of the theatre she could feel the dried perspiration on her skin. *How the hell does Beyoncé stay so fresh?*

'Don't worry,' Cat said. 'I've got this.'

'For the love of God,' a man, two rows ahead, cried, 'this is a children's production!'

An hour and a half later, they stood between rows of shampoo and toothbrushes at a nearby chemist. Frankie was yammering on about what a terrible idea this was while Cat raided the shelves. She had already sprayed Frankie with deodorant, after unceremoniously shoving her hands up her top, and dabbed her lips with three different shades of lip gloss.

'Ha! Got it,' she announced, holding a small, white tube in front of Frankie.

'Haemorrhoid cream! You have got to be kidding me.' Frankie jerked back.

'If it's good enough for Sandra Bullock, it's good enough for Frankie Rose.' She popped the cap and inched towards Frankie. 'Show me those puffy eye bags of yours, Frankston.'

Cat put her credit card on the counter and Frankie tore open a packet of jelly beans. 'So, what's the plan, Cat?'

'Okay, he happens to be in the area for a work thing. So, the good news is, perhaps he does have a steady income after all.' Cat winked.

'Now's not the time, Cat.'

Cat waved her off. 'I've arranged a meeting outside The National Hotel.'

'And it's just a phone exchange? Nothing more?'

'Nothing more.' Cat collected her paper bag of cocoa butter, haemorrhoid cream and Colgate and ushered Frankie out the door. The night was balmy, but Frankie was feeling the chill.

'What do I even say to him? Is "Who's the hussy?" too direct?'

'I'd probably lead with something a little more neutral, like, "Pick me, choose me, love me!"'

'Okay, *Grey's Anatomy*, let's just get this over with.'

They parked around the corner from the pub. Cat handed Frankie Sunny's phone and then held her firmly by the shoulders. 'Remember, keep it simple: "Here's your phone back." Nothing more.'

'Here's your phone back,' Frankie echoed.

'And then get the hell out of there!'

'And you'll be waiting here?'

'And I'll be waiting here.'

Frankie closed the car door behind her and slowly walked to the top of the street, peppered with vintage terrace houses. At the corner she glanced back, to see Cat hold two thumbs up and mouth, 'Go get 'em, tiger.' Frankie patted down her white cotton tank top, threw her shoulders back and headed into the pub. She spotted him straightaway, standing with his back to her. He was wearing a burgundy shirt and suit pants. *Damn it*, she thought before she could help it, *he looks even better from the back*. Feigning confidence and mild indifference, she took long, exaggerated strides towards him. Pulling up inches away, she unceremoniously tapped him on the back.

'Hi there, Frankie.' Sunny turned around and pulled her into a hug. *No kiss? Hello friend zone!*

'Sunny.'

'You're such a doll for dropping off the phone. But I have to say, I almost didn't follow up. It's been pretty liberating being uncontactable.'

Frankie took a step back and, with an outstretched arm, held the phone before him. 'Here's your phone back,' she uttered tonelessly and began to make her exit.

'Thanks, Frank. So, how have you been?'

'My friend's waiting for me.'

'So, you're not going to tell me how you've been? Geez, you're a hard one to crack.' He laughed tensely. His brow furrowed and then his lips parted, as if he was about to say something and then decided against it.

'I should really get going. I think I heard Cat's waters break.' Without so much as a shake of his hand, she turned on her heel and raced back to safety.

🐢

Frankie found Cat waiting idly at the corner in her Mini Cooper.

'Quick! Get in!' Cat yelled through the open window. Frankie fell into the car as Cat slammed on the accelerator.

'What's going on? Oh my God, did your waters actually break?'

'What? Don't be ridiculous. It's her!'

'Who's her?'

'Her!'

'Her? *Her?*'

'Yes, *her*! The woman from Sunny's phone! She came from the other direction as you turned away.' She threw a left and they both flung to the side. 'Nice hair flick, by the way.'

Frankie ignored her. 'And you're sure it was her? It *is* pretty dark.'

'Well, she had the same build, same-coloured hair. And ...'

'And?'

'I feel it, Frankie,' Cat leaned towards Frankie, 'in my loins.'

'Jesus, Cat. That's not a thing!'

'Don't argue with my loins, Frankie. Last I heard, yours weren't creating life.' She parked in the next side street and turned to Frankie. 'Let's go!'

'Cat, no. We are *not* going back to the pub. I smell like haemorrhoid cream!'

'Do you really think I'm going to let that goddess of a woman who just sauntered in with your boyfriend get a whiff of your puffy eyes? *Please*, this isn't my first rodeo.' Cat unclipped her seatbelt and inelegantly got out of the car.

Frankie sighed and peeled herself out after her friend. She took a moment to peer through the back window to check that Winnie was safely tucked away in his makeshift waterbed-style carrier case, so she didn't notice Cat whipping out two black, knitted balaclavas from her handbag. She slipped one halfway over her Refuse To Be Tamed hair and tossed the other at Frankie.

'Follow me.'

'What? *Balaclavas?* Cat, it is terrifying how prepared you are for this moment.'

'Claud made them!'

They crept along the street, wearing the itchy balaclavas over their hot faces, until they reached a narrow, cobblestone alley and Cat wrenched Frankie to the side, pushing her up against the wall.

'Jesus, Cat, enough with the theatrics.' She rubbed her neck.

'Just follow my lead.' She pulled the balaclava all the way over her face. Frankie rolled her eyes and begrudgingly began to shadow Cat. They moved past a small garage and wound their way through a huddle of bins, breathing in leftovers and stale beer bottles. Cat intermittently turned around to wave on a slightly mortified Frankie or put her finger to her lips, until they found a small break in the fence they could squeeze through. They crouched down between bushes, their balaclavas now pushed up onto their foreheads to allow for full viewing.

'Look.' Cat pointed towards a small table inside the bar.

Frankie squinted through the leaves. The back beer garden was dotted with groups of people chatting and milling around tables. She furiously scanned the mini-skirts and manicured beards until she spotted Sunny. Perched on a step ladder, he was facing Frankie and Cat and the likely-glowing complexion of an auburn-haired woman.

'How did you—' Frankie grabbed Cat's hand.

'My loins.' Cat pointed gratifyingly at her crotch.

'All right, Miss Marple, now what?'

They waited. And waited. Sunny and the Screensaver ordered a round of drinks and sat there talking. Forever. Sunny looked on with a seriousness Frankie hadn't seen before. The woman, legs crossed, appeared to be doing most of the talking.

'This is a complete waste of time, Cat. Why did you bring me here?'

'Just be patient. It's not like you have anywhere better to be.'

The minutes creaked past. They remained silently hunched, shifting their weight between their feet. Sunny grew more animated, gesticulating enthusiastically. And then, all of a sudden his hand was on the woman's wrist. A casual intimacy that shot a furious shiver through Frankie's gut. There she was, camouflaged among branches and bottle tops staring at Sunny, a man she barely knew but couldn't seem to ignore, with his hand on another woman's arm. The same hand that had held

Frankie's lower back as they kissed amid ornamental aquarium driftwood and infrared lights. His warm, encompassing palm now grazed the same woman who called his phone's screensaver home. Sunny tilted his head to the side, as question upon question hit Frankie. *Who is this woman? What are you thinking at this very moment, Sunny? And why on earth do I care so much? It's barely been a month!*

'Okay, so my final summation,' Cat said quietly, twisting around on the balls of her feet, 'is that it's not looking good.'

'No shit, Sherlock!' Frankie pulled away from the fence and stood up, shaking her lifeless legs and rubbing her arms. 'I've had enough.'

Cat, this time taking Frankie's lead, followed her back to the car.

'Cheer up,' Cat said, reaching for Frankie and curling her arm protectively around her. 'He's not worth it! Don't you have another train date tomorrow?'

Frankie didn't respond. She couldn't think about the impending disappointment that almost certainly awaited her on her next date.

'Just take me home, Cat.'

'At least you still have the turtle.'

—16—

The boy who cried wolf, and then cried some more

Have you heard the saying *boys don't cry*? Well, it's complete and utter bullshit. Boys can cry. Oh boy, can they cry.

Let me start from the beginning.

Three days ago I received an email from a man named Michael. He had found my copy of Kazuo Ishiguro's *Never Let Me Go* at Burnley station, told me he enjoyed it and would love to discuss it over a glass of wine. After confirming he was a male (as you know, you never know), I shrugged my shoulders and agreed. After all, I had nothing to lose. Oh yes, that reminds me – I've officially ended things with Edward Cullen, my one-month lover. You see, it appeared that he was not only passionate about Young Adult literature, but he was also passionate about other women while dating me.

Anyway, I agreed to meet Michael at Jungle Boy in Windsor. Which brings me to my date last night.

When I walked into the moodily lit room, five minutes fashionably late, I saw a handsome man sitting at a two-seater bar table, with my tattered copy of *Never Let Me Go* sitting next to him.

'Michael?' I smiled at the brown-eyed, black-haired man, dressed in a brown woollen shirt with elbow patches.

'Frankie! You look as beautiful as I imagine Ruth to be,' he replied, as I took my seat.

A literary-themed compliment – we were off to a good start.

We talked about everything and everyone, from Virginia Woolf to Donald Trump – and we shared the same views on both (heroic and horrible, as if you even had to ask). So, things were going well; great, even.

Until I ordered an espresso martini.

'What did you just order?' he said, aghast.

'An espresso martini ...'

'Oh.' Michael looked crushed, as if I had just ordered the blood of twenty innocent children.

'What's wrong?' I asked, quizzically.

'It's just, that's what my ex, Diana, used to order. We've been separated for two years,' he divulged, sadly.

And that's when it all started to go south. Rapidly.

Not wanting to discuss the ex (a big first-date faux pas), I tried to divert the conversation away, to anything, really. But it all kept coming back to the same thing.

'Do you have any pets?'

'No, Diana didn't like animals.'

'It's awful, what's happening in Syria at the moment.'

'Diana didn't like to talk about politics.'

'The weather is amazing at the moment. It's been so sunny.'

'Diana loved good weather.'

Eventually, we got off the topic of Diana. (Who, by the way, sounds like the absolute worst. Hates animals and refuses to acknowledge current events – what's wrong with this woman?) We talked a little bit more about Ishiguro's other books (we had both read most of them), and the date was thankfully coming to an end. (I tried not to act too happy to part ways.) I took out my phone to check the train timetable, and all of a sudden I heard a gasp. I looked up at Michael, his eyes now suddenly bloodshot. *Oh no*, I thought. *He isn't, is he?* He was. His eyes were welling. They were actually welling. Yes, he was. He was about to burst into tears.

'What's wrong?' I tentatively asked.

'Your phone, it's the same as Diana's.' He sniffed. I have an iPhone.

I had to defuse the situation before it exploded. So, I did what I do when I don't want my fizzed-up Coke to erupt out of its bottle: I put my hand over it. I awkwardly placed my hand on his shoulder. How was I to know that this would be his spiralling point?

Michael wailed. And I mean really wailed. In a crowded, busy bar, this thirty-five-year-old man sobbed at the top of his lungs over his ex-wife, who left him two years ago, and who didn't even like dogs.

Now, what I did next was as close to gallant as I have ever come. While everyone in the bar was staring at me and the crying man sitting opposite, I got up from my seat, went around to his side of the table – and hugged him. A full-blown embrace. And he howled and sobbed and snorted for a very painful twenty minutes, into my favourite silk top.

When he finally pulled himself together, he apologised profusely. And of course, I said it was okay. After all, I know what it's like to have your life fall apart. And I was going to let it go, I really was. Until he looked up at me, this blubbering mess of a man who had just been crying into my chest like it was a pillow, and said, 'Hey, want to come back to mine?'

Until next time, my dears.

After all, tomorrow is another date.

Scarlett O' xx

Leave a comment (379)

Cat in the Hat > Ahhhhh! I'm almost crying as much (from laughter) as Michael was.

Stephen Prince > @Nooffencebut ... I'm surprised you haven't made some senseless 'this is sexist' comment yet.

No offence but ... > @StephenPrince ... What, did you miss me?

Stephen Prince > @Nooffencebut ... I missed your stupid comments, yes.

No offence but ... > @StephenPrince ... You're an idiot. By the way, Scarlett O', I was at Jungle Boy the other night, might've been there at the same time as you.

Stephen Prince > @Nooffencebut ... You go to Jungle Boy? I love it there. Maybe we'll go there together sometime ;)

No offence but ... > @StephenPrince ... In your wildest dreams.

Jumping Josh > Loved *Never Let Me Go*!

Lici Lou > Talk about never letting go! Literally laughing out loud. Thank you for being so real.

17

The Great Gatsby by F Scott Fitzgerald
Route 86 tram to Bundoora RMIT via Smith Street

The tram held but a few travellers, spread out along the carriage, each firmly guarding their personal space. Frankie and Cat sat in the second-last row, their eyes trained on the seat that now cradled a copy of *The Great Gatsby*, unlawfully taken from The Little Brunswick Street Bookshop discount bin. 'How this classic ever ended up in there is the real crime!' Cat had told Claud as she swiped it on her way out. Frankie's mind kept trailing back to her blog, and the momentum it had picked up in the few weeks she had been writing it. She'd been receiving ego-boosting emails about how funny and brazen she was and how people loved her writing style. It gave her hope that maybe, just maybe, writing another book was not off the cards for her, just yet. *Maybe this is my year*, she thought. *If I can just keep going with this blog*.

'Why couldn't Claud come? I don't know a thing about antenatal classes, but I'm guessing he might have a role to play?' Frankie asked.

'Oh, Claud wasn't interested in attending a class weeks before I'm meant to attend it. Plus, panting females in the downward dog position isn't really his scene.'

'That's surprising, I thought it would be exactly his scene,' Frankie countered, to which Cat responded with a swift but playful elbow to her side.

'Any word from Edward Cullen?' asked Cat, without averting her gaze from the as-yet-unnoticed book.

'Nope.'

'And you're sticking to the freeze-out?'

'What do you think?' Frankie momentarily diverted her attention from the waiting book. 'He's obviously already spoken for. And I refuse to be party to that.'

'You're hardly one to talk, Bridget Jones. You're still playing the field.'

'It's not the same,' Frankie bit back. 'One: my dating escapades are merely a half-arsed social experiment to give me something to write about. Two: need I remind you that you're the one who convinced me to go for it in the first place? And three: none of these people has made it to screensaver status!'

'Whatever you say, Anna Karenina.'

The tram jolted to a stop. A father and his toddler stumbled off and were quickly replaced by a tall, lanky man who looked to be in his late twenties. He wore beige chinos and a navy T-shirt, and he clasped a phone and a book, one on top of the other, in his hand. Frankie and Cat tried not to gasp, and squeezed each other's hands. In unison they leaned forward, straining to catch a glimpse of the cover. *The Art of Racing in the Rain.*

'He's the one,' Cat gushed.

'Come on, you dog-loving bookworm, go get that book,' Frankie quietly coaxed.

The man swiped his travel card, took a suspicious peek at the gawking women and sat down two rows in front of the book. They sighed. It was too good to be true. Moving with the rhythm of the tram, Frankie and Cat resumed their journey, staring at the waiting book.

'And what about Lord of the Cries? Any word from him or his therapist?'

'Yep, he sent through a long-winded apology an hour ago. Apparently sobbing wildly over his ex on the first date doesn't give credit to his "full personality",' Frankie air quoted.

'Just be sure to let him down easy. It doesn't sound like he can handle any more rejection.'

'Him and me both, Cat. Him and me both. Is it crazy that I would have been maybe willing to give him another go? If it wasn't for his crude proposition at the end, I mean. Am I getting desperate?'

'Yes,' Cat responded without missing a beat.

The tram slowed, coming to a stop next to a cluster of shops and cafes. Frankie rose from her seat, pulling Cat up with her. As they navigated past the cute guy stooped over his book, Cat nudged him with her toe, gave him a knowing look and nodded her head in the direction of their novel calling card. The man looked back dubiously as they stepped off into the welcoming heat and eased their way onto the footpath.

Google Maps led them around the corner to a red-brick, Victorian-style shop front adorned with a sign: *Yo Mama*. Upon opening the door they were confronted by a long, very narrow staircase.

'Is this some kind of joke?' Cat called out, hands on her burgeoning belly. 'Which skinny bitch decided on this layout?'

They squeezed up the stairs, passing photos of women cradling their swollen bellies and wrinkled, shrieking newborns. Frankie felt a deep longing in her gut that she didn't know existed and that, just like a surprise twist in a novel, shocked her. *Then again*, she thought as she followed Cat slowly to the top, *everyone else seems to be telling me to settle down, find a partner and start a family. Why not my body too?*

A very heavily pregnant woman and her partner brushed past, nudging Frankie and Cat down the long hallway as they followed the arrows to the class in silence. Frankie mentally prepped for the next hour. Before entering the class, Cat pulled Frankie in tight, whispering her thanks in her ear before she opened the door.

Frankie tentatively peered around the corner, bracing herself for what lay ahead, and her heart sank. *Ads.*

'He's here,' she hissed.

'Who?' Cat shouted back.

'Keep your voice down!' Frankie pointed her chin forward, beckoning Cat to look at the horrible sight she saw before her eyes.

There, surrounded by pregnant women and their doting partners, stood Ads and – *Oh dear God*, screamed Frankie in her mind – Ads' new girlfriend. Thanks to Frankie's casual online stalking, she knew Ads and Priya couldn't have been together much longer than a year. Frankie may have known that she existed on Facebook, but seeing her in the flesh – pregnant – brought goosebumps to her own skin.

Just then, Ads looked up and caught Frankie's eye. She tried to look away, but it was too late. He headed straight for her.

This is not happening. This is not happening, Frankie chanted in her head.

'Frankie,' Ads said as he reached her, 'it's good to see you. You know, I was just thinking about you the other day.' His girlfriend trailed behind him.

Frankie inhaled sharply, Cat took her hand and squeezed. A whirlwind of emotions swept over her, so much so that she could barely breathe, let alone talk. Cat nudged her.

'Ads, what are you doing here?' Frankie uttered, and then immediately realised how stupid she sounded. *Of course* she knew why he was here.

'Isn't it obvious?' The woman stepped out from behind Ads, looped one arm through his and pressed her hand to her neatly distended belly.

This is not happening. This is not happening.

'And you are?' Cat jutted in, knowing very well who she was.

'Priya, Adam's girlfriend.'

Frankie couldn't help but stare. Priya was a petite woman, *that* Frankie knew, but Facebook hadn't prepared her for Priya's dewy bronzed skin and luscious locks, which seemed to glow, even in the low-lit room. Frankie could hear the faint click of Ads' tongue, his not-so-subtle nervous twitch.

Priya stroked Ads' hand. 'Frankie, congratulations. You two make a fine pair.' She wiggled a bony finger from Cat to Frankie.

'Yes!' Cat tugged Frankie towards her, pinched her bum and kissed her cheek. 'We're just so excited to welcome our little angel into the world. And it only took one sperm donor to do the trick,' she gushed.

'Frankie,' Ads chimed, 'a parent? The same woman who couldn't keep a pot plant alive for more than a few days?' He laughed uneasily, clicking his tongue again.

'Oh no, I'm not, we're not,' Frankie stuttered.

Priya smirked and feelings of inadequacy washed over Frankie.

'What Frankie is trying to say—' Cat began before being interrupted by a stout woman prancing into the room.

'All right, mums and dads!' the woman began, ushering people into order, 'time to get those bellies breathing!'

Frankie looked gratefully at the instructor as the pack dispersed. Cat ushered her over to a spare yoga mat, a mere six people away from Ads – *Could this room be any more intimate?* – and gave her hand a final, reassuring squeeze before balancing her delighted self on the fit ball. Frankie crouched down next to her.

'Now, never underestimate the power of a good kegel routine, ladies,' the woman chanted from the front of the room. 'We need to keep that pelvic floor tight!'

Frankie exhaled deeply and trained her peripheral vision towards Ads. Priya was stretched out on her mat, nestled between Ads' open arms. Ads stroked her legs, and she giggled at something he whispered in her ear. Frankie breathed in. Here he was, the man who used to be her future, embracing his new future with someone else. She tried not to stare, but she couldn't draw her eyes away. *Since when did you even want a family?* The question lingered bitterly in her mouth.

'Love, embrace her buttocks like so.' The instructor was now kneeling deep between Cat's knees with her arms reaching around, clutching Cat's behind, demonstrating to the class what to do.

'Oh, I'm okay, thanks,' Frankie muttered awkwardly.

The instructor shrugged, stepped away and began to guide the class through a series of low-belly breathing techniques.

'Frankston, you're so *tense*,' Cat burbled as she stretched her left leg to the side. 'How can you expect my cervix to blossom when you're grinding your teeth so loud the next-door neighbours can hear you?'

'What am I supposed to do?' Frankie hissed. 'My day has been hijacked by the man who did a hit-and-run number on my heart! And did I mention he's managed to climb to the top of the corporate ladder and knock up some two-bit beauty in the same time that I've found three grey hairs and become Period Girl?'

'I'm sorry, Frank, do you want to go?' Cat asked.

'No, no. I'm okay,' Frankie said, biting her tongue.

Twenty minutes to go, she intoned silently. *Think of your best friend's unborn child. Ignore the happy family that your ex is creating.*

'Now,' the instructor called, 'you may find the "Swaying" or the "Slow Dance" position soothing during the early stages of labour. Mums and dads, allow your partner to place her arms around your shoulders. She should rest her head on your chest and sway gently back and forth.' Frankie helped Cat into a standing position and draped her arms around her back. Over Cat's head, Frankie watched Ads as he embraced Priya, his lips grazing her forehead. Frankie's pulse quickened. *Just get a dagger and stab me through the chest already!* In an attempt to avert her eyes, she abruptly swivelled Cat around, but her foot caught on the edge of the mat and she toppled to the floor, taking Cat with her.

'Frankie!' Cat exclaimed. 'Watch out for the pregnant woman!' All eyes turned towards them. Frankie could feel Priya's smirk itching up her back.

'Oh God, are you okay, Cat? I'm so sorry, I tripped,' Frankie fussed, helping her friend onto the ball.

'Frankie, I know they're getting under your skin.' Cat whispered with a nod in Ads' direction. They watched, mesmerised for a moment, as Ads and Priya laughed together quietly.

'You know what? I have had it up to here with this class!' Frankie could feel herself losing it. There was no going back now. 'I'm really sorry, Cat,' she said as she grabbed her bag from behind the fit ball and stormed out the door, hearing Priya and Ads snicker as she left. Frankie marched down the stairs and threw herself out the front door. She pulled her phone out of her back pocket and dialled her dad's number.

'Dad,' she yelled, when he answered on the third ring. 'Guess who I just saw at Cat's antenatal class? Ads, that's who.

With his girlfriend Priya who is none other than pregnant. PREGNANT!' Frankie paused to catch her breath and listened to her dad breathing into the earpiece. 'His new baby mama! Can you believe it?' Frankie dashed down the street, gesturing wildly. 'He told me he couldn't fathom having children for at least six years! And now he's knocked up some beautiful Daisy Buchanan! Cat didn't even ask me if I wanted to leave until it was too late. Oh, and did I mention that Sunny, the guy who I've been casually seeing, was cheating on me the whole time? That's right, Dad. He made me the other woman! It's all too much. I can't seem to get anything right these days.' Frankie slowed her pace. With her phone pressed to her ear, she navigated her way through the suddenly crowded footpath, winding her way between prams and couples holding hands. 'It'll be okay. It's just been a bad case of *A Series of Unfortunate Events*. Thanks for the chat. You always know how to make me feel better. I should go. Have a good afternoon, Dad. Oh,' Frankie added, 'please don't tell Mum about this.'

She hung up the phone, opened Twitter and started to scroll.

🐦 @Adamsegler: Enjoyed antenatal class with my new baby crew @priyavinay and @catinthehat (where's Frankie)?

18

From: Lachlan Rennard
To: Scarlett O'
Subject: I fancy a date

Hey there Scarlett,

Well, aren't you the creative one! I stumbled across your copy of *To Kill a Mockingbird* a couple of weeks ago. I haven't read it since secondary school and have been loving this trip down memory lane. It's always been a favourite of mine. I mean, 'It was times like these when I thought my father, who hated guns and had never been to any wars, was the bravest man who ever lived'. It doesn't get much better than that, does it?

Finding your note in the back, however, was the real icing on the cake. How did you come up with such a gallant idea? I'll tell you what, Tinder has some stiff competition!

I would love to take you out to discuss all things Scout Finch and Boo Radley. Have you been to the Night Noodle Markets? I hear the ramen is top notch.

Cheers,
Lachy

From: Scarlett O'
To: Lachlan Rennard
Subject: Re: I fancy a date

Hi Lachy,

Thanks so much for your email. I'm so glad you've been enjoying your journey through 1930s Alabama. Isn't Harper

Lee a genius? I've had *Go Set a Watchman* on my to-read pile for far too long now!

How did I come up with this idea, you ask? Well, I happen to work at a bookstore with my best friend, Cat. Working there is like being cocooned inside one big book. After a day of rearranging bookshelves, I leave work smelling like the pages of a paperback. It was actually Cat's idea to find some way to use books to find a boyfriend (or a new member for our sad little book club of two).

Did I mention Cat's expecting? In fact, I just accompanied her to her first ever antenatal class. The same antenatal class that my ex and his NEW and PREGNANT girlfriend attended. Oh, and just randomly, there was this other guy that I was dating, just BY THE WAY. I'm totally over him, but just thought I should let you know that HE CHEATED ON ME! Well, to clarify, I was the other woman. He had a girlfriend the whole time! The nerve. Am I right?

Look, I'm sorry for ranting. I'm not usually one to Harper on (get it?). Despite every attempt by my mother to encourage me to 'talk about my feelings' and tell me that 'a problem shared is a soul renewed', I prefer to hide my thoughts in a tiny box and lock it in the Fort Knox I call my heart. Sorry, it's just been one of those days. Oh, and I just downed an entire bottle of red.

But there's nothing like a bowl of miso to cheer a girl up. Next Thursday work for you?

Frankie (my real name) xxx

From: Lachlan Rennard
To: Scarlett O'
Subject: Re: Re: I fancy a date

Looks like you have a lot on your plate at the moment. Perhaps we should leave things for now.

Lachlan

From: Scarlett O'
To: Lachlan Rennard
Subject: Re: Re: Re: I fancy a date

Lachlan,

I have no idea what got into me the other day. I'm mortified by my totally inappropriate and unjustified over-share. And I definitely don't usually drink during the day (alone). I completely understand if you're no longer interested in meeting up.

But for the record, I really am totally over my ex.

Let me know if you change your mind.

All the best,

A deeply ashamed fellow bookworm x

—19—

Once a chreader, always a chreader

So, for those of you who don't know, I was recently cheated on. Well, sort of, anyway. I found out that the guy I was seeing was very much involved with someone else. I was, dare I say, inadvertently the Andie Hardy to his Amy Dunne. The Megan Hipwell to his Rachel Watson. In other words, I was the 'other woman'. So, I did what any proud woman would do. I went all *Gone Girl* on his arse and went back to being the *Girl on the Train*, searching for love wherever I could find it.

I've been contemplating a lot about how someone could cheat on another person. Trying to understand how you could do that to someone you like, sometimes even love. Which got me thinking. Is cheating on a person as easy as cheating on a book? Is someone who is capable of chreading (cheat reading), also capable of plain old cheating? If so, lock me up and throw away the key, because I'm guilty as charged!

You know those books that you really should love? Think the *My Brilliant Friend*s of the world. Everyone's talking about how good it is, and it has all the makings of a solid, long-term book relationship. It's rich, loving and generous-hearted, but for some reason it's just not doing it for you. You're looking for something more exciting. Perhaps with a little more romance, passion, risk (and maybe even a saucy sex scene or three). So, you decide to pick up *Something Borrowed*. It's nothing serious, just some lighthearted fun. You read the first chapter, relishing the excitement of it all. But you can't keep this up forever. You reluctantly put down the book and begrudgingly return to *My Brilliant Friend*. After a while, you find yourself reading both books simultaneously, a page here, a page there, trying to keep up with both plots. But a balancing act like that will never last. Eventually *Something Borrowed*, that happy-go-lucky fling, ends up sleeping beside you, dog-eared, on your bedside table. *My Brilliant Friend* is pushed aside, onto the floor, like the rejected, perfectly nice book that it is.

So, my question is … in my situation, am I the *Brilliant Friend* or the *Something Borrowed*?

Both seem pretty terrible to me.

Until next time, my dears.

After all, tomorrow is another date.

Scarlett O' xx

Leave a comment (905)

Emma Alicia > This is so on-point. I love your literature-to-real-life comparisons.

Sarah Josh > I didn't realise you were cheated on. Hope you're okay, hun xx

---

No offence but … > Not sure what you're getting at, but if you're condoning cheating, I might have to stop reading this blog.

> **Stephen Prince** > @Nooffencebut … Did you read this blog? She was the one being cheated on!! PS I would never cheat on you ;)
>
> ---
>
> **No offence but …** > @StephenPrince, you would never get the chance.

Wuthering Heights by Emily Brontë
Lilydale train line towards Flinders Street

💬 Frankie: Cat, where are you?

💬 Cat: One minute away, I promise.

💬 Frankie: Let's get this SIFUB show on the road!

Ever since Frankie 'accidentally' posted a very unflattering photo of Cat on Facebook when they were twenty (eyes half-open, shirt pulled up, poppy-seed-in-teeth unflattering), they had been holding SIFUBs, or Sorry I Fucked Up Brunches. When one of them did something out of line, they had to shout the other to the world's best brunch. Croissants, avocado toast, bircher muesli and, of course, mimosas. There was no holding back.

Frankie had been waiting at Great Eggspectations, their traditional SIFUB restaurant, for the last fifteen minutes. She had already apologised to Cat for abandoning her mid-labour relaxation technique and Cat had already forgiven her. But neither were ones to pass up an opportunity for an all-expenses-paid SIFUB. Frankie checked her watch again. *Where the hell is Cat?* She had been tardier than ever lately, running a perpetual twenty minutes behind schedule.

'Frankie, haven't seen you in a while. Who's the guilty party this time?' said Tommy, glancing at Frankie's peace offerings on the table. 'Doughnuts *and* Dickens. It must have been pretty bad.'

Tommy, who always smelled of warm lattes, owned Great Eggspectations. He had come to look forward to Frankie and Cat's infrequent visits, which always followed the same pattern. First, obscenities were thrown around, quickly followed by the two devouring an obscene amount of food, trailed by long embraces and 'I love you's'.

'Oh you know, just the usual abandon-your-pregnant-friend-at-her-first-antenatal-class,' Frankie confided.

'Ouch,' Tommy winced.

As if on cue, Cat, wearing a baby blue knitted dress with matching knitted earrings, came bustling into the restaurant shouting her apologies for being so late.

Cat slapped a kiss on Tommy's cheek before sitting down. 'The SIFUB usual please, oh gracious host!'

She grabbed greedily at one of Frankie's strawberry doughnuts and took a big bite. A blob of jam dropped, unnoticed, down the front of her knitted dress. Frankie smiled and dabbed it with her napkin.

'So, what's news, Frankston? Anyone else found another book?' Cat asked, devouring the rest of her doughnut in two swift bites.

'I received an email yesterday from some guy. But I scared him away with my insane rambling.' Frankie sighed.

'That's my girl.'

Tommy ambled back over, balancing a large tray piled high with plates and glasses. He placed each item majestically on the table as Frankie and Cat cheered in delight. He then collected his regular tip, a Nutella doughnut, and sauntered back to his post at the front of the cafe.

'I dropped *Wuthering Heights* this morning, but, to be honest, I'm not in the mood to go on any more dates. Even for the sake of the experiment. I'm just sick of this nonsense with Sunny. I know I should be over it, and I am, I really am. But I'm just so damn mad at him for playing me around like that. I feel like such an idiot.' Frankie bit into a piece of toast, smeared generously with blackberry jam.

'So, tell him! I don't know why you're still ignoring his calls. Next time that loser rings, answer and give him a piece of your mind!' Cat said through mouthfuls of muesli.

'I'm taking the high road, Cat.'

'The high road is the one most travelled. And do you know what that means? It's bloody boring.' Cat poured more honey over her yoghurt. 'If you're not going to tell him off, at least do something to give yourself closure,' she added, sucking on the spoon of honey with raised eyebrows.

'What do you mean?' Frankie asked, shifting uneasily in her seat.

'You know, a dose of good old-fashioned revenge.'

'Cat, this isn't high school. I'm not going to concoct another revenge plan with you.'

'Why not? He deserves it! He made you the *other woman*, Frank. Plus, remember how good it felt when we dyed Richie Lucas's hair blue?' Cat sneered, grabbing at the warm croissants.

'Yeah, yeah. I remember. Okay, what sort of revenge are we talking? Nothing too damaging. Just something a little cheeky.'

'I like cheeky. I can work with cheeky.' Cat smiled. 'What about a Facebook hack? Or some form of skywriting?'

'Too big. Way too big. Maybe we can leave him a voicemail pretending his phone bill is overdue?' Frankie offered meekly.

Cat scowled. 'Frankie, that's literally the worst idea I've ever heard.' But then a smile crept over her face. 'Claud once signed me up to a *Fifty Shades of Grey* subscription for a year as a joke,' Cat said.

'What does a *Fifty Shades of Grey* subscription even come with?' Frankie laughed.

'Signed copies of the book, handcuffs and a lot of leather. I actually quite enjoyed it in the end. Well, except for the suspenders Claud knitted for me. They were itchy.' Cat winced. Frankie laughed. 'Okay, so what does Sunny hate?' Cat nudged.

'Racism? Arrogant people? Caged turtles?'

'Boring! Anything else?'

Frankie took a bite of her banana pancake, thinking. Then she looked up at Cat with a smile.

'You want how many bananas?' Trixie, the fruiterer, asked.

'Two hundred, please,' Cat repeated.

'Okay, then. What are you doing? Making the world's biggest banana cake?' Trixie laughed.

'Something like that.'

Frankie sat on a crate in the fruit store, nervously scrolling through her Instagram feed. Flushed pomegranates, luscious broccoli heads and auburn pumpkins surrounded her, and the sweet smell of syrupy grapes and tart oranges filled the room.

'You're lucky I got a big delivery in today. I usually don't stock that many bananas unless it's a special order,' Trixie said as she began to pile large handfuls of bananas from the shelves into a trolley.

'Trix, you're a legend!' Cat slapped her on the back.

'No problem, love. Do you have far to walk? That's a heavy amount of bananas,' Trixie asked.

'Nah, not at all. It's actually just around the corner.' Cat smiled.

'So, that comes to a hundred and forty dollars,' Trixie said, pressing numbers on a calculator.

'Cat, it's really expensive.' Frankie came to stand next to the bursting trolley. 'I'm beginning to have second thoughts.'

'It's worth it.' Cat whipped out her credit card. 'And it's on me.'

Cat swayed her hips as she walked down a bustling Lygon Street, pushing the trolley filled to the brim with two hundred bananas. She had been singing, out of key, Gwen Stefani's 'Hollaback Girl'. Only, she failed to recall anything other than the B-A-N-A-N-A-S part.

'Cat!' Frankie blurted, walking beside her trolley-wheeling friend. 'You are driving me bananas. Enough with the singing!'

Cat ignored her and began to sing louder.

'Okay, stop! There's his car.' Frankie pointed to the bright red Honda Civic parked just off Lygon Street.

'Ha, cute number plate.'

'That's his name,' Frankie said.

'His name is Sunny Day?'

'Yes.'

Cat stopped alongside the car and turned to look at Frankie. 'His surname is Day and his parents named him Sunny?'

'Yes.'

'That's almost as ridiculous as naming your child after a train line, Frankston. Maybe you two *are* destined to be together?'

Frankie rolled her eyes.

'Okay, so what's your plan?' Cat asked.

This was typical of Cat, throwing them face-first into drama and leaving the finale up to Frankie. Frankie assessed the situation, caressing her chin thoughtfully for effect. 'His sunroof's broken, so we could climb in through that.'

'Excuse me? Your skinny arse might fit in there, but there's no way I'm getting all this down that tiny hole,' Cat said, pointing to her hips.

Frankie rolled her eyes and kicked off her shoes. She attempted to jump up onto the car and failed to get her footing, sliding immediately down the side. 'It's too slippery. Give me a boost.'

Cat balanced the trolley against the car, then wrapped her arms around Frankie's waist and pressed her against the warm car. On the count of three, Cat lifted as Frankie leapt. She landed, clumsily, on the top of the car with a loud thud.

'We did it!' Frankie exclaimed, already out of breath. She curled her legs up beneath her and clawed her fingers underneath the sunroof. She jiggled the roof, creaking it half-open. 'Damn it. It won't open all the way.'

'Just shimmy in, Beyoncé style! You need to make sure you get the bananas in every little crevice,' Cat instructed from the road.

Frankie took a deep breath and slid herself, feet-first, into the small hole as far as she could go. She sucked in her stomach and wiggled her body in a vain attempt to manoeuvre further in, but … she was stuck.

'This is hopeless,' she croaked.

'Come out and try again.'

'I can't. I can't move up and I can't move down. I'm stuck,' Frankie said, squirming frantically. Her feet were erect on the leather seats, her arms pressed awkwardly outside.

'Okay, put your hands up and I'll lift you out,' Cat said.

'No, no. There's no time. Sunny could come out at any minute. Just hand me the bananas and I'll throw them in. Let's just get this over with!' Frankie could feel panic rising as the sides of the sunroof pressed painfully against her hip bones. She anxiously looked around and then grabbed a handful of bananas from Cat's outstretched arm. She dropped them carefully into the car, so that they fell softly on the seat. As each banana landed, it seemed to say, 'Take that' 'You cheating' 'Scoundrel of a' 'Human' 'Being'. Passing pedestrians stared on at the scene unfolding in this quiet, residential street. *We must look like crazed lunatics,* Frankie thought, suddenly feeling deeply embarrassed.

'This is like some ridiculous scene out of *The Secret Seven,*' Frankie grunted uncomfortably, as she shovelled bananas into Sunny's car.

'I know, isn't it great?' Cat chirped.

'How many do you think we've put in now?' Frankie asked, squeezing another banana into the car.

Cat peered inside the trolley of bananas, shuffling them around with her hands. 'About half. So, only a hundred more to go!'

Frankie looked around nervously. People were staring at her; well, at the half of her poking out of a Honda Civic like a drunk teen at prom.

'Frankie,' Cat said, suddenly dancing on the spot.

'Yeah?'

'My bladder.'

'What?'

'I need to pee. Now.'

'Hold it, Cat! Let's just finish off the bananas and then we're out of here,' Frankie called down.

'Frankie. I'm pregnant. If I don't find a toilet in the next two minutes, there will be urine dripping down my legs. And trust me, you do not want that,' Cat said. 'I'll be two minutes. I'll just run back to Trixie's.' Cat was now jumping up and down, holding her crotch.

Frankie stared in mortified disbelief as Cat raced around the corner, her curly hair bouncing up and down. Without Cat's protective presence, Frankie felt all the more vulnerable. And stupid. *Who do I think I am? The Count of Monte Cristo, returning to enact an elaborate plot of retribution? I have got to stop letting Cat talk me into these things!*

'Are you all right there?' asked a freckled man on a bicycle who had pulled up beside the car and was looking at her curiously.

'Fine, fine. Just enjoying some fresh air.' Frankie acted out an exaggerated yawn, stretching her arms out wide as she nervously kicked bananas with her feet.

'Okay, enjoy!' The man cycled off.

Cat, where are you? She desperately tried to dislodge herself again, shimmying left and then right, but to no avail. She jiggled up and down, hoping the friction of her body against the car would set her loose.

'Frankie?'

Frankie jumped at the sound of a familiar voice and then slowly peered over the side of the car.

'Uh, hi Sunny.'

—21—

The Secret History by Donna Tartt
Frankston train line towards the city

One hand on his hip and the other shielding his eyes from the glare of the sun, Sunny peered up at a stranded Frankie. In a vain attempt to disguise the madness unfolding around her, she crossed her arms in front of her torso. But there was no hiding this predicament.

'What's going on here, Frankie?'

Where the hell are you, Cat? 'Uh, I can explain.'

'I can't wait to hear it. Want to come down and tell me?'

'I'd love to.' Frankie didn't move.

'You're stuck, aren't you?'

'Yep.' Frankie dropped her arms and hung her head.

Sunny clambered up onto the car and positioned himself opposite Frankie. Placing both hands under her arms, he helped her twist and turn her body. Together they managed to unwedge her hips so she could put one of her feet on top of the passenger seat and push her way up while Sunny gently guided her out. She flopped onto the roof of the car, butt pointing sky-high for a moment before commando crawling forward until she was lying as flat as a pancake on the bonnet.

Sunny peeked down through the half-open sunroof. He gave a long grimace, a shake of the head and propelled himself off the car.

'What the hell, Frankie!' he yelled as Frankie slowly sat up, then lowered herself to the ground. 'Bananas? I'll never get the smell out! I may as well sell the piece of junk now!'

Safely back on the ground, Frankie tried to regain her composure, her mind racing. *What's that thing Cat does? Power posing!* She stood akimbo, clumsily thrusting her hands on her hips.

'Sunny, you've been served.'

'Served? What's this all about?' Sunny was clearly running out of patience. 'I don't hear from you in weeks and all of a sudden I arrive home to find you wedged in the roof of my car!'

'Don't pretend you don't know exactly what's going on,' Frankie retorted, tapping her foot for good measure.

'Believe it or not, I'm going to need you to shed some light on the situation, Frankie.'

'Have a look at the screensaver on your phone and tell me again you have no idea what's going on here.'

Sunny squeezed his temples with his forefinger and thumb. Frankie looked on, eyebrows raised in a challenge.

'Frankie, I can explain.'

'Oh, I'm sure you can,' Frankie said. 'I bet you've woven this story a hundred times over!'

'It's really not what it looks like.'

'It's exactly what it looks like. Just how many women do you have dangling for your amusement? Two? Three? Five?' Frankie bent down to pick up her bag and slipped on her sandals. She swivelled around and called over her shoulder, 'Good luck with the bananas,' and marched down the street.

'Frankie.' Sunny jogged up behind her, grabbing her shoulder and spinning her around so that they were face to face. 'I'm telling you, you've got it all wrong!' He looked into her eyes with an earnestness that not even Frankie could ignore. She exhaled loudly and brushed Sunny's hand off her shoulder.

'You have one minute,' she said, waggling her index finger.

They took a seat on the kerb next to Sunny's car. With her arms laced around her knees, Frankie looked out to the road. She channelled her best chilled apathetic vibe, sitting at a safe distance and keeping her eyes averted. She leaned casually to the side, as if to say, *This better be good, but I don't really care about what you say either way because I'm supercool and laid back.*

Sunny shifted uncomfortably, and eventually spoke. 'The woman in the picture was my girlfriend.'

'Was? Oh, so you've broken up? Then why were you with her the other night? I saw you two together at The National.'

He froze, his jaw tightening. 'That's impossible.'

'Oh yeah?' Frankie was not backing down. 'Then who was she? And don't you dare say a long-lost relative. I saw the way you were looking at her.'

Sunny shook his head. She could see his frustration – or was it guilt? Hurt? – building. 'She was a colleague. We were meeting about a big potential project. Not that I should have to justify myself to you.'

'Oh, that's rich.'

'Look, Frankie, I didn't want you to find out like this,' Sunny started, 'but, well, you're right. The girl in the picture, we never broke up.'

'Gotcha! You sneaky bastard! I knew it!' Frankie shot up, glaring down at Sunny. 'I'm outta here, Sunny. No need to say another word.' She thrust her bag over her shoulder and stormed along the footpath. She was going to find Cat and kill her. *It was her damn banana plot that led to this fateful run-in. And where the hell has she got to anyway? And fuck the supercool chick routine!*

'We never broke up because she died!' Sunny yelled after Frankie. She froze, not daring to turn around. *Well, I didn't see that one coming.*

'She passed away a few years ago. I know I should change the photo, but I can't bring myself to.'

Frankie took a long, deep breath and then turned to see Sunny standing with one foot resting on the footpath and the other on the road, head lowered, hands hanging limply by his side. His face was ashen. It was what she imagined Henry de Tamble would have looked like the first time he realised he would never see Clare Abshire again.

'Jesus, Sunny ...' Frankie shuffled, tail between her legs, towards Sunny, placing her bag, along with her ego, back on the ground next to him. 'I'm so sorry.' She rested her hand on his arm, squeezing lightly.

They sat back on the edge of the worn nature strip, and it was now Frankie who shifted nervously. Another woman, she was prepared to deal with. This, however, was not quite as clear cut. The weight of the woman's huge ghostly shoes bore down on her.

'I know. It's high time I moved on, right?' Sunny broke the silence. 'It's been five years. *Five years.* But in today's world, changing the picture just seems so final. You know?'

'Oh, I totally get it,' Frankie said, but she felt overwrought. She came here prepared to castrate him, not console him, and she couldn't stop her next words from falling out of her mouth. 'My family had a cat. Terribly gluttonous thing. He literally ate himself to death. I didn't change my Facebook profile photo for over six months.'

'Oh yeah, that's totally the same thing,' Sunny said, montone.

Frankie cleared her throat a little too loudly, looked to the ground and then dared to probe. 'What was the story with you two?'

'We were together for about eighteen months before she died.' Sunny stopped. 'We were in love. And then she was gone. In an instant. It's just not the sort of thing you expect to have to deal with in your twenties. Or ever. You can't prepare yourself for that kind of grief.'

'I know I said I get it because of the whole cat thing, but I really don't get it. I can't even begin to fathom that kind of loss.' Frankie itched with nerves. Her body ached for him, and a little for herself as well. She felt hot with her confusion, and her regret.

Sunny smiled, placing his hand on her thigh. 'Those were some dark days, Rose. Some really dark days. She'd be disgusted to know that I'm still pining after her. She was always one to grab life by the horns.' He looked over Frankie's shoulder, peering into the car. 'What the hell were you thinking with the bananas?'

'Revenge plot gone wrong?' Frankie shrugged, feigning innocence. 'Look, if I'd known the truth, I would have gone a little easier on the rotten ones.'

'You're one of a kind, Frankston Rose.'

They sat in silence on the grass, staring out across the road, watching a handful of cars putter past and dogs mark their territory during their afternoon walks. Their shoulders barely grazed one another.

'You know what?' Sunny took out his phone. 'If you can update that Facebook photo of your cat—'

'William Shakespaw.'

'If you can update William Shakespaw's photo,' he repeated, switching on his phone, 'so can I.' And he stretched his arm out, angling the phone towards them.

'That's really not necessary,' Frankie said, trying to push the phone away, but Sunny resisted, snuggling in closer.

He put his arm around Frankie's rigid frame. 'To new beginnings. Say, "William Shakespaw!"'

🐢

Frankie burst through the front door of The Little Brunswick Street Bookshop. She found Cat standing in front of their new The Book Was Better stand, copies of *The Time Traveller's Wife*, *One Day* and *My Sister's Keeper* in one hand, her phone in the other. Seb stood in front of her, silently stacking books into a precariously positioned pyramid.

'Well, it's even worse than we thought,' Frankie announced.

'What do you mean?' Cat asked, eyes not diverting from her phone.

'Who on earth are you messaging?' Frankie leaned over to look at Cat's phone screen.

'I'm making a "Hot Men Who Knit" Instagram page. Featuring Claud, Claud and more Claud.' Cat faced her screen towards Frankie, revealing the new Instagram page flooded with pictures of Claud knitting at work, knitting by the fire, knitting on the bus, knitting in the kitchen (bare chested).

'Claud is going to love that.' Seb rolled his eyes. 'So, Miss Rose, where were you for the better half of the morning?'

Frankie paused and craned her neck to check for any life within the folds of the bookshelves. *No sign of customers.*

'Cat,' she eventually whispered, 'she's dead.'

'Who's dead?' Cat replied without making eye contact.

'The Screensaver.'

'What?!' Cat and Seb screeched. 'When? How? Oh my God, this is *terrible*.' Cat finally dropped her phone and turned to face Frankie.

Frankie shuffled a pile of invoicing receipts left discarded on the counter, still processing the afternoon's giant bomb detonated by Sunny. There was still so much more she wanted to know. *Needed* to know.

'She died five years ago. He said he's trying to move on. He even changed his screensaver today – replaced it with a photo of the two of us. How's that for your modern-day romantic gesture?'

'Did he say how she died?' asked Seb.

'Nope, he said he wasn't ready to go into the details.' Frankie sighed. 'He still seems so torn up about it.'

'Well, that's understandable.' Cat nodded. 'And just to be clear, you don't suspect that he *murdered* her?' Cat narrowed her eyes. 'Does he exhibit any anti-social behaviour? Any voyeuristic tendencies? A fixation with fire?'

'Cat, he's not a serial killer. You really need to let the sociopath thing go.'

'And what about the woman from the pub? His accomplice, perhaps?'

'Ha! A colleague, apparently.'

Frankie picked up a packet of glittery bunting from the floor and began nervously hanging it on the Blind Date with a Book display. This was some nightmare of a plot twist. 'Oh God. What the hell am I going to do?'

'This doesn't have to be the end of the world. Okay, she's dead. And yes, five years later she's still his screensaver. But at least you know they can't get back together.'

'But don't you get it?' Frankie turned to face Cat. 'All the bad stuff is automatically deleted when you die. I'll always come up second best. Striving to live up to the perfect dead woman!'

'Tell that to Bateman.'

'Seb, please don't bring Patrick into this.' Frankie started to pace in tiny circles. 'He couldn't even bring himself to delete her from his phone. How do you expect him to delete her from his life? Not that I would expect him to. I just can't live up to it. I'll never be able to top her.'

'You can top anyone, Frank,' Seb offered kindly, but unhelpfully.

'So, what are you going to do?' Cat interjected.

'I have no idea. Pay for his car to be cleaned?' Frankie stopped and raised an eyebrow at Cat. 'Thanks for that, by the way. Abandoning me mid-banana rampage. That's the last time I let you talk me into one of your harebrained plans!'

'Ah, you're welcome, Frankie. Car filled with hundreds of bananas? It's freakin' brilliant.'

'Why didn't you come back? Where the hell did you go?' Frankie asked.

'The bathroom at the grocer's was clogged, so I had to walk all the way to Seven Seeds. By the time I got back, you were already talking to him. It looked intense, and, you know me, I hate to meddle.'

They passed the afternoon like all good bookstore retailers: trading recommendations with customers and, where possible, stealing away to read – for consumer research, of course. But Frankie couldn't help letting her mind wander through the events of the morning. A dead girlfriend. A partner in mourning. A photographic gesture. Where did she stand with this onion of a man? Restless, she picked up her phone and started to tap away furiously.

'What are you doing?' Cat called from across the store where she was reorganising the travel books.

'I'm trying to find some answers.'

'Answers to what? Don't tell me you're on WebMD again. I've told you, that extra fold of skin is totally normal.'

'I'm not googling my symptoms, Miss It-Must-Be-Cancer, Please Play "Another One Bites the Dust" At My Funeral,' Frankie said dismissively. 'I'm trying to find information about Sunny's girlfriend.'

'Do you even know her name?'

'Not yet,' Frankie muttered as she scrolled through Sunny's Facebook feed (thank God Cat had talked her into requesting his friendship after their first date), looking for posts about his deceased lover. 'Aha! Hazel D.'

'Jeez, you work quick.' Cat joined Frankie, craning over her shoulder. 'But no listed surname? This could be tricky.'

The front door swung open and, right on time, The Little Brunswick Street Bookshop's most punctual customer walked in. Even when she was smiling, Mad Matilda always looked angry, and she would stomp into the bookstore every afternoon at 3.30, like clockwork. Cat murmured a greeting over her shoulder and then watched as Frankie weaved her way through the labyrinth of the internet, scrolling through obituary and coroner archives, looking furiously for any mention of a twenty-something with the corresponding first name or initials.

Hazel D death notice
Nothing!

Hazel D dies unexpectedly
Nothing!

Hazel D, Sunny Day's girlfriend, dies
Nothing!

Forty-five minutes later, she still had nothing.

'I give up!' Frankie slammed down her phone, ignoring the sceptical stares from a customer slinking through the children's section. 'It's like she never even existed.'

Then Frankie was recoiling in horror. 'Oh, shit!' She threw her phone across the table.

'What is it?' Cat said, startled.

'He's calling!'

'Who? Sunny? Answer it!'

'I can't. I'm not ready to speak to him. It's all too heavy!'

'Jesus, Frank, you're being ridiculous.' Cat scooped up the vibrating phone and answered cordially, exchanging some pleasantries before passing the phone to an unimpressed Frankie.

'What's up, Sunny?' she said, totally, one-hundred-per-cent supercool laid-back chick again. Cat looked on in suspense, subconsciously nodding along with Frankie's 'uh-huhs' and 'mmm hmms'. After a few minutes, Frankie put the phone down and bent to collect the pre-order logbook from under the desk. She began to casually search for the latest entry.

'So?' Cat breathed.

'Oh, sorry,' Frankie said nonchalantly. 'I'm seeing him tomorrow night.'

'Tomorrow night?'

'Yep.' Frankie casually cross-checked deliveries. 'He said he would cook for me. He asked if frozen banana cake would do.'

'Frozen? What does that mean?'

'He said, and I quote: "Revenge is a dish best served cold."'

Not the Hemingway to my heart

Sir Thomas Beecham reputedly once said, 'Try everything once except folk dancing and incest.' Well, Sir Tommy, let me preface this by saying: I'm so, so sorry.

I'll start from the beginning. A few weeks ago I left my much-loved copy of Jeffrey Eugenides' *Middlesex* on the Hoddle Street bus. A flock of giggling schoolgirls skipped onto the bus as soon as I stepped off, and I assumed (to my horror) that one of them would take my adored novel. But to my surprise, a couple of days ago I received a delightful email from a man named Ernest. He had found my book, loved it and wanted to meet for a date. Well, how could I say no to that? Especially with his Nobel-Prize-winning name. It was fate. Or so I thought.

Before I go on, here's a quick side note on the Edward Cullen situation. It turns out he's less of a cheating Tom Buchanan than I previously feared, and more of a grieving Captain Norval Chase. You see, he lost the love of his life. And by lost, I don't mean left behind in the supermarket to later pick up from the lost and found, like I did with my copy of *Lady Susan* yesterday. I mean bereavement, fatality, demise, passing, death. As you can tell, I am totally sympathetic as well as incredibly overwhelmed by this scenario. I thought about cancelling my date with Ernest on account of all the feelings, but:

1. A girl's got to eat.
2. It turns out I'm starting to feel like myself again. Like I have purpose, meaning to my existence, because, as much as I love to read, I love, *need*, to write even more and this blog is helping stitch me back together.
3. Could I really turn down an opportunity to discuss the brilliant work of Jeffrey Eugenides?

Hence, I decided to keep my date with Ernest.

But the date was, to be frank, a slow *Death in the Afternoon*. He informed me that he regularly attends Israeli folk-dancing classes in Elsternwick, and invited me to come along. After much convincing by my best friend (who is a strong advocate for all forms of exercise, dance and dating), I decided to reply, *Why the hell not*? I trained into Elsternwick, dropped a few books on the Sandringham line on the way, and then found Ernest standing outside an old warehouse, as promised. He was carrying my scruffy book in one hand, and a neon orange water bottle in the other. As always, my first question was, 'So what did you think of *Middlesex*?' To which he replied, 'Genius. Pure genius.' We were off to a good start.

The Israeli folk-dancing class was entertaining, to say the least. Loud Middle Eastern music pounded from speakers high on the walls, deep into my veins. The room was about ten degrees hotter than it was outside, leaving everyone covered in a thick layer of sweat. We danced in circles, learned steps such as The Grapevine, The Cherkassia and The Yemenite and shouted 'Yalla!' 'Oi!' and 'Hey!' after every few steps. Ernest told me I was a natural, and to be honest, I really was.

But don't get too attached. The trouble started when we began partner dancing. Ernest grabbed my clammy hand in his and pressed me close to his sticky body. We began to shout over the music, talking about everything from Calliope Stephanides to the intricacies of gender to our shared passion for all things Pulitzer Prize-winning. He told me about his over-bearing mother and I offloaded about mine.

That's when things started to get a bit dicey.

'My mother's third cousin also changed her name after a life-changing experience at a Balinese ashram,' he said.

'Oh really?' I urged him to continue.

After a while he butted in again. 'My mother's third cousin also conceived her child on a train carriage.'

'My mother's third cousin has the same name as your mother.'

'Let's see that photo again? My mother's third cousin looks identical to your mother.'

You see where this is going? Turns out I was on a folk-dancing date with my third cousin, once removed.

Well, when Jeffrey Eugenides supposedly said, 'No matter how long you've been at it, you always start from scratch', I can only assume he was talking about my love life.

Until next time, my dears.

After all, tomorrow is another date.

Scarlett O' xx

Leave a comment (121)

Cat in the Hat > LOL. That Sir Thomas Beecham is one fine fellow.

Jane Ostentatious > My colleague told me to read your blog and they do not disappoint. This is HILARIOUS! Ah, to be tragically single in Melbourne.

No offence but ... > This strikes me as pretty racist. Was it necessary to mention the ethnicity of the folk-dancing?

Stephen Prince > @Nooffencebut ... Another classic/ridiculous comment from your PC-self.

No offence but ... > @StephenPrince, another grating comment from your annoying self.

Stephen Prince > @Nooffencebut ... Let's go for a drink at Two Wrongs and grind each other's gears?

No offence but ... > @StephenPrince IN YOUR DREAMS

Harry Potter-Fiend > A thousand LOLs. This should be a book.

—23—

Frankie stood before Sunny's door and took a deep breath. It calmed her a little but she still couldn't help but play anxiously with the bottle of pinot in her hands, flicking the corner of its label back and forth between her index finger and thumb. She fixed her low-cut black top and pulled up her jeans. Despite Sunny telling her it was completely unnecessary, she had spent the day on her hands and knees scrubbing his car, and after three showers she still reeked of bananas.

She sighed at the memory of that look in Sunny's eyes when he told her about Hazel D. She had never seen such pure loss. It was what she imagined Dexter Mayhew felt when Emma Morley died. *Okay, you can do this,* she thought. *You—*

'I thought I heard creepy breathing outside my door!' Sunny's door flew open, and Frankie jumped back in surprise.

'Ah, sorry. I was just about to knock. This is for you,' she said quickly, thrusting the wine bottle into Sunny's hands.

'Pinot, my favourite. Come on in.' Sunny placed his hand casually at the bottom of Frankie's back and gently ushered her inside.

The strong smell of melted cheese and freshly baked dough filled Frankie's insides. Sunny's apartment was painted a vivid blue, and the dining table was scattered with large sheets of butcher's paper covered in scrawled sketches.

'Wow,' Frankie said.

'I told you I was messy.' Sunny shrugged.

Frankie was drawn to one particularly colourful drawing, a beautiful yet confronting image of a hand holding a bleeding heart in front of a pine tree adorned with fairy lights and colourful lanterns, over which was written *ONCE UPON A TIME, A MAN GAVE HIS HEART FOR CHRISTMAS* in big black letters. She touched the rough butcher's paper and looked at the illustration casually draped next to it. *KIDNEY-CROSSED LOVERS*, it read, on top of a beautiful image of what looked like an intertwined Romeo and Juliet, one single, bleeding kidney uniting them in an embrace.

'What are these? They're amazing,' Frankie said, unable to tear her eyes away.

'Oh, just something I've been working on. Don't judge too quickly, they're very much a work in progress,' Sunny said dismissively.

'Did you draw them? They're beautiful!'

'Yeah. I just whipped them up. They're at the conception phase now.'

Frankie glanced over at Sunny, who was pottering about his poky kitchen. His shoulders were rigid and he seemed, if not nervous, exposed.

'They're brilliant. I didn't know you could draw,' Frankie said.

'I was an Art Director at AKDB until last year, when I quit to do my own thing.'

'An Art Director at AKDB? Isn't that one of the biggest advertising agencies in Australia?'

'Might be!'

'How did I not know this?' Frankie said.

'You never asked,' Sunny replied, and Frankie instantly felt guilty.

'I can't believe you had the balls to quit a place like that,' Frankie said quietly.

'I love drawing, and problem solving and thinking up big ideas. But I'd had enough of thinking up those ideas for tooth-paste and banks. You know? I mean, I know that you have to do some of that stuff to pay the bills, but I wanted something bigger than that. More consequential. So, I pitched an idea for a pro-bono concept for Organ Transplant Australia. It's a charity I'm really passionate about, because of, well, Hazel.' Sunny paused, and Frankie's heart skipped a beat. 'My Creative Director loved it, but she wasn't willing to do it for free, even though they're a multi-million-dollar business. And Transplant Australia didn't have the funds for it.' Frankie could hear a slight bitterness in Sunny's voice. 'So, the next day, I put in my notice. And I've been in talks with Transplant Australia ever since.'

'That's incredibly brave of you.'

'Not really.' Sunny tried to wave her off. 'It's just something I had to do. You know, to be able to look at myself in the mirror every day.'

'You have such vision, Sunny,' Frankie said, running her eyes across the sketches, each taken from the pages of various books. 'So, is this ... has this got to do with how she died? Hazel?' Frankie cautiously said her name, and watched as Sunny's forehead creased at the sound of it.

'Ah, I think the pizza is burning. I better take it out of the oven before I set my house on fire again. That's another story!' Sunny dashed into the kitchen, leaving Frankie staring at his drawings, Hazel's name still on her lips.

157

'This pizza is a-*mazing*.' Frankie bit into a slice covered in mushrooms, capsicum and olives. 'I can't believe you made this.'

They were sitting at Sunny's rustic wooden table, a pile of papers and sketches swept to the side to make room for them.

'It's the only thing I really know how to make. But I make it well, if I do say so myself.' Sunny smiled in between mouthfuls.

'You really do. And I know my pizza. I'm not sure whether I've told you, but it's my all-time favourite food,' Frankie said.

'I figured, when you ordered a family-sized pizza to your apartment the other day,' Sunny laughed.

'Hey! They were desperate times, my friend. If being dubbed Period Girl doesn't call for a family-sized pizza, I don't know what does.'

'So, how's your writing going?' Sunny asked.

Frankie sipped at her wine and thought about telling him about the blog. He'd probably find it funny. *Maybe another time.* 'Non-existent.'

'Why? Come on, Frank. I read your last book. It was brilliant. Truly. And I hate romance fiction.' Sunny smiled.

'You read *A Modern Austen*? When?'

'The day I found out you wrote it.'

Frankie's heart quickened as she covered her face with a slice of pizza. 'You didn't, did you?'

Sunny put his hand on top of Frankie's, gently pushing the pizza to the side. 'You should be proud of your work. It was so good, Frankie. Really. Your writing, it's like art.'

'Don't talk to me about art, Mr Art Director. These drawings, they're actually amazing.' Frankie gestured towards the sketches pinned up on the walls, trying to distract him, and herself.

'They're nothing. Just roughs. You should see my oil paintings,' Sunny teased.

'Your oil paintings? You're full of surprises, Mr Day. Can I see them?' Frankie asked.

'Well, there's one hanging in my bedroom that you might get to see later.' Sunny winked.

Frankie's heart began to race as her eyes flashed towards a door which loomed in the shadow of the short hallway leading off the living room. 'So, these ideas,' Frankie said, collecting herself. 'You said you've pitched them to Organ Transplant Australia?'

'Yeah, I've had a few meetings with them, and they loved the concept apparently. I have a good feeling about it all. Finally. They've been using facts and figures to try to engage with people for years, and it's not working. I've been trying to get them to see that we need to move people. Really get them thinking, feeling. I'm hoping some captivating, big illustrations with emotional messaging tied in with true, bloody, graphic imagery will do the trick. It's just a matter of them scraping together enough money to get the ball rolling. I'd do it for free, but it's not cheap producing ads,' Sunny said.

'What's the next step?' Frankie asked.

'Well, I met with the head of Transplant Australia the other night. Actually, just after you gave me my phone back,' Sunny said with a smile. 'That's what the meeting at The National was all about. The woman I met with, the Marketing Director, seemed really keen. It was my first big breakthrough. We both got pretty excited.'

'Ah, right,' Frankie said, trying not to cringe at the memory of hiding in the bushes spying on him. 'That's great, Sunny. Really exciting.' She couldn't help but smile at seeing him so passionate, so alive.

'Anyway,' said Sunny, scooping up their empty plates, 'it's time for dessert!'

159

After eating one too many chocolate brownies, Sunny reclined on the bright red couch in his living room and watched Frankie thumb through his bookshelf, her fingers tracing lightly over each novel.

'John Green, Rainbow Rowell, Cassandra Clare, Veronica Roth, Stephenie Meyer you literally have the biggest collection of Young Adult books of anyone I know.' Frankie laughed.

'You are such a book snob,' Sunny said, throwing a pillow at her.

'I am not,' she countered, tossing the pillow right back. 'I just think there's more to literature than Young Adult. Especially if you're a thirty-two-year-old man.'

'I disagree. I can give you five reasons right now why YA books are better than any other genre,' Sunny said, stuffing the pillow underneath his head.

'Okay, Mr Day. Five reasons, now. Go!' Frankie challenged.

'One: they're literary treasures,' Sunny started, which Frankie countered with a dismissive 'Ha!'

'Let me finish,' Sunny said. 'Too often YA gets disparaged by haughty book critics, such as the one in this room …' Frankie rolled her eyes as Sunny continued, 'which crushes my soul. Think award-winning books like Angie Thomas's *The Hate U Give* or Lois Lowry's *The Giver*. Are you telling me you don't think highly of these brilliant, timeless books, Frankston?'

Before Frankie could answer, he went on. 'Two: they're trail blazers. I mean, Nevo Zisin in *Finding Nevo* wrote brilliantly about the intricacies of gender, religion and sexuality! Three: they comment on pop culture and current affairs – think *Dear Martin* by Nic Stone, about a kid who's arrested for reasons he can't grasp. Four: they're aspirational and full of ambition, unlike the depressing books you like to read. And five: two words – Harry Potter.' Sunny finished his speech with a bow of his head.

'Wow,' Frankie said.

'Wow, what?'

'I never thought someone's passion for YA books could be so sexy.' Frankie smiled.

'So, does that mean you'll read one?' Sunny asked, one eyebrow raised.

'Definitely not.' She tried to hide her smirk as her eye caught something on the bottom shelf. 'Oh! Here's your copy of *Winnie-the-Pooh*.' She picked out the book, more tattered than her copy, almost every page cornered over. It looked more loved than any book she had ever seen.

'It's beautiful,' Frankie said, turning each page gently.

'How is Winnie, anyway?' Sunny asked.

'He's fine. He's at home in his tank, probably feasting on turtle pellets. Cat insisted on babysitting tonight.'

'She doesn't mind being away from Claud?'

'To be honest, I think she wanted to get away from him. Those two have been acting very strangely recently,' Frankie said.

'Probably the anxiety of expecting their first,' Sunny offered.

Frankie slid the book back onto the bookshelf, pushing it in a little too hard. A photo frame from the top of the tall shelf came tumbling down, the glass shattering at her feet.

'Shit, Sunny, I'm sorry!' Frankie said, picking up the frame. And there, staring right back at her, was a photo of Hazel and Sunny, embracing in front of the Eiffel Tower.

'Oh my God. I'm so, so sorry,' Frankie repeated, kneeling to pick up pieces of glass.

'Don't pick them up with your hands, Frankie. I'll grab a broom,' Sunny said with a hint of gravity in his voice as he stood abruptly from the couch.

'No, no, it's okay, I've got it. I'll do it.' Frankie piled the shards carefully onto her hand, but not carefully enough—

'Shit!' she exclaimed as she cut her finger. She stuck it into her mouth and sucked.

'Are you okay?' Sunny asked, rushing over to her. 'Let me see.'

'I'm fine. I'm fine. It was just a light cut. I'm so sorry, Sunny. I had no idea that frame was there,' Frankie said.

'It's fine,' Sunny said, aloof.

Frankie apologised again, her voice quivering.

'I'll just get another photo frame. It's not the end of the world,' Sunny breathed.

'I'm just so sorry,' she said. 'I can't imagine what it was like to go through something like that. You don't deserve it. Nobody does. I wish she was still in your life. So you wouldn't have to date idiots like me because of some tragedy beyond your control.'

Sunny looked down at their legs, just touching at the knees. He ran his thumb along the seam of her dark blue jeans. 'It's not like that, Frankie,' he mumbled, his eyes still averted. 'I mean … losing Hazel was the worst time of my life. And I *will* tell you about it more, when I'm ready. But I'm not the sort of guy who settles. I would never get into a relationship with someone if I didn't think they were anything but amazing. And I've thought you were amazing since you kissed my nose in the bookstore.'

Frankie's body prickled with goosebumps. 'Sorry,' she uttered.

'Frankie?' he said gently.

Frankie looked up.

'You have to stop apologising for being you,' Sunny said.

'Can I kiss you instead?' she asked.

'Yes, that I'll allow.'

Her cheeks grazed Sunny's stubble as she leaned in and touched her lips to his. Sunny lifted Frankie off the floor and she wrapped her legs around his torso. She laughed into his neck as he carried her into his bedroom and put her gently on the bed. He kissed her again, with more fervour than he had before, and soon both their shirts were discarded on the floor. Sunny looked down at her and breathed in deeply. He moved his finger softly along the edge of Frankie's bra strap, near her collarbone, but instead of pushing it off her shoulder like she expected him to, he continued to run his finger over her chest, tracing her constellation of freckles.

'I really love hanging out with you,' he whispered through kisses.

Frankie pulled away. Her heart skipped a beat, but no words formed in her head. So, she did the only thing she could think to do: she closed her eyes and pulled him into her arms.

Frankie lay next to a sleeping Sunny, allowing herself to be soothed by his shallow breaths. She looked over at him and grinned, stroking her hand lightly through his messy hair, the curlier pieces at the base of his neck flexing beneath her fingers. Frankie hadn't felt like this in a long time. In fact, maybe ever. There was something so intimate, so exceptional, about what had just happened between them. With Ads she always felt so secure, so confident in what was to come, but with Sunny it was different. He was full of surprises, each one better than the last. She peered over at the clock on the bedside table beside her, sitting next to a copy of her book. 1.12am. She couldn't sleep. She looked at Sunny's beautiful oil painting, hanging on the wall in front of her. Its colours formed what looked like the Melbourne skyline, but instead of buildings, it was made of tall trees. At the bottom of the painting, in thick black letters, were the words, *Can't we just start at the beginning and do it again?*

Frankie sighed and smiled. A part of her couldn't help but wonder whether the words, the whole painting, were about Hazel. She couldn't stop thinking about the beautiful, auburn-haired girlfriend – and felt such a pang of sadness for Sunny, but also a twinge of jealousy. How could Sunny ever love her more than he loved Hazel? Not that they were ready for love yet; not even close.

Frankie rolled onto her side, peering over the edge of the bed. She brushed her hand along the carpet, feeling for her phone. Finding it entangled in the strap of her bra, she pulled it towards her and switched it on.

  💬 Cat: Can I feed the turtle chocolate? PS Have you slept together yet? x

  💬 Frankie: No and yes. xx

Frankie clicked open Mail. Sitting at the very top of her inbox was a new email with the subject: *I found your copy of* Man's Search for Meaning *on the train.*

Frankie gulped and read the email. It was good. Very good. He would make great material for her blog. Frankie looked over at Sunny sleeping calmly beside her, and felt a twang of guilt. She had found someone she really, truly liked. And wasn't that the whole point of her train experiment? Shouldn't she end it all now, before anyone got hurt? But her blog was starting to gain momentum. She now had a couple of thousand subscribers, and a local indie e-magazine had reposted her last entry, captioning it: 'Reading between the lines ... Literally! Ever heard of speed dating on trains? "Book Ninja" leaves her favourite paperbacks on trains in search of "the one".' She was almost too afraid to believe it, but something inside her said this could be the stepping stone to getting back into writing. Her blog was no longer about finding love, and more about finding a new career. Before she had time to change her mind, Frankie quickly wrote back to the man at the other end of the email.

I'd love to meet. Where suits you?
Scarlett (AKA Frankie).

It's not a real date, she told herself. *I'm not going into it looking for love – just good content for my blog. It's fine. Totally fine.* She heard Sunny shift in his sleep, and she pushed away the shame.

—24—

The Stalker in the Rye

Okay, here we go again! A few nights ago, I collected my silk top from the dry cleaner, armed myself with tissues and a bottle of Valium (just in case) and braced myself for another train date.

Before you ask, yes, I'm still seeing Edward Cullen. Then why go on this date? (#brokenrecord) Well, as the revered philosopher Samantha Jones once noted, you're a free agent until he says he loves you. (Plus, since being burned in the past, when shit starts to feel real, I prefer to run for the hills/ self-sabotage/suppress any deep emotions. Yep, I'm a walking contradiction. Please forgive me.)

This brings me to Jai. He reached out to me after discovering my copy of *Man's Search for Meaning*. (If you take anything from this blustering blog, it's read this book. Already read it? Read it again.) According to our email correspondence, Jai is a school teacher with a penchant for historical fiction and Latin dancing. And he is very much looking for love.

We met on the roof of Bomba, a tapas bar crammed among the hustle and bustle of Lonsdale Street. I don't usually do tapas. I like my food burly (#bangforyourbuck), but finding my blind date sitting in a corner with a selection of tiny treats spread out as an offering (bless his cotton socks) suddenly made this bite-sized food a little more palatable. Points for thoughtfulness, but make sure to keep them coming!

First impressions? Jai had delicious loose locks, bright eyes and a stubble-framed smile. He rose to greet me and had hands the size of entree plates. Now let's get to the crux of the date. Conversation flowed freely. And in most cases, you'd say, 'Great. Conversation flowed freely!' But in this particular instance, I mean that Jai happily broke down all conventional first-date boundaries. Yes, conversation went from polite, to upbeat, to deep, then quickly to let's-tone-it-down-a-notch-Jai. Here's a little rundown.

1. Polite Jai
We discussed pets and professions. I gushed about Winnie and he showed off pictures of his French Bulldog. He gave me funny insights into parent–teacher conferences, and I steered him away from any discussion of internet memes.

2. Upbeat Jai
I can now reenact the first three steps of the rumba. Boy, did I get schooled!

3. Deep Jai
I know that he is very close with his mother. *Very* close. Still keeps in touch with most of his high-school teachers. Knows the entire soundtrack to *Les Miserables*. Would like three children by the time he is thirty-five (better get a wriggle on then, Jai), and is afraid of bats.

4. Too intense, Jai
No, I can't tell you the last time I ovulated. I don't know if I have a family history of hip dysplasia. And I appreciate that you've done your research, but how do you know I regularly take the Route 86 tram?

It took a matter of ninety minutes for our date to quickly spiral from cute and quirky to intense and inappropriate. After brushing off an examination of my dental cavities, I casually popped the last of the hors d'oeuvres in my mouth, muttered an excuse and got the hell out of there. Since ending the date THREE DAYS AGO, I have received thirty-eight (unsolicited) messages from Jai. Here are some of the highlights.

Jai: Hey Frankie, you sure are a strong, independent woman not letting me taxi you home! I can see you made it in safely. Thanks again for the great night. Jai x

Jai: Morning Frankie, how did you sleep? I've been awake most of the night consumed by thoughts of you. It's not often you meet somebody who's easy to talk to AND easy on the eyes. When can I see you next? Jai x

Jai: Hey Frankie, I know you just arrived at work and I hate to bother you, but I was scrolling through the upcoming Comedy Festival line-up and wanted to know if you're free to see Tommy Little on March 22nd? Jai xx

Jai: Sorry, that sounded ridiculous. March? I'm getting ahead of myself.

Jai: I can see you've checked your phone since my last message. Have I offended you? Jai xx

Jai: What are you watching? Jai xxx

Jai: I can't stop thinking about you.

💬 Jai: My therapist tells me I come on too strong, but when I see a good thing I can't risk letting it get away. I think we have a really special connection. Let me take you out one more time! Jai xx PS You looked really beautiful in that dress this morning. Red really suits you.

📞 [21 February, 4.12pm]: Missed call from Jai

📞 [21 February, 7.42pm]: Missed call from Jai

📞 [21 February, 8.05pm]: Missed call from Jai

📞 [21 February, 8.43pm]: Missed call from Jai

📞 [21 February, 10.27pm]: Missed call from Jai

📞 [22 February, 4.18am]: Missed call from DO NOT UNDER ANY CIRCUMSTANCE ANSWER THIS NUMBER

💬 DO NOT UNDER ANY CIRCUMSTANCE ANSWER THIS NUMBER: Are you okay? I think you might have slept through your alarm. I'll ring the doorbell just in case.

💬 DO NOT UNDER ANY CIRCUMSTANCE ANSWER THIS NUMBER: My heart bleeds for you.

💬 DO NOT UNDER ANY CIRCUMSTANCE ANSWER THIS NUMBER: Please just tell me what I did wrong.

It turns out Jai has been, ahem, 'lovingly' stalking five or so women after swiping them on Tinder. Over the last seven months, he has been on a dating rampage, showering women with platitudes and flowers, and peeking through curtained windows. His dating activity is now being closely monitored by police. They are currently debating whether he needs to be placed on a predator watchlist.

Sometimes being single isn't so bad after all.

Until next time, my dears.

After all, tomorrow is another date.

Scarlett O' xx

Leave a comment (1434)

No offence but ... > @StephenPrince, he sounds like you. A STALKER!

Stephen Prince > @Nooffencebut ... OUCH.

Cat in the Hat > I'm legitimately scared for you.

Fat Foodie > I want to hear more about the tapas. Details please?

—25—

Birdsong by Sebastian Faulks
South Morang train line towards South Morang

The Course of Love by Alain de Botton
Hurstbridge train line to Flinders Street

Frankie took a step back on the platform as the train, now carrying a copy of Emily St. John Mandel's *Station Eleven*, chugged away from the station. She had arrived a few minutes early before meeting Cat in order to slip onto a few extra trains, deposit a book on an empty seat and fly out as the doors started to close. She was trying to extend her reach, though she wasn't quite sure why. *It's more about the blog than the dates*, she kept telling herself. As she watched the train take off out of sight, she felt the sticky sensation of being watched. She spun around on her toes, karate hands in the air. Nothing. Just regular commuters milling about.

Frankie made her way over to her platform, subtly slipping *Little Fires Everywhere* by Celeste Ng on a waiting bench as she passed. She looked around for Cat, then leaned up against a cool, brick wall to wait. It was another one of those unpredictably hot Melbourne days; it began with a warm, light drizzle and was easing its way into a balmy summery afternoon.

She stood near two young women, both of whom had dark, liquid lines rimming their lids and thick bangs framing their petite faces. Bits and pieces of their conversation floated over the sounds of travelling trains.

'—bought me flowers.'

'Oh, how sweet!'

'No, it's too much.'

'… Freddy …'

'Swiping right—'

Frankie spotted Cat weaving through the crowd and watched with a smile as her friend cupped a sloppy green drink in one hand while furiously trying to push back stray curls from her eyes, poking the strands back into the large bun sitting askew high on her head. Frankie looked at her watch.

'Well, look at that! Record time, Cooper. Only six-and-a-half minutes late!'

'You know I can't start a Hump Day without a hit of All Kale the Queen.'

'Whatever you say, mama,' Frankie replied, planting a kiss on Cat's cheek.

The train pulled up, only two minutes late, and they piled on with their fellow travellers. Cat pushed her way to the closest priority seat and collapsed onto it, her knitted T-shirt stretching across her growing belly. She sipped her drink and raised her eyebrows expectantly at Frankie. Frankie checked the seat availability on the train and, once satisfied that she wouldn't be an encumbrance, slipped down next to Cat.

'Well?'

'Well, what?' Frankie asked.

'Don't play games with me, Franklin Roosevelt.'

Frankie looked around her, searching for the answer to the mystery she called her best friend.

'It's time,' Cat prodded.

'Time for what?'

'For me to spend some quality time with your boyfriend.' Cat held up her hand, blocking Frankie's protests. 'Ba ba ba!

I won't take no for an answer. We can't take any more chances with this one. I need to see once and for all if he's worthy of your time.'

Frankie stared at Cat. 'Firstly, Sunny is not my boyfriend,' she said, then after pausing for effect, added, 'and secondly, let's be honest, Cat, I think you've already done just enough damage for one relationship ...' She mimed peeling a banana, taking a large bite out of the imaginary fruit.

'Damage? Well, I never!' Cat blew her cheeks out and stuck her chin in the air. 'So ungrateful, dear Frankie. *So* ungrateful.'

Frankie smiled; Cat's puffed-out cheeks got her every time.

'I love you, Cat, but even you must realise it is totally and utterly unnecessary for you to spend any prolonged period of time with Sunny. I mean, *I've* barely spent any time with him!'

Cat blew out her cheeks again and crossed her arms with a loud *hmph*, but her feigned anger didn't last long. 'You know, I'm just so protective of you, Franks,' she said before they reached the next stop. 'I can't stand the idea of anybody messing you around. I just want to make sure he's the real deal,' she said tenderly as she dipped her hand in her oversized shoulder bag, pushing its contents around noisily.

'I know you do, Cat.'

'Shit,' Cat hissed, flinging her head back. 'I left my phone at home and Claud insisted I text him as soon as his new short-tipped knitting needles arrived. He has been itching at the bit to get his lace knitting skills down pat. He'll be so disappointed!'

Frankie smiled and handed over her phone. The image of burly Claud pored over his delicate creations, bringing garments to life so lovingly, never ceased to bring joy to her day. As Cat tapped away ferociously on her iPhone, Frankie leant back in her seat, moving to the beat of the train.

When they arrived at their stop, Frankie and Cat eased their way up from their seats. As soon as their feet touched the platform, Cat whirled around with a suspiciously large grin plastered to her face.

'Don't you just love Wednesdays, Frankie?' she said blithely as she glided towards the ticket post.

And then Frankie felt her phone vibrate. As she pulled it from her bag and saw a message from one Sunny Day, she flashed a look at a bounding-away Cat and opened it.

💬 Sunny: Sounds fun. See you then xx

Eh? thought Frankie. *What arrangement did I make with him?* She scrolled up through her messages to check.

💬 Frankie: Hi hot stuff, want to come to a morning rave tomorrow with my best friend (arguably the more beautiful and sophisticated of the two of us) tomorrow morning? Pick me up at 6.30am? Kisses, Frankie xoxo

Frankie caught up with Cat and grabbed her by the shoulder, bringing her to a halt.

'What the hell, Cat!' she cried, waving her phone around in the air. 'You texted Sunny from my phone?'

'I'm sorry, I couldn't resist, Frank,' Cat said. 'Please give me a chance to suss him out and make sure he's not some cad with only one thing on his mind!'

'You're unbelievable.'

'Oh, thanks, Frankie.' Cat rubbed Frankie's back affectionately.

Frankie pulled away abruptly and picked up the pace. 'I'll meet you at the shop,' she called back as she power walked the hell out of there.

'The nerve. Absolutely no boundaries. Hot stuff? She will rue the day. Rue *the day*!' Frankie grumbled under her breath. She arrived at the bookstore, thrust her key in the lock, and with a final curse on the day she laid eyes on *Catherine*, she threw open the door. Upon entering, she closed her eyes and breathed in the thick smell of paperbacks, taking a moment to let the spirits of the great books wash over her.

No sooner had she placed her bag under the counter than she heard the ominous rattle of the front door opening. Expecting to see Cat grovelling at her feet, she jumped at the sight of her parents walking into the store. Well, not so much walking, but rather Putu racing towards her daughter, tugging a reluctant Rudolph along by the arm. Frankie quietly groaned.

'Mum, Dad, how lovely to see you,' Frankie uttered through gritted teeth.

'Hello, my beautiful little bookworm.' Putu, still clutching her husband, used her free hand to smother Frankie in a deep bosom hug. 'Your father and I just couldn't wait until we saw you on the weekend! Rudolph, tell your daughter the exciting news!'

Frankie only barely stopped herself from rolling her eyes. 'Mum, I'd love to chat, but you can't just barrel through the door, interrupting my *work* day, whenever the feeling strikes. I don't have time right now.'

Putu looked around the empty store. 'Darling, please, I'm sure the books can take care of themselves for a few moments. This is a family matter.'

It took all of Frankie's inner will not to throw herself across the counter and seize her mother by the throat. 'Fine,' she growled. 'You have two minutes,' she added, nodding at the store's *Alice in Wonderland*-themed clock to make sure her mum knew she was serious.

Putu straightened, threw her tousled hair behind her shoulders and prodded Rudolph, who was absentmindedly flipping through one of the Enid Blyton satires, *Five Go Gluten-Free*. 'Your father and I have decided to move to Richmond! Isn't that right, Ruddy?'

Frankie looked from her glowing mother to her tranquil father. *To Richmond?* Putu and Rudolph currently lived a safe forty-five (on a good day) minutes away in Eltham. And sometimes even that felt almost too convenient.

'Richmond?' Frankie tensed. 'You're moving to Richmond? Where? When?' *Please say in twenty to thirty-five years.*

'Ruddy, do you want to tell her?' Putu couldn't wipe the smile from her face. She beamed up at her husband, who simply patted her back in reply. 'In two weeks! We just landed the most adorable two-bedroom, one-bathroom, verandah-out-the-front Victorian.' Putu clasped her hands, jiggling on the spot.

'And I assume you're well over in the other side of town?' Frankie prayed to God, Allah, Buddha and her dead dog Bratwurst. *Please, let this be a short Airbnb kind of move.*

'We'll be two streets away from you! Oh, it will be so fun. We can have girls' nights and pop over to veto each other's outfits before parties. Oh!' Putu's hands threw to her chest. 'I could even come and hang out with you and Cat at the bookstore. You'll just be a hop, skip and jump away now!' Putu clapped her hands excitedly, but Frankie's head had started to pound. She loved her mother, but she could, under no circumstances, live closer than fifty kilometres to her. How could her father have allowed this to happen? She glared at Rudolph, who was now snoring on the chair in the children's section.

Mouth still agape, Frankie's mind raced frantically for a tactful response. 'This is so ... different.'

'I know!' Putu practically squealed with delight.

Cat flew through the door. 'Well, if it isn't my absolute favourite pod of people!' Putu instantly embraced her, then pulled back and gazed at Cat. Without a word, she placed her hand firmly on Cat's belly, closed her eyes and began to chant under her breath. After a few moments, she opened them, and looked deeply into Cat's eyes. 'My beautiful creator of life! I'm so happy to see you.'

The back door creaked open, and in blew Claud, knitting needles in one hand, pen and paper in the other. He reached the growing group and stopped, clearly unnerved by the scene unravelling before him. 'Rudolph, Putu, how nice of you to drop by.' It was no secret that he hated Putu's impromptu visits, which left a trail of destruction and distraction behind her. 'Is there a book I can help you find?'

'Darling,' Putu ignored the question, 'looking exceptionally handsome as always.'

Claud blushed. He had never quite gotten used to people commenting on his perfect bone structure and chiselled jawline.

He turned to grab a pile of books from the shelves that lined the bottom of the counter.

'Oh I wish I could stay all day and gossip with you two,' Putu winked, 'but we better get a wriggle on. We're going to scour that little second-hand furniture shop down the road for some snazzy lamps. Now that we're such hampsters!'

'Hipsters.' Frankie rolled her eyes.

Putu went to nudge Rudolph awake. 'You just let me know when's a good time to send my feng-shui lady over to yours. She'll be in the area in the next two weeks, *neighbour*.'

And just as quickly as they had arrived, they were gone. Then Frankie remembered the messages. She moved to face Cat. 'Cat, what on earth were you thinking inviting Sunny behind my back?'

'I'm sorry, it's the—'

'Baby hormones?' Frankie bit. 'Don't bring your banana-sized, unborn baby into this!'

'Okay, okay.' Cat threw her arms up in defeat. 'I'm just worried about you. I need to know that he's good enough for you.'

Frankie eyed her meddling but genuinely concerned friend and was defeated; she could hardly hold a grudge against her. 'Fine,' she conceded. 'But you better not make me look any worse tomorrow! And absolutely no more virtual contact.'

👍 Cat Cooper is now friends with Sunny Day.

—26—

Girl (and boy) on a Train

I did it. I caved. I agreed to see Tom again. (Remember Perfectly Lovely But No Spark Tom? Great conversationalist, terrible kisser?) My best friend had engineered a date with Edward Cullen the next morning, and I desperately needed something to take the edge off (#commitmentphobe). Plus, when your affections fluctuate between: 'I feel it in my bones' and 'He's calling, but I'm watching *Outlander*', it doesn't help to confirm whether the grass really is greener on the other side.

Saying yes to another date with a guy who seems charming, intelligent and attractive but doesn't get your juices flowing, is like telling yourself you'll just read *one* more chapter before bed. You know you'll regret it in the morning, but you just can't resist finding out what happens next. Plus, when a guy texts, 'Be the Willem to my Jude (HAVE YOU READ *A LITTLE LIFE* YET?!?!). Meet me on the last carriage of the 8.17pm South Morang line heading to Flinders Street tonight,' you just don't turn down that kind of offer. I'm only human, after all.

So, I threw on a simple black dress and a pair of hot pink espadrilles, and charged my train card. At West Richmond station I slipped a copy of *Eleanor Oliphant is Completely Fine* with my contact details onto an empty bench and waited tentatively at the end of the platform.

Stream of consciousness between 8.12 and 8.17pm:

1. What did Edward Cullen mean when he said he really loves hanging out? The use of 'love' and 'hanging out' in the same sentence seems extremely misleading. Are we buddies or lovers? Casually dating or something more serious? Could he *love* me or just *love* the idea of me? Please for the love of God, somebody tell me what he means!

2. What does 'the one' even mean?

3. If Tom were a character in a Jane Austen novel, who would he be? Colonel Brandon (an Austen thorough-bred, but just a touch on the serious side), Henry Tilney (the AAA effect: audacious, affectionate, articulate) or John Knightley (the slow burn)? At this point, I think I'd be satisfied with anybody other than Mr Collins (my cousin) #settling.

4. Pizza.

Eventually the train pulled up, the doors opened and there, in the last row of the carriage, stood Tom, waving enthusiastically. I approached (*casual hair flick*) and sat next to him. And then my heart melted just a little bit. In his hands he held a flask hidden in a brown paper bag, and a packet of jelly babies. It was as if all of my Christmases had come at once. I immediately took a swig and a large handful of lollies and relaxed back into my seat. Perhaps Tom wasn't so predictable after all?

After catching up (nope, still haven't read *A Little Life* and I hate myself for it) and getting just a little bit wasted on his portable gin-and-tonic, we suddenly found ourselves entranced by our fellow commuters. We started to muse about who they were and where they were going, about what made them tick and what made them want to hurl things against a wall.

There was the old lady with her hair wrapped in a clear plastic, waterproof headscarf who was – obviously, to us – originally from Russia, loved watching *Bold and the Beautiful* re-runs and had a secret sex dungeon in her basement. The twenty-something leaning against the door who wore thick black eyeliner smudged under his eyes and too-tight skinny jeans – he enjoyed attending doof-doof festivals and reading children's poetry in his spare time. And our favourite, a middle-aged man in a pinstriped suit with a little extra weight around his waist – accountant by day and life-drawing nude model by night.

And before I knew it, we had arrived back at my stop. We had travelled to the end of the line and back around the City Loop without noticing. Could Perfectly Lovely But No Spark Tom be lighting a bit of a flame under this lurve train? Destination: Spanner in the Works-ville.

Suddenly sobered by (without being too cocky or presumptuous) the thought of an impending kiss, we tentatively exited the train. I awkwardly said, 'Looks like this is my stop,' and he replied, 'Pretty, isn't it?' We looked around and took in the bleak concrete surrounds. And then he cupped my face. Yes, while standing half a metre away from me, he took my face in his hands. He gazed deeply into my bug-eyed expression of doom and leaned forwards. I braced myself for the slobbery drool, the stiff body language, the overly polite use of tongue.

I am happy to report that it was a marked improvement on our first kiss. Less tense, a little more passion and just the right amount of saliva (with a side of guilt).

Did I want it to be the end of the line for us?

Until next time, my dears.
After all, tomorrow is another date.
Scarlett O' xx

Leave a comment (273)

Ruby Lulu > No need to get your knickers in a knot: Edward Cullen clearly just means 'You're amazing and perfect in every way, please never leave me, marry me and bear my children.'

Danielle Marin > How have you not read *A Little Life*?

> **Bookish Babe** > @DanielleMarin AGREED

No offence but ... > Why would you mention that the old woman had to be from Russia? This blog is becoming more and more racist by the day ...

> **Stephen Prince** > @Nooffencebut ... Was waiting for one of your ridiculous comments. They make my day.
>
> ---
>
> **No offence but ...** > @StephenPrince, Get a life, Stephen.
>
> ---
>
> **Stephen Prince** > @Nooffencebut ... Get a life yourself ... what's your real name?
>
> ---
>
> **No offence but ...** > @StephenPrince, Stephanie.
>
> ---
>
> **Stephen Prince** > @Nooffencebut ... Pretty :)

— 27 —

Pride and Prejudice by Jane Austen
Route 78 tram towards Richmond

Frankie groaned and flung herself out of bed, walking bleary-eyed to her front hallway to answer the loud call of the buzzer.

'What?' she snapped at the intercom.

'Rise and shine, beautiful,' Cat called from the other end. Frankie rolled her eyes and reluctantly pressed the button to let her friend up. She opened her front door and curled up under a blanket on the couch, preparing herself for the bubbliness that was Cat at 6.20 in the morning. Right on cue, Cat pranced in wearing a shiny, neon-blue knitted two-piece, all 'Good morning, sunshine!' and 'Listen to the three new things I observed on my way over here!' But she also handed Frankie a large takeaway cup of coffee, so Frankie almost forgave her.

'No matter how good this coffee is, I still hate you for friending Sunny on Facebook after I specifically told you no more virtual contact,' Frankie grumbled as she sipped on the steaming coffee.

Cat kissed Frankie on the cheek. 'I'm sorry, I'm sorry, I'm sorry. You're such a trouper.'

Frankie merely sighed.

'But Frank, can I tell you what I'm actually really excited for?' Cat said.

'To plant more fruit in Sunny's car? To sleep with your K-Pop instructor again?'

'Ouch and double ouch. No, to spend some quality time with Sunny! It's been a long time since I've seen you remotely interested in a guy. Dare I suggest you might even be willing to close "the gap" just a tiny bit?'

'Thanks, Cat. Now, don't say any of that stuff to Sunny. Or I'll kill you.'

Cat mimed locking her lips and throwing away the key.

'And don't tell him about the blog, either. He doesn't know anything about the train dates. And don't mention Ads, or my mum, or that we stalked him that one time, or—'

'How about I just do what I usually do, and only talk about myself? That will avoid me accidentally divulging last night's sneaky pash.'

'Perfect.'

'Now, go get ready. He'll be here in five!' Cat said, half pushing, half dragging Frankie off the sofa.

'Okay, okay. What does one wear to a morning rave, anyway?'

Ten minutes later, Frankie returned wearing bright green leggings, a tight white tank and a pink headband. Cat was sitting on her couch, stroking Winnie, and Sunny was sitting cross-legged next to her. He was wearing a skin-tight, bright purple morph suit, which showed off every curve and bulge of his beautiful body.

'Sunny!' Frankie laughed. 'What on earth are you wearing?'

'It's what all the kids are wearing to morning raves these days,' Sunny smirked, stretching out his purple-clad legs.

'Can you just imagine how sexy I would look in one of those?' Cat shimmied. 'And before you say anything, there's no need to remind me, Frankston – I've already apologised for the bananapocalypse. Told him it was all my idea.' Cat threw Sunny a knowing look.

'You don't look half-bad yourself either, Frank.' Sunny grinned.

Frankie brushed her hair from her face and smiled back.

'Oh, look at you two love birds. You remind me of a young Elizabeth and Mr Darcy.' Cat put her hand on her heart.

'Who?' Sunny asked.

Masses of people dressed in loud colours piled into the Melbourne Cricket Ground as Frankie, Sunny and Cat approached. A loud, thumping beat reverberated around them, which Frankie could feel all the way through her veins and into her heart.

'Tickets?' a young girl with green spray-painted hair asked at the door. Cat pulled out her phone to be scanned, and in return the girl handed over three shot glasses filled with thick green liquid. 'Here's your complimentary wheatgrass shots,' she sang.

Downing their drinks and grimacing at the taste, they filed through the archway and gawked at the sight that unfolded before them. The stadium was packed to the brim with thousands of people, all huddled together on the grass, dancing. Masses of glitter dropped, seemingly from nowhere, carried on the cool breeze slipping through the open roof. They found their feet moving involuntarily to the beat of the loudly pulsating music.

'Come on, let's go!' Cat grabbed Sunny and Frankie's hands, pushing towards the centre of the crowd.

'This! Is! So! Fun!' Cat shouted in between breaths. She had been periodically shimmying and twirling between blueberry-eating recharge sessions. Cat looked over at Frankie, who was jumping up and down rigidly on the spot. Sunny was doing the same, awkwardly, beside her.

'Come on, guys! You have to let loose!' Cat rolled her hips towards them. 'Frank, imagine what good material this is for your blog.' Cat smiled, and then froze as Frankie glared at her.

'I mean, if you were to ever write one! I've been begging Frankie to write one for years but she just refuses to listen,' Cat said quickly to Sunny.

'I've been trying to get her to write too. She's so talented, isn't she?' Sunny said.

'She sure is, my friend. But now's not the time to talk about Frankie's talent. Now's the time to dance!' Cat said, sashaying violently. Frankie followed suit, dipping her face away from Sunny.

Rain started to fall lightly. One, then two, then three drops touched Frankie's face.

'It's just a bit of rain, Frank!' Cat shouted as Frankie crossed her arms. 'Live a little!'

'I'm just going to take a breather,' Frankie said.

'I'll come with you,' Sunny said quickly.

'Come back here when you've finished breathing, and you're ready to dance!' Cat called after them.

Frankie pushed past the crowds of energetic ravers, Sunny following closely behind, his breath prickling her neck. She was almost at the exit when she heard him call her name. She turned around to see him flinging his arms around and wiggling his hips.

'Wait, I love this song!' he shouted.

'You're kidding me. Beyoncé?'

'It's only the best, most profound song of all time. I mean, whoa oh oh, whoa oh oh. Come on! It's magic.' Sunny grabbed her hands, pulling her forward and back, twirling her round and round.

'You've got moves, Sunny!' Frankie laughed, throwing her head back and finally relaxing just a little.

'One year of tap-dancing classes will do that to you,' Sunny replied.

'You're full of surprises, Mr Day.'

She let him spin her round as thunder swelled loudly above them and the sky began to open. The rain swiftly transformed from a drizzle to a downpour, hitting them harshly like a cliffhanger at the end of a chapter. But nothing could stop them; they gyrated, they turned and twisted and spiralled as the rain hit them harder and harder. The crowd around them began to disperse, in search of cover, until it was just them and the hardcore ravers dancing in the downpour. And at that moment, Frankie felt freer than she had in years. She didn't care that her life wasn't exactly where she had hoped it would be, she didn't mind at all. Because at that moment, she was happy. Truly, uncomplicatedly happy. She whirled into Sunny's embrace, slung her arms around his neck and kissed him in the rain. It was her very own Elizabeth Bennett and Mr Darcy moment – even if Sunny didn't know who they were.

'There's no slowing Cat down is there?' Sunny said, following Frankie into her apartment. They were both soaking wet and out of breath, having sprinted home in the rain.

'She *loves* a good boogie. When my first boyfriend broke up with me, she took me to a salsa club and didn't let me stop dancing until the pain went away. I couldn't walk for two days.'

'She's a good friend,' Sunny said.

'She's insane. But she's loyal as hell.' Frankie smiled.

'I can tell.'

'How so?'

'This morning, when you were getting dressed, she told me if I messed with you she'd slit my throat. She kept running her finger across her neck whenever you weren't looking.' Sunny laughed.

'Oh God, I'm so sorry. She's a little overprotective.'

'Actually, it's kind of endearing.'

Frankie cracked open the lid of Winnie's tank and nudged him affectionately just as a large crack of thunder erupted, making her jump.

'I can't believe it's storming,' she said.

'That's Melbourne for you.'

'You must be freezing. Do you want to shower?' Frankie asked, admiring the way Sunny's morph suit clung even tighter to his incredible body when wet.

'No, that's okay, you go first. You're drenched,' Sunny said with a smile, pulling at the rim of Frankie's top, which was now translucent, revealing the shadow of her bra. He took a step closer, placing his open palm on her stomach, the tips of his fingers grazing her bare skin.

'I'm fine too. I'll just change.' She hesitated for a moment, the heady feeling from just an hour ago lifting. 'I'm sure I've got something for you to wear too. A wet morph suit is never a good idea.' Frankie laughed, looking him up and down. 'I'll be right back.' Somewhat reluctantly she took a step back, Sunny's hand falling from her body.

She closed her bedroom door behind her, leaning against it. Eyes squeezed shut, she breathed in deeply then peeled off her wet clothes, throwing them into her laundry basket on her way to grab a towel. She quickly dried off, then threw on some blue jeans and a black T-shirt, before opening her bottom drawer. Ads' drawer. She hadn't touched it in two years. Well, except for the few tragic nights she had taken out his jumper and smelled it. That and a pair of jeans were the only things of his she had left, but this time, as she carefully unfolded them, for the first time, her heart didn't tighten. She slammed the drawer shut with her foot and walked back into the living room. Sunny was sitting on the couch in nothing but his briefs, his morph suit balled up in the corner.

'Sorry, it got cold,' he said.

She cautiously placed the fresh clothes in front of him.

Sunny slid the jumper over his head. 'Should I be worried that you have men's clothes in your apartment?'

'Not at all. They're just my ex-boyfriend's.'

Sunny raised an eyebrow, about to ask a question, but Frankie butted in before he got the chance.

'They're old. I should've thrown them away a long time ago,' she said, sitting down next to him.

'Can I get you anything to eat or drink?' Frankie asked.

'I'm actually pretty hungry. That wheatgrass shot surprisingly didn't quite hit the spot. What do you have?' Sunny smiled.

'I've got a packet of Skittles, a Kit Kat and a slice of cheese.' Frankie laughed.

'I'll go the Skittles.' Sunny smiled.

'Skittles it is!'

'Thanks, Hazel.'

Frankie froze.

'I mean *Frankie*. Thanks, Frankie.' Sunny pushed his hand awkwardly through his hair.

Frankie walked to the kitchen silently and grabbed the Skittles. As she stood for a moment, staring at the colourful packaging, it hit her. *He's not over her. He'll never really be over her.* How could she have thought she could take Hazel's place? Beautiful, auburn-haired, blue-eyed Hazel. She was probably a doctor. Or a social worker. She probably died heroically, saving people's lives. She—

'Frankie, I'm sorry. I don't know why that happened.' His voice startled her, and she spun around to see him standing in the doorway.

'It's fine,' she said, stuffing five Skittles into her mouth and holding out the packet.

'It doesn't seem fine.' Sunny took the packet and put his other hand on hers.

'It's okay. I completely understand.' Frankie half-smiled at him, and tried to believe it.

'Can we sit?' he asked quietly.

When they were seated on the couch, Sunny looked at her, his eyes pained. 'Hazel died unexpectedly, just over five years ago.'

Frankie took a deep breath, suddenly unsure about everything. 'We really don't have to talk about this.'

'It was a huge shock to everyone, including me,' Sunny said. 'And the worst part is, she could have been saved. If more people opted to donate their organs, it might have been okay ...' His voice trailed off and he stared somewhere far away, back in time.

'What happened?' Frankie dared to ask after what seemed like forever sitting in silence.

'We were on holiday, driving around the South of France. It was so romantic. I'm talking croissants and baguettes for days.' Sunny's eyes glazed over. 'Hazel was too scared to drive on the right-hand side of the road. I, of course, thought it was the most fun thing in the world. Just a part of the adventure! On our last day we drove from St Tropez to Nice. I begged Hazel to drive. We were only ninety minutes from Toulon. I told her she should live a little.' Frankie shuddered. 'Half an hour in, she got confused on a turn and swerved over to the wrong side of the road.' Sunny paused, stiffening at the memory. 'We hit a truck. I blacked out and woke up in hospital with a punctured lung and a broken arm. The next thing I remember is being told that Hazel had died.' He paused, breathed and shattered before her eyes.

Hazel. His love. Dead in an instant. Without so much as a farewell. Frankie grappled with what she was hearing, struggling to comprehend what he had been through. 'Sunny, I'm sorry. So, so sorry. I don't know what to say. I can't begin to fathom the pain you've been through. The loss.'

'That's why I'm so passionate about working with Transplant Australia,' Sunny said quietly. 'Maybe I can do something to make up for it.'

'Make up for it?' Frankie repeated, then awkwardly placed her hand on his shoulder. 'It wasn't your fault. You couldn't have known what would happen.'

He shook his head. 'I should never have pushed her to drive. She wasn't comfortable. The guilt. It's something I'll have to live with for the rest of my life,' he said, chillingly monotone.

'Sunny. It wasn't your fault. You cannot blame yourself,' Frankie said again, and then when he didn't respond she continued to ramble. 'I'm so sorry you lost the love of your life, Sunny. I can't imagine the trauma you must have been through. Must still be going through.' She looked down to see herself patting his shoulder uncomfortably, as if he were an uncle she saw once a year at Christmas.

'Thanks, Frankie. And just so you know ...' He took her hand and wrapped it around himself, leaning into her. 'I truly believe you can have more than one love of your life.'

Frankie tensed. 'I have a gap,' she blurted.

'A what?'

'A gap. Well, that's what Cat and I call it. My feelings are all bottled up in here,' she pointed to her chest. 'And when I try to express them to, say, you,' she pointed the same finger into Sunny's chest, 'they fall out on the way into the gap.' She pointed to the air between them. 'I think it's this constant fear I can't seem to shake. This fear of being disappointed, hurt, misunderstood.' She stopped, and fidgeted with her hands. 'Um, I thought I should tell you something, you know, personal, because you just opened up to me,' she added.

'That wasn't personal, Frankie.' Sunny laughed. 'We all have a gap. Some of us are just better at filling it than others.'

Frankie shifted an inch away, taken aback by Sunny's quick dismissal. 'Oh. Well, you can ask me anything, then,' she uttered. 'I forced you tell me something you weren't ready to tell me. You can ask me anything you want.'

He watched her for a moment before he said, 'Anything?'

'Anything.'

'Why don't you write anymore?'

'Have you seen the reviews?' Frankie half-laughed. 'That's why I don't write anymore. Not anything real anyway.'

'I don't believe that,' Sunny said evenly. 'I think you're afraid. Just like you're afraid to open up around me, to let yourself fall. Writing's who you are. It's every particle of you. It's like if I told Katniss Everdeen she was terrible at fighting. She wouldn't care. She would continue to shoot those arrows with everything she's got.'

'Well, lucky for me, this isn't life and death,' Frankie said.

'Frank, I've read your stuff. It's amazing.'

'That's contrary to popular opinion,' she bit.

Sunny stood up. *It's over,* Frankie silently berated herself.

'Where are you going?' she called out to him. He picked up a pen and the notebook on her dining table.

'Here,' he said.

'What's this for?'

'Write something. Anything. I'll show you it's not scary.'

'I can't just write something!' Frankie said, pushing the notebook away.

'Why not?'

'Because. That's not how it works.'

'Come on, Frankston. Just write something. I promise I won't judge you.' Sunny waved his hands in the air.

'Okay.' Frankie sighed. 'But don't look.'

Sunny turned his back to her as Frankie stared at the notebook resting in her hands. Tentatively, she peeled open the cover, cracking the book's spine. A fresh piece of paper. Frankie looked up at Sunny. His back looked so firm, the edge of his shoulder blades protruded slightly through his jumper. She clicked her pen and, before changing her mind, quickly scribbled something down.

'I'm ready,' Frankie said, slamming the notebook shut and handing it to him.

'What does it say?' he asked.

'Open it.'

I think I'm falling for you ... but I'm worried
you won't be there to catch me.

PART TWO

'You don't need scores of suitors.
You only need one ... if he's the right one.'
Little Women, Louisa May Alcott

—28—

From: Miguel Oliveira
To: Scarlett O'
Subject: The Alchemist is find me

Hola charming Scarlett,

I am satisfyingly surprised to find the book of yours *The Alchemist* on the tram number three. Paulo Coelho is an old favourite of mine and very near to my emotion, due to the circumstance that we share the mutual hometown (Rio de Janeiro).

I will going to leave the book on the tram seat for another traveller to find and read, but my excitement became the better of me. Luckily I picked up the book of yours and read it over, because I find the note of yours next door to my favourite quote about my heart finding its treasure.

What a unique idea Scarlett, you have! You will try to find the love of the life with the assistance of a book. This is a very romantic motion and it is one that really echoes with me. This is similar to something from of a film.

I will take you out on a date if you agree. This is my history: Miguel is my name and I relocated to Australia from Brazil two months ago to audition for *Cirque du Soleil*. I do not make acceptance, therefore I am now preparing full time in acrobatics for auditions of next year. In the downtime of mine I am a poet, and I read to you some poetry of mine on our date. What you think? Tomorrow evening?

Kind regards,

Miguel

The Bronze Horseman by Paullina Simons
Route 246 bus to Clifton Hill

Frankie woke slowly. She rolled onto her back and stared at the oil painting, as she had become accustomed to doing. She let the soothing reds and purples slowly float her awake, her head softly pounding as her mind ran through the events of the night before. Blurry memories of pasta, sex, lots of wine and an absurdly tense game of Scrabble flooded her brain.

'Still pining over your loss?' Sunny said huskily, half-opening his bright blue eyes. He lay comfortably beside her, his arm slung snugly over her waist.

'I said it last night and I'll say it again, MILF is not a word.' Frankie pouted.

Sunny laughed and kissed her lightly on the forehead. 'I love it when you're competitive.'

Frankie's heart wavered at his touch and even more so at those first two words. They had been together four months, and even though they now spent more time with each other than they did alone, they were yet to say those three little words. *I love you.* Cat told her she should just get it over and done with. 'Just say it!' she would whine. And it had been on the tip of Frankie's tongue, on the cusp of trickling out without warning, more often recently. But she was scared. Was she really ready for that sort of commitment?

'MILF is not an acceptable Scrabble word,' she said again.

Later, Frankie opened drawers and rifled through cupboards. 'Have you run out of muesli?' She danced around barefoot in Sunny's kitchen, wearing nothing but one of his loose-fitting grey T-shirts. She loved the feeling of her exposed feet on his cool kitchen tiles, which were so different to the warm wooden floorboards she had at home.

Sunny draped one of his arms around her waist, pointing to the bench with the other. 'It's just there. Like it always is.' She leaned into him as he kissed the nape of her neck, then picked up the box of muesli, buried her hand inside, took a handful and guzzled it down.

'Are you sure you don't want milk with that?' Sunny asked.

'I told you, I prefer it dry.'

'You're such a little weirdo.' Sunny kissed her again. 'So, up for a Scrabble rematch tonight?'

'Please! Anyway, I have K-Pop class tonight.' Frankie smiled.

'K-Pop? Is Cat still into that?' Sunny said, pouring himself a glass of orange juice, arm still wrapped around Frankie.

'Yes, thirty-six weeks and going strong. Although now she mainly just sits in the corner and watches me do this.' Frankie wiggled her bum, backing into him.

'You've got moves, girl.' He laughed. 'So, tell me. Are you going to try writing anything today?' he prodded.

Frankie flinched. *The blogs.* She couldn't tell him. Not now. 'What time's your meeting with Organ Transplant Australia? How are you feeling about it?' Frankie scoffed down another handful of muesli.

Sunny furrowed his brow, opened his mouth and then closed it, deciding not to push it. 'I'm feeling bloody nervous. God, I just hope we get the final go-ahead.' Sunny looked down at his watch. 'And it's in an hour! Shit, I have to shower.'

'Mind if I join you?' Frankie's eyes shone.

'I guess that would be all right.' Sunny picked her up casually and carried her over his shoulder, with Frankie in fits of laughter.

'Stop it,' Cat snapped. Her swollen legs were resting heavily on the seat in front of her, a copy of *Belly Laughs* balanced precariously on her profoundly pregnant stomach. Frankie and Seb were setting up an Authors You Didn't Know Were Jewish stand next to her, with Frankie stopping every few seconds to rub Cat's tummy.

'I can't help it. You're just so huge.' Frankie continued to prod gently at Cat's belly in wonder.

'Oh gee, thanks, Frank.'

'Yeah, now your stomach's even bigger than your head!' Seb scoffed, wrapping a copy of *Catcher in the Rye* in a bright red ribbon.

'And why are you here again, Sebastian?' Cat snapped, not in the mood for his games. She had become more and more irritable with him the more pregnant she became.

'Like I've told you a bajillion times, it's school holidays so I work here now.' Seb balanced the ribboned book on top of a copy of *I Feel Bad About My Neck*.

'Oh, so I'm paying you to insult me?' Cat retorted. Seb rolled his eyes and continued stacking books in silence.

'Such a big yummy tummy. I can't believe there's a tiny human in there.' Frankie stroked her friend's belly in awe, ignoring Seb and Cat's tiff.

'Stop it. You're freaking me out.'

'An itty-bitty little person is stewing in your womb.' Frankie moved her hand in circular motions on top of Cat's stretched, knitted sweater.

Cat gulped, sniffed and then let out a small howl.

'Oh God, Cat. I'm sorry. I didn't mean to upset you!' Frankie moved her hand back by her side, awkwardly running her fingers over the embossed cover of *Indignation*.

Cat let out another giant wail, tears suddenly streaming down her face. Now deep into her third trimester, she was well and truly ready to explode. Frankie clumsily patted Cat's arm, awkwardly smiling at the customers who were now gawking at the blubbering mess that was her best friend.

'I'm not ready to have a tiny human!' For the last nine months Cat had been so swept up in antenatal classes, knitted onesies and *What to Expect When You're Expecting* (the book *and* the movie), she had seemingly forgotten that at the end of this wild ride, out would pop someone she would be stuck with for the rest of her life.

'I'm not done living my own life. I don't want to look after anyone else just yet,' she lamented.

Melvin, a regular, slightly cantankerous customer who dog-eared the pages of the books he was browsing (he was yet to buy a single book in the eight months since he had started frequenting the store), peered over at them. Frankie raised her eyebrows in a challenge.

'Oh, Cat.' She rubbed her back soothingly. 'You can still have a life. Your life will just be different, that's all.'

'I hate different!' Cat wailed.

'But think about all the amazing differences that will come, Catty. You will have created an incredible child who will love you unconditionally. And you will love them categorically back.'

'But what if I'm not enough?' Cat whimpered.

'Well, you'll have Claud,' Frankie said.

'And me!' Seb butted in.

Cat grimaced.

'And you'll have me too. And together, we'll all love that little baby until it's so absolutely smothered by us that it'll join a motorbike gang, dye its hair purple and get a nipple pierced in rebellion.'

'Thanks, Frank. That makes me feel *so* much better.' Cat snorted.

'Cat, come on,' called Seb, 'I know I give you a rough time, but seriously, there's no-one that would make a more awesome mother than you. Heck, you'll probably be reading the poor sucker *The Exorcist* as a bedtime story. I wish you were my mum!'

'I'm way too young to be your mother, Sebastian.' Cat pretended to frown, but her eyes gave her away.

'Are you three about done?' Melvin grumbled, shoving a copy of *The Anatomy of Melancholy* towards Frankie. 'Can you put this one on hold for me?'

Frankie sighed and took the book, planning to return it to the shelves as soon as he left.

'Enjoy the afternoon,' Cat said sarcastically.

'Enjoy the baby. See this,' he said, pointing to his bald head. 'It was full of luscious locks before I had a son two years ago,' and with that he stormed out.

'Bastard,' Frankie muttered, turning around to see Cat's open hand held out in front of her.

'What?'

'I guessed he would buy philosophy. Pay up.' She grinned, tears still staining her cheeks.

Frankie laughed and reached for her wallet. She would happily give Cat all her money if it meant she would return to her normal, cheery self. Rummaging through her bag, she felt her phone vibrate against her palm.

'Hello?'

'Frankie, is that you?' a husky female voice said from the other end of the phone.

'It is. Who's this?'

'Frankie! It's Marie from Simon & Schuster. Long time no speak. How are you, darling?'

'Marie, oh hi, how are you? Sorry, how unexpected. Just give me a minute.' Frankie shot up from her seat, gesturing wildly at Cat, and ran out to the storage room at the back of the store, closing the door behind her.

'Hi Marie. How are you? It *has* been a while. Two years or so!' Frankie laughed awkwardly as her mind raced. *Why is she calling? Oh God, have there been even more terrible reviews for* Something About Jane?

'Oh, I'm so sorry about that. It's been crazy busy here, as you can imagine. Anyway, I'm sure you're wondering why I'm calling. I've just read your "book dating" blog and, Frankie, it's brilliant! Hilarious, pithy, witty – it's a sidestep from your romance writing, but I love it. I think it could be a great book, Frankie. A bestseller, even. I don't want to get ahead of myself, but I'm thinking a movie deal too,' she chattered animatedly.

'My blog?' Frankie said, shocked.

'Yes, *The Book Ninja*. I think we can come up with a better name, something a little catchier, but I really do love the content. Is it all true? Have you really been on all those horrible dates? What a world we live in!'

'How did you find my blog?' Frankie probed.

'Oh, an anonymous source sent it to me. Said it was the best blog they'd read in years. And Frankie, I have to agree. I'm just upset I didn't find it sooner. It's marvellous, Frankie. Marvellous!'

Frankie sat on the wooden stool in the corner of the room, a cool sweat trickling down her spine.

'So, what do you say? Let's set up a meeting and make this happen! I'd love to work with you again, Frankie. Email me when suits and we'll take it from there. You still have my email, right?'

'Uh, yeah. Okay. Okay, sure,' Frankie murmured.

'Great, I've got to run. Like I said, crazy busy! But email me and we'll catch up soon. Looking forward to it, Frankie!' Marie sang.

Frankie hung up. Her head was swimming. *How does Marie know the blog is mine? And if she knows, what's stopping Sunny from finding it too? And who is this anonymous source?* Frankie rolled her eyes. *Of course.*

'Catherine!' Frankie stormed back into the bookstore, startling two young customers browsing the new Witchcraft and Magic section, dressed head to toe in black.

'Yes?' Cat, composure regained, replied innocently, not bothering to look up from her book.

'Did you or did you not send the blog to my editor?'

'Guilty.' Cat put up her hand, bashfully. 'But before you get mad, let me explain.' She stood awkwardly, revealing her swollen belly in all its glory. 'I know you're in denial about how bloody fantastic the blog is, but it's good Frankie, it's really good. Have you read the comments you've been getting?' Cat whipped out her phone and started scrolling. '"Have not cried this much from laughter in years," "This is my life," "Your blog is the highlight of my week." Thousands of people are obsessed with it and you're talking about shutting it down? You need to publish it, Frank. This is what you've been waiting for, your next big break. It's a no-brainer.' Cat threw her arms in the air.

'Like I've told you before, Catherine, although you refuse to listen, I don't care about how well it's doing, I'm pulling the plug tonight. No more blogs, no more dates. I can't lie to Sunny anymore. He's become too important to me,' Frankie said, although dreams of a newly published book suddenly danced before her eyes. She had been following the comments and flood of new readers to her blog, too. And she had to admit that it was exhilarating.

'So, tell him,' Cat urged. 'If you explain how successful your blog is, he'll be supportive. You know he will be. He's the one who keeps telling you to write again.'

'That might have been true a few months ago, but I'm in too deep now. I can't just call him up and be all, "Oh hey, honey. I've been dating multiple people behind your back for months so I can write a blog about my hilarious experiences. You're cool with that, right?"' Frankie bit sarcastically.

'That's exactly what you should say,' Seb said smoothly.

Frankie jumped. 'Seb! How long have you been standing there?'

'Long enough to know that you've been offered a book deal. And quite frankly, you'd be senseless to turn it down. This is your dream, Frankie.' Seb put a hand on her arm. His grey jumper hung loosely on his arms, his red, scruffy hair bunched up around his eyes. But his usually vivid eyes seemed tired.

'Like I've told both of you, I'm deleting the blog,' Frankie said, unconvincingly.

'Well, then you're being an idiot,' Seb said, and Cat nodded in agreement.

'What about if you publish it anonymously? Under "Scarlett O"'? Or, why not just tell Sunny the truth? Tell him it was just for the publicity, nothing more.' Cat sat back down.

'That's a great idea, pregos,' Seb said.

It worried Frankie when the two of them got along. She took in what her friends were saying, for a moment letting herself imagine what it would be like to be published again. Maybe if Frankie explained it to Sunny like that, he might understand.

'And you can still delete the blog. Just save all the files,' Cat said, excitedly.

'But you need to go out with a bang. Your last date needs to be even better than creepy stalker Jai. As entertaining as he is,' Seb said. Jai had (very unwelcomingly) visited the bookstore a few times and had met Cat and Seb, before Claud banned him indefinitely for being, well, a creepy stalker.

'Seb's right.' Cat shuddered. 'As much as it pains me to say so. If you're going to shut down your blog, you need one last, incredibly horrific dating hurrah. Then you can delete the blog, sign the book contract and live happily ever after with Sunny, a published book and my beautiful baby.'

'Well, there *was* one great email I received yesterday,' Frankie said cautiously.

'Yes?' Cat and Seb said simultaneously, staring eagerly at her.

Frankie filled them in on the Brazilian poet turned acrobat, knowing what would come next.

'Yes! This is perfect! When's the date?'

'I haven't set a date! I wasn't going to respond. Because, you know, I'm not dating anyone else anymore. But he may have suggested that we meet tonight.'

'You've got to see him tonight, Frank. This isn't about Sunny; it's everything to do with your future writing career. You can explain it all to him later,' Cat said soothingly.

How will I ever make this up to Sunny? Frankie thought. She felt desperately torn between her desire to give herself truly and irrevocably to Sunny and her curiosity and need to see this experiment through. Could she actually be on the precipice of something great? Seb and Cat looked like a couple of dashboard bobble heads, nodding furiously in encouragement. Frankie rolled her eyes, took out her phone and scrolled to the email from Miguel. She typed a quick response agreeing to see him, and before she had time to change her mind, clicked send.

'Okay, I'm seeing him tonight. And I feel sick about it. I hope you're both happy.'

What am I doing? she agonised silently. Over the last few months, guilt over the dates, the blog, every little deception that now weaved through the foundation of Sunny and her relationship, had started to weigh her down. But that didn't stop the blog from also feeling so right or from garnering attention. And now, with hundreds of new readers each day, Frankie had become more and more anxious that Sunny would discover her dirty little secret. She had been close to blurting it all out so many times, but she was too scared that she would lose him as a result. And now, if a publishing deal actually became a reality (*could it?*), then Sunny would find out about her indiscretions regardless. *This blog is no longer about romance and all to do with me getting back into writing. Something Sunny's been telling me to do all along. Surely he'll be happy for me?* Frankie stressed, cracking her knuckles. *That's it*, she told herself. *Tonight is the last date. The very last. Then—*

'Hello, my darling Sunny,' Cat cooed as the door jingled open.

Frankie's eyes shot up from her phone screen. Sunny was standing just metres away from her, and he looked distraught. *Shit.*

'What's wrong? How'd it go today?' she exclaimed, rushing over to kiss him.

'Terribly.'

Frankie's heart stopped.

'Just kidding! It couldn't have gone better,' Sunny said excitedly, his face instantly transforming. 'They've decided to fund the entire campaign. Billboards, online ads, even TV commercials – the whole whammy! And they want to set it live before Christmas. I actually can't believe it. I've been working towards this for so long.'

Frankie's heart skipped as she flung her arms around him. 'I'm so happy for you, Sunny,' she gushed, and she was. She tingled with excitement at the thought that all of his efforts, all of the pain that he had managed to weave into something so beautiful, so important, had finally come to fruition. She had never felt such pure, vicarious joy before. *Is this what it feels like?* she asked herself. *Is this what it's like to truly be in love?* She buried the thought deep inside.

'Frankie,' Ads yelled into the phone, laughter, music and background chatter muffling his voice. 'I got the promotion! You can officially call me Junior Partner Ads, from now on,' he said proudly.

Frankie took a final look at the Goodreads tab before shutting down her laptop. The words 'insipid' and 'trashy' rattled through her head. 'Wow, Ads, that's fantastic!' she managed to utter. 'Well done.'

'You've got to get over here. The team is having a few celebratory drinks at the Arbory.'

Frankie hesitated, pivoting on her chair so that her back was to the blank computer screen. 'Sounds fun, but I've got that deadline tomorrow. I better not.' Frankie cleared her throat.

'Oh, shit, I forgot.' Frankie heard Ads pull away from the phone as he ordered another round of drinks. 'Okay, well don't wait up!'

'Love yo—' Frankie managed to whisper before he hung up.

Sunny kissed her lightly on the forehead, his stubble softly grazing her skin, drawing her back to him. Frankie's chest tightened suddenly as she remembered the email she had just sent to another man, setting up a date for tonight.

'I'm so proud of you,' she said, burying her face into his chest. She could feel tears forming in her eyes, as happiness and shame battled within her.

'Get a room!' Seb scowled. Frankie kept her head buried in Sunny's chest, inhaling his soothing scent.

'What's up, man? You don't look so great.' Sunny looked Seb up and down.

'I'm glad someone's finally noticed. No, I'm not okay. I've been bitten hard by the love bug.' Seb fell dramatically into a big, orange armchair by the side of the counter.

Frankie pulled her head away from Sunny, glad for the distraction. 'Oh?' she said, surreptitiously wiping her eyes. 'Celeste? You told her you loved her?'

'No, not yet.' Seb yawned, reclining deeper into his chair.

'I barely know anything about this Celeste Fitness, and you've been dating her for months. She's never even been to the store! When can I meet her? Tell me everything about her.' Frankie poked Seb's arm.

'Oh, Frank. She's perfect! The epitome of sunshine on a rainy day. A sweet drop of water in a desert. I've never met anyone like her before. Smart, sharp, jaw-droppingly beautiful, side-splittingly hilarious, and *well read*.' Seb's cheeks grew as red as his hair as he described his crush. 'The problem is: I want to do something to really impress her. Orchestrate the perfect plan to tell her she's the love of my life.' His eyes glazed over.

'Oh, Seb, young love, you're making me blush!' Frankie replied, massaging his bony shoulder. 'But the setting doesn't matter. It's all in the words. Just tell her when you next see her at school. With conviction, of course.'

'Frankston Rose! It's not like you to be so unromantic,' Sunny said sarcastically, and then added: 'Sebastian, I know just the way to tell a girl you *love* them,' dragging out the word that made Frankie's spine quiver.

'Oh? And how do you suppose I do that, Sunny Day? We can't all have chiselled good looks and ridiculous, punny names like you, mate.'

'Three words, Seb. Grand. Romantic. Gesture,' Sunny said huskily, counting the words out on his fingers. Two teenage girls, who were browsing through magazines while not-so-subtly ogling Sunny, stopped dead in their tracks, lusty drool bubbling at the corners of their small, pink mouths.

'Like kissing her in the middle of a packed train to avoid a fine?' Frankie laughed.

'Exactly like that! Are you telling me you would've given *Hunger Games*-loving me the time of day if I hadn't pulled out a show-stopper like that?' Sunny winked.

Frankie smiled at the memory and leaned into his big embrace.

'All right, Romeo and Juliet, let's bring this back to me and my problem. What sort of grand romantic gesture are we talking?' Seb pushed his hand through his hair impatiently. Frankie had seen him pine over many a woman (most were fictional literary characters of course, but the angst was always very real) but she had never known him to be torn up like this.

'All right. If you're really ready to say the L word, you have to pull out the big guns.' Sunny cracked his knuckles. 'She goes to your school, right? Why not fill her locker with rose petals, skip class and take her for a spontaneous picnic by the

Yarra? There's a great, quiet little place along the river where everyone used to go to get to third base.'

'Gross. You've totally done that before. And I don't think that's her style.' Seb rubbed his temples.

'Ooh! What about walking the length of the country for her like in *The Unlikely Pilgrimage of Harold Fry*?' Cat butted in.

'Yeah, sure, you'll do anything to get rid of me, Cat,' Seb spat back sarcastically.

'A romantic treasure hunt like Amy's in *Gone Girl*?' Cat suggested.

'That was hardly romantic, Cat. It was more psychotic,' Frankie added.

'Same difference.'

'What about something so old-fashioned and traditional that it becomes romantic?' Frankie proposed.

Seb raised his eyebrows in anticipation.

'Like, fill a classroom with hundreds of candles and write an adoring speech about all the things you like about her. You can't lose with a timeless gesture,' she finished dreamily.

'Yeah, something like that could work,' Seb mumbled, suddenly embarrassed.

'A timeless romantic gesture, hey? Would something like this float your boat?' Sunny flipped Frankie around so she was facing him, dipped her deeply and kissed her passionately, right in the middle of the bookshop. Cat and Seb called out, 'Gross!' and 'Get a room!' but Frankie didn't care. Her senses prickled, she could feel herself falling even deeper. And then, all too quickly, Sunny pulled away.

'I should get going,' he said abruptly. 'See you tonight?'

'Yep,' she managed to say.

'No!' Cat interrupted. 'Frankie, you have plans tonight, remember? You promised we'd go to K-Pop and then you'd come to my house to help me with my *women's issues*,' Cat said, staring at her until the dreaded penny dropped. She shrugged at Sunny, not trusting herself to speak.

'Okay, well, you'll have to make it up to me tomorrow night, then,' Sunny said.

Frankie nodded, but before she could reply she was pulled sharply down by Seb, who had exited the chair and crawled behind the counter, and was now ferociously tugging Frankie to join him.

'What on earth are you doing, Seb?' Frankie hissed. He was making swift hand motions towards the door, and his face had gone from pink to an unnatural yellow.

Jai, he mouthed. Frankie twisted her head towards the door and froze as she saw her failed-date-turned-stalker sauntering towards them. *Shit. Shit. Shit. What is he doing here? Where the hell is Claud when you need him? What am I going to say to Sunny?*

'Frankie, what *are* you doing?' Sunny asked as she threw herself down behind the counter with Seb, her heart racing a mile a minute. *Everything is about to unravel. I can't let him find out. Not like this!* Cat, Seb and Frankie took a collective deep breath as Jai approached the counter.

—30—

Dead Famous by Ben Elton
Route 16 tram to Fitzroy Street, St Kilda

'Jai, what can I do for you?' Cat said nervously.

'I'm looking for my darling Frankie,' he replied, smoothing over his dark hair so that it clung to his forehead. 'I saw—'

'Jai here,' Cat interrupted before he could say anything further, 'is Frankie's stalker.'

Sunny looked from Cat to Jai, fists clenched by his sides as Frankie poked savagely at Cat's swollen ankles.

'I am not her *stalker*,' Jai huffed. 'Frankie was just confused when she called me that. If I could just explain it to her ...'

'Well, she's not here. Come with me, Jai.' Cat waddled across to the other side of the counter, linking arms with Jai and guiding him slowly towards the door.

Sunny poked his head over the counter, gazing down at Frankie. 'You have a stalker?' he asked gruffly.

'Sunny, I can explain.' Frankie stood up cautiously, dragging Seb up with her. She reached for Sunny's hand but he pulled away.

'I can't believe you kept something like this from me. This is just typical. Who is he?' Sunny asked defensively. Frankie glanced at Seb, who shrugged. She took a deep breath. *This is it. It's time to come clean.*

'Well, you see, a few months ago—' Frankie started.

'A few months ago!' Cat came running back. 'When Frankie was Period Girl. Remember? You two had only just met,' she interjected.

'How could I forget?' Sunny said coolly.

'Well, a few people saw her video and became obsessed with her. It didn't last long, but Jai couldn't let the whole thing go. We haven't seen him in months, really. But he did love to lurk around here every so often. He's harmless. We must've forgotten to tell you about him!' Cat said, all in one breath. Sunny watched Frankie closely, but she looked unswervingly at the floor.

'So, that's it? Just a crazed fan?' He raised his eyebrows.

'That's it. How ridiculous is that? So, no need to worry, I told him where to go.' Cat laughed a little too hard.

Sunny didn't look convinced. A subtle change in his features showed a transition from concern to distrust. 'If he comes back again, you two let me know. You really should report him,' Sunny said, lightly brushing Frankie's arm.

Frankie, Cat and Seb all nodded compliantly.

'I should get going. I need to get that final proposal done by the end of the day.' He bent down to kiss Frankie goodbye.

As Sunny strolled out of the bookstore, Cat, Frankie and Seb finally exhaled.

Frankie groaned, dropping her head in her hands. 'I am a horrible human being.'

'You'll tell him the truth soon. After tonight's date,' Cat encouraged.

Sunny: I hope you're okay, Frank. Any other stalkers I should know about?

Frankie: Only the one. I'm fine. I promise.

Sunny: Okay, Period Girl x

DO NOT UNDER ANY CIRCUMSTANCE ANSWER THIS NUMBER: I still love you.

Frankie tied her hair into a loose ponytail and adjusted her denim jacket. Taking a deep breath, she tried to ignore the pangs of guilt stabbing sharply at her stomach like tiny ninjas. She was standing outside the Milk the Cow fromagerie in St Kilda, where she had agreed to meet Miguel. She wrapped her arms around herself, in part to keep warm but also in comfort. She was seriously considering backing out, but then the tantalising thought of a successful book deal, a way to redeem her writing career once and for all, pushed her through the large wooden door and into the fiery warmth of the bar.

She glanced at her watch: five minutes early. She sat at a free, cosy table in the corner of the room, placed her own tattered copy of *The Alchemist* in the centre and then opened the menu. *Just get some good material and get the hell out of here. Shouldn't be hard with a poet-turned-acrobat with a precarious grasp of the English language.* She took out her mental pen and paper, ready to take notes.

'Frankie?' a tanned, tall and ridiculously good looking man asked in a seductive accent.

'Miguel? Nice to meet you.' Frankie stuck out her hand to shake his, but instead he leaned over and kissed her twice, once on each cheek. Caramel curls fell carelessly, framing his perfectly symmetrical face, and Frankie felt herself flush before his piercing blue eyes.

'Sit down, you're making me nervous.' Frankie giggled.

'I am so happy I meet you,' Miguel said as he took a seat. *God, even his terrible English is sexy!*

'Good to meet you too, Miguel. What did you think of *The Alchemist*?' Frankie nervously tore at a napkin under the table.

'I read it before, you remember? It is my favourites. That's why I think, maybe, this might be fate.' Miguel's eyes twinkled. *Damn it.* Frankie's stomach was in knots.

'Of course. Shall we order?' Frankie raised her hand in the air gracelessly, attempting, in vain, to get the attention of the waitress. Finally, a strikingly tall woman with a dazzling nose piercing glided towards them and asked for their order.

'We'll have the Cheese and Wine Flight. If that's okay with you, Miguel?' Frankie asked.

'Yes, for of course. Cheese and wine, how you say, go together like the Romeo and Juliet?' Miguel smiled and Frankie heard the waitress clear her throat. After jotting down their order she slowly backed away, not taking her eyes off Miguel.

'So, Miguel, you're an acrobat?' Frankie asked.

'Yes, you ever met an acrobat before, Frankie?' The flickering candlelight enhanced his best features.

'Never. What made you get into this field?' Frankie said, deadpan. *Do not flirt!* she silently commanded herself.

'A park? I am not go to a park today,' Miguel replied, confused.

'Sorry!' Frankie gasped. 'Your job. What made you choose acrobatics?'

'Ever since I was child, I want to be acrobat. I think acrobat is the, how you say, sex of the circus,' Miguel said, expressionless.

'That's beautiful.' She stifled a laugh, making a mental note to keep that little piece of magic for her blog.

'As you are.'

At that point the waitress interrupted, carrying a large tray of aromatic camembert, Stilton and brie and three different types of red wine.

'Ah, this appears delicious.' Miguel licked his lips, then sucked on a piece of cheese. 'You like to see trick?' *Wow, he even makes cheese slurping look seductive.*

Frankie shrugged, trying her hardest to remain polite but unimpressed.

Miguel winked and downed the glass of wine in front of him. Then he stood up, flexing his arms above his head and baring a thin strip of tanned abdomen in between his jeans and white shirt.

He put out his hand for Frankie, which she reluctantly took hold of, and walked her to the back of his chair, stroking her palm. Frankie pulled her hand away quickly. Miguel pushed his chair in and began to move the table opposite him backwards.

'What are you doing?' Frankie asked.

'I make room for front aerial,' Miguel said, as if it were the most obvious thing in the world.

'Right here?' Frankie asked.

'Yes. Where else?'

Frankie looked around the intimate restaurant, at couples huddled over plates of cheese and crackers, clinking wine glasses and licking shared spoons. Miguel leaned over and tapped the violet-haired woman sitting behind him on the shoulder, informing her, in broken English, that she should 'abandon for protection reasons'. She narrowed her eyes and grudgingly scooted her seat back.

'Are you ready?' Miguel purred, but Frankie avoided eye contact. He counted to three under his breath and then he was off, gracefully pushing his body forward, holding his sturdy arms out in front. His hands lightly skimmed the ground before vaulting his body over the top of himself and landing elegantly on two feet. The entire restaurant erupted in applause, and he gave a small, humble bow.

'That was brilliant,' the violet-haired woman gushed, her cheeks turning a similar colour to her do. Wolf whistles roared from the back of the restaurant, diners held their forks in midair, mouths open, and Miguel beamed proudly back at them all.

Frankie fell back into her chair, embarrassed by all the attention her date was attracting. She cut herself a slab of camembert and spread it generously over a cracker, then slathered it with quince paste and shoved it into her mouth. *Is this guy for real?*

Miguel, having dismissed calls for an encore, sat back down opposite her, watching her as she ate, seemingly entranced. Frankie tried to focus on the cheese and biscuits, avoiding his burning gaze.

He cleared his throat. 'You are beautiful girl. You are my ocean pearl.'

'What?' Frankie replied, choking on her cheese.

'I poet, remember? I wrote you poem, my Frankie.'

Frankie sighed. *This is for the book. This is for the book.*

We meet because of Paulo Coelho, Miguel recited.
Your heart, may I borrow?
We love the same books.
Feijoada, for you, I want to cooks.
Frankie, your eyes, they are beautiful like mine.
You are to me, a book spine.
I am the pages and you hold me tight.
We go home to mine later, all right?

Frankie took a gulp of wine.

'That was incredible,' the waitress, suddenly appearing, said breathily. But Miguel didn't take his eyes off Frankie, who was guzzling her third glass of red with averted eyes. He leaned over the table and tickled her arm with his fingers. Frankie shivered.

'So, tell me what you like about *The Alchemist*,' Frankie said, suddenly feeling the wine rush to her head.

Miguel cooed, recalling all of his favourite parts. Frankie, desperate to steer the conversation towards more neutral territory, chimed in, quoting scenes, recollecting the first time she read the book while travelling around Europe. Miguel told her how he fell in love with Santiago's journey when he first read it in high school. Even with his halting English slowing them down, Frankie felt alive while discussing literature, a surge of electricity igniting scholarly sparks between them. Her heart raced while she deliberated *Brida*, *Eleven Minutes*, *Aleph* and *The Pilgrimage*, so swept up that she forgot where she was, whom she was with. Until Miguel placed his hand over hers, and suddenly a bubble of remorse burst inside her chest.

'I should get going,' she said quickly, pulling her hand away.

'Okay,' Miguel said, laying a wad of cash on the table. As he guided her out of the restaurant, his hand on the small of her back, they received a few solo claps from diners who had witnessed his earlier performance. Stepping out onto the street, Miguel stood uncomfortably close to Frankie.

'Well, that was fun. Acrobatic tricks performed in the middle of a restaurant; you don't see that very often. I wish I had your flexibility! I can't even do a star jump.' Frankie laughed awkwardly.

Miguel didn't return her laugh. Instead, he raised an eyebrow and whispered, 'Do you trust me?'

'Uh, I guess.' And with that, Miguel lifted Frankie off the ground and tossed her above his head, twirling her in a full circle over his arm. Frankie squealed in both surprise and hysteria. He put her down smoothly, then straightened her jacket on her shoulders.

'Well ...' she stumbled, stunned.

Miguel laughed and moved closer. Pressing his thumb to her lip, he moved his mouth towards hers.

Frankie ducked her head. 'Ah, I'm sorry. I really have to go. Thanks for a nice night. Catch you around,' she said, already running in the opposite direction.

🐢

Frankie tiptoed in through Sunny's front door, her head spinning from the copious amount of wine she had consumed. She spotted a chocolate meringue sitting in the centre of his kitchen table, a post-it note stuck haphazardly to it.

> *Thought you might be hungry after a night of*
> *helping Cat with 'women's issues'.*

Frankie pushed a toxic sensation to the back of her mind and took a bite. It powdered, leaving a trail of crumbs down her sweater. She slipped off her ballet flats and tiptoed towards his bedroom. She heard him before she saw him. A soft, shallow breathing that she had come to know only as his. Tentatively, Frankie pushed open the door. He lay on top of the blankets, wearing nothing but a pair of red boxers, his sculpted stomach moving up and down as he breathed. *God, he is beautiful.*

Frankie crept inside, slid off her clothes and skimmed into bed beside him. She wrapped her arms around his big body, softly placing her leg over his, nuzzling in, not able to get close enough. She kissed his neck, inhaling his scent.

'I love you,' she whispered, careful not to wake him. The words felt clunky in her mouth. But for the first time in forever, Frankie was happy.

Then why did she have tears rolling down her face?

From: Jai Reddy
To: Scarlett O'
Subject: Now this is what you call a poem

An ode to Frankie
By Jai Reddy

Skin so fair, hair so lush,
I'd like to nick a lock from your brush.
The scene was set in fair Verona,
I cannot lie, you give me a boner.

You have set my heart alight,
I just want to hold you all night.
In your denim jacket you look so ethereal,
I can't deny that you are wife material.

Thoughts of you afflict my mind,
By my love, I am blind.
If distance makes the heart grow fonder,
Then I am glad to such lengths my heart did wander.

Marley and Me by John Grogan
Lilydale train line away from the city

Frankie dashed up the stairs of her apartment building. The store opened in half an hour and she still needed to shower, change and drink coffee. Very strong coffee. Today was a Tuesday. And she hated Tuesdays. Tuesday was team-bonding day. After wrapping up the weekly finances, Claud would make each of them share their professional highs and lows from the last week while doing mindfulness knitting. After attending a leadership seminar called 'Keeping Your Employees Happy but Productive', he was all about 'talking about our feelings' and 'rejuvenating our minds through the power of needles and thread'. Tuesdays also meant that there were still four more days until Friday, when the real team bonding started. Nothing said 'We're a happy little working family' like a bottle of red (or gin-and-tonic, hold the tonic) and hot chips from the pub down the road.

And then there was that other feeling accompanying her creeping dread. Regret? Guilt? Or just a lingering lactose over-load? Arriving at her front door, Frankie leaned forward and banged her head against the dry wood. *It's okay*, she told herself. *It was just for the blog. It's over now.* She shoved her key in the lock, threw her head back and faked embracing the day.

Frankie flipped on the kettle on her way to wish Winnie a good morning.

'Hey little guy,' she cooed, sliding open the lid and sprink-ling a handful of pellets in the corner.

'Late night, hey?' Winnie lay curled up near an ornamental log. Frankie rubbed the back of his shell. Winnie didn't move. Frankie tickled his back feet. 'That always gets you moving.' Nothing. 'Winnie? Winnie?' Frankie jumped back, hands flying to her mouth. '*Winnie!*' She grabbed her phone with shaking hands and dialled Sunny's number, pacing in circles while she waited for him to pick up.

'Miss me already?' She could hear his smile through the phone.

'You need to get over here. It's Winnie!' She peered through the glass tank, looking hesitantly for any movement in the tank. 'I think he's dead.'

Twenty minutes later Sunny walked through the door. His hair was scruffy, his stubble rough. *Oh, he's so dreamy in the morning.* Frankie shook her head. *Winnie, think of poor, sweet, potentially dead Winnie!* Sunny squeezed her hand and planted a warm kiss on her cheek. With a final embrace, he pushed past her and headed over to the living room.

'What do you see?' Frankie called from behind the alcove at the entrance. She listened to Sunny pad through the apartment and the clunk of the tank being propped open. Rustle. Splash. Click. Shuffle. Frankie leapt back as Sunny suddenly appeared back in front of her. He pulled her into a long hug, rubbing her lower back. 'I'm so sorry, Frank. We lost him.'

They sat side by side on the couch, clutching two steaming cups of coffee, both staring blankly at the shoebox resting on the coffee table in front of them.

'I can't believe he's gone.' Frankie sniffed.

'There'll never be another turtle quite like him.' Sunny nodded, gazing at the makeshift coffin.

'How could this have happened? He was so young, so sprightly, for a turtle, and then – poof – gone.'

'Sometimes these things just happen. There's no way of explaining it.' In that moment, Sunny spoke as if he were worlds away. Frankie looked at him. *Are you still talking about Winnie?* she couldn't help but wonder.

'I just can't believe it.' She inhaled sharply. 'You don't think it was the trip to the onsen that did it? What if it was too steamy for him? Was he out of water for too long? He was never quite his slow-moving self after it. Oh God,' she cried. 'What if we accidentally fried his insides and he has been slowly boiling to death ever since!' Frankie jumped up from the couch, but before she could get any further away, Sunny had stood and enveloped her in his arms.

'You were a great mum. And he loved all the excursions you took him on. He had a beautiful, exciting life thanks to you,' he murmured, rocking her gently. Frankie felt her whole body relax as she rested against his firm chest.

'I'm going to be so late,' she said finally, and reluctantly pulled away, wiping stale tears from her cheeks. Without looking at Winnie, she opened her phone to call Cat – and saw three Snapchat notifications, all from Miguel. 'I'm just going to give Cat a buzz,' she muttered and closed the door to her bedroom quickly behind her.

Clicking into Snapchat, a photo awaited Frankie: Miguel doing the splits. The caption read, 'Doing a divide to awaken my physique core.' Next, a short video of Miguel swinging upside down from rings hanging from the ceiling of the gymnasium was captioned, 'Higher body brawn is most important.' Finally, a photo of Miguel with a woman standing on his shoulders and another woman wrapped around his torso, arms splayed, entitled: 'Women's magnet ;)'.

'Shit.' Frankie frantically tapped out of the app and dialled Cat's number.

'Frankston,' Cat answered breathlessly, 'I'm mid-squat. Where the hell are you?'

Frankie divulged the sad news, choking back tears. They went back and forth between Cat insisting she stay home and Frankie asserting that she would be fine in an hour. Cat hung up on her after her third protest. As she attempted to compose herself before joining Sunny, she heard a shrill voice echo from her front foyer.

'Sunny, my darling!'

Her mother. Again. Frankie sighed loudly, overcome by a very physical sensations of repulsion and frustration. Ever since her parents had moved to Richmond, they were always dropping by unexpectedly, and always at inopportune times.

'Mum, what a surprise,' she quipped as she entered the living room to find Putu sensually rubbing Sunny's shoulders and Rudolph sitting on the couch. Sunny stared at her with a your-mum-needs-to-stop-touching-me look.

'We were just in the neighbourhood and thought we'd swing by to see our favourite daughter!'

'Mum, I'm your only daughter.' Frankie planted a kiss on the top of her father's head and went to give her mother a lack-lustre hug. 'This really isn't the best time.'

Putu looked coyly from Frankie to Sunny. 'Oh, to be young again!'

'Mum,' Frankie wrapped her arm around Putu's back and swivelled her to face the door, 'we've spoken about this.

You cannot keep turning up unannounced. I'm running late for work. You have to leave. And please stop molesting Sunny.'

Putu brushed her daughter away. 'My dear, sweet cabbage, let me just say hello to that scaly grandson of mine.'

Frankie tensed. She threw her head back. *Heaven above, Winnie! Take me with you!*

'Putu, did I tell you how much I've been enjoying the Himalayan goji berries you bought me? I can just feel my body exploding with antioxidants,' Sunny interjected. He nodded to Frankie, who slowly backed away, receding into the safety of her bedroom. She closed the door quietly and quickly pulled on a pair of jeans and a cream woollen jumper. She heard the front door click open and then closed, and she exhaled. *How did I get so lucky with Sunny?* But the thought was followed by a sharp, guilty sting. She shook her head, grabbed her coat and joined Sunny, who was now sitting on the couch alone.

'Thank you,' she said, running her palm over his rough cheeks. 'For everything.'

'I just hope you're okay. Please, Frank. Open up to me, tell me how you're feeling.' Sunny gazed longingly into her eyes.

'I'm fine.' She brushed him off, letting her hands fall to her side.

Frankie was crouched in the front window, absentmindedly rearranging a display of children's picture books next to a sign announcing upcoming Book Week celebrations. *Koala Lou, Loni and the Moon, Under the Love Umbrella, No One Likes A Fart.* Sitting among these sweet and hilarious and poignant stories, she suddenly yearned to be young and unencumbered by adult worries and complications, but her thoughts were interrupted by Cat's exasperated rant about how from *Snow White* to *War and Peace* to *The Kite Runner*, too many mothers are conveniently killed off in literature. 'What kind of example is it setting for our children?' she yelled.

Before Frankie could even form a response, her phone buzzed on the floor next to her. Another Snapchat notification from Miguel: this time the photo – which featured him juggling a lemon, pear, grapefruit and orange – was captioned, 'Apple all the days keeps doctor abroad'. There was a sudden thump on the window and Frankie recoiled as the glass reverberated around her. She looked up and saw Sunny waving back at her. He wore a black suit and tie, held a box under his arm and clutched a garden pot from which a burnt orange marigold poked out.

'What are you doing here?' Frankie mouthed. Sunny beckoned for her to join him on the footpath, and so Frankie squeezed her way back into the store, called a quick 'Be right back' to Cat, and went outside.

'What's going on?'

Sunny kissed her. 'It's time for Winnie's funeral.'

'It's the middle of the day. I can't just leave.' Sunny looked over her shoulder into the store, and when Frankie turned she saw Cat and Claud step into view. Cat had draped a long black throw knit (handmade by Claud) around her shoulders, and Claud held up two handbags. Seb popped his head out from between the shelves, giving Frankie the 'I've got this' thumbs up.

'It's all been arranged,' Sunny said. He took her hand and guided her down the street, with Cat and Claud close on their heels.

They had walked about four blocks when Sunny directed them through a labyrinth of alleyways and narrow streets until they pulled up at a small community garden. Covered in lush, green grass, it was peppered with various plots filled with sprouting vegetables. Sunny opened the white picket gate.

'Can we even be here?' Frankie took a tentative step forward.

'Live a little, Rose.' Cat winked, marching, with a slight waddle, through the place like she owned it.

Frankie followed Sunny to a small hole dug at the bottom of the garden. It sat among a cluster of pink daisies, under the canopy of a large oak tree. Sunny crouched down and placed Winnie's box in the hole, then stood and wrapped his arms around Frankie, pulling her towards him tightly. They all stood back, solemnly gazing at Winnie's resting place.

'Would anybody like to share some words?' Sunny addressed the solemn little group.

Cat stepped forward. 'Today we come together to bid farewell to our lovely little companion, Winnie. While he was a turtle of few words, he was undoubtedly a wise and beautiful soul who enriched each of our lives considerably.' She clasped her hands gravely in front of her. 'I loved how Winnie always held intense eye contact, especially when chewing on dried grasshoppers. He really had an amazing way of making me feel both cherished and threatened at the same time. We'll miss you, dear Winnie. Rest in peace, you morose little guy.' She pressed her hands to her lips and awkwardly bent down to touch the box. Before gracelessly standing up, she pushed a small pile of dirt over it.

'Thanks, Cat. That was really heartfelt,' Sunny said emotionally. 'Frankie? Would you like to say anything?'

Frankie glanced hesitantly at Sunny. She didn't think she could hold herself together. She wasn't ready.

'I'm good,' Frankie said coolly.

'Come on, Franks. You can do it.' Cat nudged Frankie towards the grave. Frankie glared back.

She cleared her throat. 'Winnie,' she said softly, moving her hands from behind her back to rest on her hips, then clasped them together under her chin. 'Winnie, well, what can I say? Um, as one of my heroes once wrote, "the very first moment I beheld you, my heart was irrevocably gone". Rest in peace, my friend.' Tears rolled uninhibited down her cheeks as she hunched over and delicately dropped a handful of dirt on the box. Sunny traced his thumb lightly over her cheek, catching her tears, then picked up the small spade lying at their feet. They watched on as he shovelled the dirt over the grave, listening to the soil hit the box with a sobering thud.

'What the hell is going on here?'

Frankie, Cat, Claud and Sunny spun in the direction of the brash voice. A stocky man with flushed red cheeks and black beady eyes stood in the entrance to the garden. 'Who the fuck are you lot?'

'I thought you said we could be here,' Frankie hissed through the side of her mouth.

'Sorry, mate.' Sunny slowly stood up, inconspicuously brushing soil from his pants. 'Just admiring the oak here. Never seen one so tall. Any idea how old it is?' he asked casually.

'Admiring with a shovel, eh?' the man bit back.

They all glanced down at the spade and back at the man.

'I've had one too many carrots go missing from my veggie patch. So, I told my wife, it's the last straw! When I catch those little punks loitering around and pinching my herbs, they're going to wish they were never born.'

'Look, mate, honestly, we were just having a walk around. No harm done.' Sunny put his arms up in innocent surrender.

The man looked across at the pile of disturbed dirt. 'Is that so?' he said coldly.

'We're in mourning.' Cat moved forward. 'We just lost our turtle.'

'I don't care if your grandma just died and you've all lost the will to live. This is *my* garden and I can't have strangers roaming through it stealing kale to pop in their next green smoothie. And don't even get me started on that hole!' He was gesticulating aggressively.

Frankie could feel Sunny slowly creeping to the right, his hand resting on her back. She felt him prod her lightly and she took a step towards him.

'We really meant no harm. We were just admiring your handiwork. Green smoothies just don't do it for us.' He took another step.

Frankie hit Cat, whose mouth was agape. She regularly found herself in heated debates with those who failed to see the value of vegetable drinks.

The man observed the now slowly moving group, but he refused to relent from his position blocking the entrance.

'You know,' Sunny said, 'I can't even imagine how infuriating it must be to find your tenderly-cared-for crops ripped from the ground.'

Frankie glanced at Sunny moving towards the man, who was looking less enraged and suddenly a bit confused. 'In fact, I pass this garden on my way to work every day and often think to myself that I've never seen a more lush area,' Sunny continued. 'I like to think about who might look after the plots, imagining that they must be friendly, loving folk. That's why I brought my two sisters and brother-in-law here.' Sunny gestured at the motley band behind him, who now stared at him wide-eyed. Claud took a step forward. 'They're visiting from out of town and I just had to bring them to see the best-kept secret Melbourne has to offer!' The man shifted from one foot to the other, clearly unsure of where Sunny – now just a metre away from him – was going with this.

'Oh yes, the best-kept secret in Melbourne,' Cat blurted out sceptically. She clutched her bulging belly and looked around nervously. 'I'm surprised it hasn't received a write-up in *Time Out* yet.'

'You might think this is ridiculous,' Sunny charmed, 'but I actually brought that pot of marigolds with me as an offering to the garden. I wanted to surprise the owners with a little anonymous token of my appreciation for their efforts in making our fine city more beautiful and sustainable.' He placed his hand on the man's arm. The man looked at Sunny's hand hanging peacefully on his arm and then back at a smiling Sunny.

'What's Sunny's game plan?' Claud whispered through a cracked grin.

'No idea. Just watch and get ready to move,' Frankie replied.

'We were hoping to plant the flowers before anybody noticed. But you sprung us!' The man jumped as Sunny shouted the last part while waving his hands in the air.

'You were, were you?' the man said, clearly unsure.

'Oh yeah, random acts of kindness and showing gratitude, it's all the rage these days! I was hoping to surprise you and your neighbours. Are you happy for me to leave the flowers in your trusty care?' Sunny checked his watch. 'My sister has diabetes and the other could pop out a little human at any minute – if I don't get them both fed soon, there'll be hell to pay! Women, eh?' He elbowed the man playfully. 'Come on, ladies, let's leave this fine man to his vegetables.' Sunny marched through the gate and over the road.

When the group was safely around the corner, Sunny turned around, smiling broadly. 'Not bad, hey?'

Frankie broke into peals of laughter. All of the guilt, sadness, fear and worry that had pent up inside her over the course of the day was suddenly bursting out of her in the most unexpected way. Sunny gazed at her, an unmistakable tint of adoration in his eyes.

Cat waited patiently for Frankie to regain her composure, but Claud frowned. 'What just happened?'

'What did I tell you?' Sunny chirped. 'Works every time!'

'What works every time?' Cat gawked. 'What the hell was that?'

'Usually we mirror each other's behaviour: we meet kindness with kindness, anger with anger,' Sunny began, assuming the role of professor, momentarily unrecognisable to Frankie. 'But by flipping the narrative and, like today, meeting hostility with warmth, you can conjure up some surprising outcomes.' He nodded decisively.

'Learn all that from one of your Young Adult books, Sunny?' Cat quipped. 'And to think I was this close to faking labour.'

'Don't worry,' Claud laced an arm around Cat, 'your time to shine will come.'

They meandered back to the bookstore in silence, each absorbing the events of the day. Frankie stole a look at Sunny. His forehead was now pinched into a slight furrow. He was so calm on the surface, but Frankie was beginning to see the depths to which his feelings, and complicated and impassioned thoughts, ran. *Oh God, could he actually be perfect?*

'You make the most terrible days suddenly doable,' she said quietly, nuzzling against him as they walked.

'And you make them incredibly special,' he replied, then stopped and kissed Frankie deeply, leaving his scent tattooed on her skin.

—33—

🗨 Cat: CHECK TWITTER NOW.

🗨 Frankie: Why?

🗨 Cat: LENA DUNHAM JUST TWEETED ABOUT YOUR BLOG!

🗨 Frankie: OH MY GOD!! Ahhh my blog is going crazy! It just hit 5000 new followers! Ahhh!

🗨 Cat: This is insane. You are my idol, Frankie Rose.

—34—

Lena Dunham just tweeted about me

Hey there, new readers. Thanks for following my blog because LENA DUNHAM tweeted about it.

This is without a doubt one of the most exciting things to ever happen to me. And that includes the time two Kit Kats came out of the vending machine when I only bought one. *The* Lena Dunham (AKA the voice of our generation) just tweeted about my tiny little Australian blog. MY blog!

A couple of years ago I stopped writing altogether (no need to re-live the diarrhoea-related reviews of my second book). Writing was such a big part of my life that when I quit, I felt like I sort of lost a bit of myself too.

I only recently put fingers to keyboard again, when starting this blog. And I really feel like I'm finally regaining a sense of who I am. I guess that's why I've continued this experiment for so long. Yes, I've found my Edward Cullen, but there's still some cosmic force pulling me to this silly little blog. And that force, I just realised, is called passion. And I'm just getting started.

As *the* Lena Dunham (who just tweeted about my blog; did I mention that?) has sagely advised, if you feel as though you were born to write, you most likely were.

Until next time, my dears.
After all, tomorrow is another date.
Scarlett O' xx

PS Did I tell you LENA FUCKING DUNHAM TWEETED ABOUT ME?!?!?!

Leave a comment (4950)

Cat in the Hat > I was THE original reader!

> **Stephen Prince** > @CatintheHat SAME!

Lena Lover > I LOVE LENA DUNHAM!!!

Talya Klein > *GIRLS* is my life!

Little Women by Louisa May Alcott
Glen Waverley train line to Flinders Street Station

> Seb: I've taken your advice.

> Frankie: What advice?

> Seb: Romantic grand gesture. I'm going to declare my undying love to Cel' if it's the last thing I do.

> Frankie: Go get 'em, tiger!

Frankie was propped over the side of her bed, the light of her phone slowly drawing her awake. Her blanket was pulled up to her neck, trapping in body heat. Sunny moaned, eyes half-open, and wrapped his arms loosely around her. Frankie felt a tingle travel up her spine as she leaned back into his embrace.

'What are you doing?' he asked, his voice gravelly.

'Just messaging Seb,' she said, clicking send on her last message.

'Should I be jealous?' He nuzzled into her neck. Frankie laughed and threw her phone back to the floor, flipping over to face him. She inhaled him, throwing her bare legs over his and planting a trail of kisses down his neck and over his collar bone.

'So, what are we doing today?' she murmured between kisses.

'This?' he replied huskily, pulling her swiftly on top of him. Frankie giggled into his chest. For the first time, she didn't want to leave this bed or this man all day, until Paddy's party later that night. Paddy was an old high school friend of Sunny's. They liked to get together every few weeks for a *Marvel* movie marathon and to discuss their latest food obsessions, podcast recommendations and how much their favourite sports teams sucked. Their relationship was the epitome of a bromance, and Frankie found it exceptionally endearing. In fact, the handful of times Frankie had met Paddy, she had gravitated to him immediately. His cheeky grin and gangly way of walking made him instantly likeable. Sunny had been so animated chatting about the party over the last few days; he was looking forward to catching up with some overseas friends that he hadn't seen for almost fifteen years, since his gap year trip to South America. Frankie grinned, thinking how handsome he was when he got excited.

'What are you thinking?' Sunny tilted Frankie's face towards his.

'That you're cute.' She smiled.

'You're not too bad yourself,' he replied, and then he kissed her.

Frankie was draped lazily along her couch. After dragging herself out of Sunny's arms so that he could focus on work, Frankie decided to spend the day on herself. A copy of *Love and Friendship* was open beside her, and she was simultaneously reading while painting her nails a cherry red, vigilantly turning the pages, careful not to smudge the fresh polish. Frankie already loved today. It wouldn't be extravagant, but often the best days weren't. Her day would be filled with not leaving the apartment, intermittently swapping between reading and watching episodes of *The Handmaid's Tale*.

Just then, the intercom buzzed. Frankie groaned. *If it's my mother, again, I swear I'm moving.* This would make it her third unannounced visit in the last week. Frankie sighed and mustered all her energy to stand up from her comfortable position on the couch.

'Yes?' she snapped into the intercom, bracing for her mum's lyrical reply.

'Frankie? It's me, Claud.'

'Claud?' Frankie tried to keep the surprise out of her voice.

'Sorry, sorry to bother you,' he mumbled.

'No, not at all. Come on up.' She pressed the intercom button. *Is something wrong with Cat?* she worried, pacing in front of the door, waiting for Claud to appear. *Is the baby okay?*

'Claud?' She flung open the door as soon as she heard him arrive. She took in his dishevelled hair and bloodshot eyes. 'Is Cat okay?'

'Yes, yes, she's fine,' he muttered, walking into her apartment and taking a seat on her couch, pushing her book and nail polish to the side. Frankie sat beside him.

'I'm sorry to barge in like this,' Claud said. He ran a hand through his thick, shiny hair, which looked uncharacteristically wild and unkempt – a far cry from his usual neat and tidy appearance.

'Claud, what's happened?' Frankie placed a hand on his. This level of affection felt foreign. Even though she had known Claud for over a decade, she had never really found common ground with him. He was always so serious, so nervous about little things, so content with knitting his way through life. But right now Claud looked the very opposite of content. His clenched fists were white, his usually glowing skin a pale yellow. Frankie's heart suddenly ached for him, and she wanted desperately to help.

'It's Cat,' he mumbled.

'What about Cat?' Frankie asked, shifting nervously on the couch.

'I'm worried she's not as invested, in the relationship. In our relationship.' Claud fidgeted. 'I just … I have to know. And it won't change anything. I'll support her through thick and thin. But Frankie, does Cat … does she still love me?' Claud stared at Frankie in suspense.

'Claud, that's really something you should ask Cat.'

'I've tried, God how I've tried. But you know how she is. Especially lately. If I ask her this, if I doubt her, well, I'm scared I'll lose her forever.' Claud shuddered.

'Isn't it better to know, though?' Frankie asked.

Claud gulped.

'Claud, can I ask: do *you* still love Cat?' Frankie inquired cautiously.

Claud gaped back at her for what felt like forever. His perfectly chiselled face contorted, his startling blue eyes piercing through her. He looked like he was about to erupt into a pool of tears.

'Of course! I love her more every single day,' his voice cracked, 'even after all these years, she still manages to surprise me.' Frankie awkwardly placed her arms around Claud and hugged him. He buried his face in her shoulder and, she couldn't believe it, cried.

Frankie assessed her reflection in the mirror. She was wearing a black faux leather mini skirt paired with tights, ankle boots and a cream pullover. Her hair fell in loose curls around her face and she wore a stain of bright red lipstick to match her nails. Her bright green eyes sparkled beneath the slick of mascara she was wearing, and a faint splattering of freckles covered her nose. Who was this dazzling, carefree, happy woman standing before her? Frankie was filled with anticipation for tonight. She was looking forward to spending time with Sunny's friends, to seeing a different side to the man she was growing so fond of. *Tonight will be great, it will be wonderful*, she told herself. And tomorrow she would tell Sunny about the blog. This was it. She exhaled, suddenly panicky at the thought.

'Wow.' Sunny leaned against the bedroom door frame, having just arrived. His eyes trailed up and down Frankie's body.

'Wow, yourself,' Frankie gushed back. His hair was still a little damp from the shower and he smelled of freshly sprayed cologne. He wore an ironed blue shirt and tailored chinos. Frankie wanted to jump him, right then and there.

'No time, babe. We're already running an hour late,' Sunny said. *Am I that transparent?* Frankie sulked and crept over to him, standing on her tippy toes to kiss him lightly on the jaw. He grabbed her hand.

'Come on. Let's go before I let you seduce me again.'

Frankie smiled, satisfied to know that she had ruffled his feathers.

'So, do you think your friends will like me?' Frankie asked. She had her hand on Sunny's lap as he drove them to the party in Thornbury.

'You've already met my friends and they love you,' he said. Her heart bounced at the word love. *They love me, but do you?*

'I haven't met all of them. Just Paddy and Richie.'

'They're the hardest to impress. If *they* love you, trust me, they'll all love you.'

'So, who's coming from overseas?' Frankie rushed to say, feeling nervous.

'Oh, just a handful of the guys we met on our travels when we were eighteen.' He smiled. 'They were all so wild back then. But then, so was I.' Sunny smirked as he pulled up at a red light. Frankie gazed out the window, watching a group of rowdy teenagers in short skirts and heavy make-up sing down the street, drinking from paper bags.

'I would have loved to have known eighteen-year-old you.' Frankie grinned.

'I would have rocked your fifteen-year-old world, Frankston.'

'Gross.' She laughed.

'Tell me what you were like at fifteen,' he pressed.

An image of Frankie's gawky, blemished skin flashed before her eyes. She could practically hear her mum chanting mantras and admonishing her dad from the other room. Frankie felt her heart quicken. 'There's really nothing to tell,' she blurted out.

'Frank, when will you start letting me in?' Sunny said, uncharacteristically annoyed.

Frankie tensed. 'I, ah ... I liked reading when I was fifteen,' she uttered.

'How interesting,' Sunny responded, a little too sarcastically.

Nineties music pulsed from the quaint terrace house. Three men stood in the front garden, laughing and smoking. A beautiful brunette woman wearing a slinky red dress was passionately kissing a short blonde woman in the alcove by the front door.

'I feel like I'm in high school again.' Frankie looked dubious.

'Welcome to Paddy's house parties.'

Sunny led Frankie in through the front door, not letting go of her hand. The music was loud and a haze of smoke filled the rooms. Bottles of vodka and cans of beer were scattered across spare tables, alongside bowls of corn chips and lollies.

'Day! Nice of you to show up.' Paddy slapped Sunny hard on the back. He was wearing a T-shirt that said, *This guy can party*.

'Mate, what a turnout. I didn't expect there to be so many people here.' Sunny brought him in for a hug, letting go of Frankie's hand.

'Nice to see you, Frankie.' Paddy kissed her cheek.

'You too, Paddy. Thanks for having me.' She fidgeted with her skirt, all of a sudden feeling out of place. She had expected quiet music, cheese and wine, not public make-out sessions, red plastic cups and – was that weed she smelled?

'Can I get you a drink?' he asked.

'That would be great,' she replied, following Paddy into the living room. He cracked a beer for Sunny and poured a glass of white wine into a plastic cup for Frankie.

'How have you been?' he shouted over the music.

'I've been good. What about you? Sunny tells me that your football team is doing terribly?' Frankie laughed as Paddy immediately started to rattle on about why he thought his team was 'in the shits', and how they could improve. As she looked around the room she saw a game of beer pong playing out in the corner, and someone throwing up into a rubbish bin while a golden retriever walked aimlessly around eating discarded chips off the floor. *Where am I?*

Sunny tapped her on the shoulder. 'Frankie, this is my very old and dear friend, Miguel.'

Frankie turned around, and froze.

'Frankie? How very enjoyable to see you again.' The tanned, curly-haired Brazilian kissed her hand. Frankie couldn't move, she couldn't speak. *Shit, shit, shit.*

'Again? You two have met?' Sunny looked at Frankie curiously.

'Yes, indeed.' Miguel smiled. 'We meet on Monday. We went on date to nice cheese-and-wine restaurant. I had such good time, Frankie. So happy I get to see you again.' Miguel stroked her arm. Frankie blanched.

'Sorry. I must have heard you wrong. You two went on a *date*? On Monday night?' Sunny said, confused. A young woman in a purple dress with a plunging neckline walked by Sunny and grabbed his arm, asking him if he remembered her. He nudged her away.

'Yes, we went on date on Monday. Frankie, she very sexy. Very modern woman. I one of many men she goes on date with from her book experimentation. I hope she choose me though, I hope I special to her.' He winked at Frankie, and a shiver ran down her spine.

Sunny stared at Frankie as if he had never met her before.

'Sunny, I can explain,' she said meekly. Sunny's face was turning a deep red, a giant crease forming in the centre of his forehead.

'You went on a date with Miguel?' Paddy frowned, but Frankie couldn't take her eyes off Sunny, who seemed to be slowly shattering before her. She reached out to touch his arm but he jerked back like she was poison.

'Please, Sunny, I can explain. Just listen to me.' Frankie's voice was breaking.

'I sorry.' Miguel shrugged, confused. 'I didn't know you two in relationship. Why you go on date with me and other men if you in relationship with beloved Sunny?' he asked, rubbing salt in the wound. *Shut the fuck up, Miguel.*

'Mate, are you all right?' Paddy rubbed Sunny's shoulder, shooting daggers at Frankie. Sunny was as still as a statue, breathing deeply, staring straight into Frankie's eyes. She reached for him again, but he just scowled, turned his back on her and walked away. Just like that, he was gone.

—36—

The door slammed shut behind them. Sunny trudged into his apartment, unceremoniously dumping his jacket on a chair next to the kitchen table. Frankie placed her handbag on the coat stand in the narrow hall, and found him fiddling with his phone charger at the kitchen counter, his back to her.

'Please, can we talk this through?' Frankie dared to approach him, resting her head between his shoulder blades. He stiffened. 'Please, Sunny. Let me explain.'

He twisted around, the force sending Frankie sailing two steps back. Sunny stared down at her and she felt herself retreat within. She couldn't bear to see his eyes so dark, so full of disappointment and hurt. He didn't say a word.

'Sunny, let's sit and talk. Please let me make this better.' Frankie hung her head low. She heard Sunny exhale deeply and, begrudgingly it would seem, walk over to the couch. Frankie sat down after him and watched as he crept to the very edge of the sofa, moving as far away from her as possible, as if she were a contagious rash. She stared at the space between them, her heart screaming in her chest.

'Sunny ...' Frankie started. 'Yes, I went out with Miguel. But not because I liked him and definitely not because I don't care deeply for you. Because I do. You have to know that. And as soon as I agreed to meet Miguel I instantly regretted it.'

Sunny continued to look at the floor, his chest rising and falling with large but quiet gulps of air.

'The whole Miguel thing was just a ruse. The week I met you, Cat and I concocted a plan to use books to find me a boyfriend.'

That seemed to get Sunny's attention. He looked up at her, confused.

'It sounds ridiculous, I know. But I was in a rut. Personally and professionally. I hadn't been on a decent date in months, I hadn't written a word in God knows how long. I needed something to help shake things up.' She tried to string words together to explain her plot, but saying it out loud made it all sound that much more insane. That much more unfair to Sunny. 'You were barely on the scene back then. It was just supposed to be a silly experiment! An innocent ploy to meet some interesting people who loved to read. Fodder for my blog—'

'Your blog?' Sunny interrupted. 'You've kept this from me for months, but have been telling the entire internet?'

Frankie looked away. 'Yes,' she whispered.

'How many were there?'

'How many what?'

'You know exactly what I'm asking here, Frankie,' Sunny growled.

Frankie averted her eyes as she confessed.

'Fourteen! You've been out with *fourteen* different men while we've been dating!'

'Well, technically one of them was a woman, which hardly counts.'

'I'm really not in the mood for cute, Frankie,' Sunny said.

His tone was so unfamiliar to Frankie, so jarring to her senses. *How did I let everything unravel like this?*

'Frankie, I just don't know what to say to you. And right now, I can't think of a way to repair this. We've been together four months – *four* months,' he repeated, the magnitude of her mistake stirring furiously around them, 'and you never said a word. And not only that, I've been pushing you to write again all this time and you lied to my face about not daring to pick up a pen.'

'Sunny, I'm so sorry. The dates, they meant nothing. You have to know that!'

'Nothing? Did anything ever happen with these guys?' Sunny whispered.

Frankie paled. 'No … Just a … kiss—.'

'I can't believe you!' Sunny boomed, throwing his fist down on the arm of the couch.

'Sunny, I'm so sorry. As soon as I started falling for you, really falling, everything else was just inspiration for the blog. And then the blog started getting some traction and I was finally writing fluidly again. I haven't felt good about my writing since my first book. My publisher's even interested in turning the blog into a book! I guess I started craving the content to fuel my writing. And I didn't want to let it all go. I know it doesn't justify any of this.' She watched him fidget with the sleeve of his jumper. 'I got carried away. I should have stopped as soon as you and I became more serious. I should have been honest with you.' She moved towards him. 'I'd been single for so long, I wasn't used to thinking about anyone but myself. I've been self-involved and selfish. I can see that so clearly now. But please, Sunny, you have to know it was just for the blog. It doesn't change anything for us.' She paused. 'You have had my true self all along.'

She regretted her last words as soon as they fell out of her mouth.

'Your *true self*?' Sunny walked to the armchair that stood diagonally across from the couch, widening the space between them further. He fell into it, leaning forward on his knees, hands clasped in front of him. The whites of his knuckles glared back at Frankie. 'How can you expect me to believe that? You've spent our entire relationship hiding things from me. Hiding in your self-diagnosed "gap", when all I've ever wanted was for you to open up to me. For you to give me a chance to know you. Really know you.'

Frankie stared at a piece of twine that had unlaced itself from the seam of the cushion leaning against her thigh. She tugged at it, feeling her own life begin to fray along with it.

'The thing is, Frankie,' Sunny murmured, 'this is merely proof of what I've feared all along.'

Frankie's head jolted up. She took in Sunny's face, his eyes creased with concern.

'You've never really let me in, have you? Despite what you say, you haven't let yourself fall completely for me. A part of you has always remained unreachable, absent. You've doubted me – us – all the way along. You just can't be satisfied.'

'That's not fair.'

'It's completely fair. You push people away, Frankie! You can't even answer a simple question about your childhood. You don't believe in yourself and you don't believe in other people! You can't bring yourself to believe that I'm not just going to up and leave suddenly, or embarrass you, or ridicule you, or doubt you.' His voice raised a decibel.

'You're wrong,' she retorted unconvincingly. *Is he?*

'Tell me you haven't spent nights lying awake nitpicking my every move, my every trait? Tell me you haven't doubted my sincerity or questioned my feelings? Tell me those dates or that blog weren't a way to secretly make sure that there wasn't somebody better suited for you out there. Tell me I'm enough.' Sunny's back curved as he rocked slowly back and forth. Frankie shook her head furiously, but couldn't help but think, *Is he right?*

'Frankie, I've tried to gain your trust. I've tried to make you see that I am exactly what I appear to be. I've given you all of me.'

'I've given you all of me too.'

'Bullshit!' Sunny shot up again. 'That's bullshit, Frankie! You've been hiding this huge secret from me for months. You've been dating other people this whole time!'

'I know, I've been so wrong about everything. But I'm scared, okay. I'm scared!' The words tumbled out of her.

'We're all bloody scared, Frankie. You don't think I'm terrified? Terrified of losing somebody I love again? It haunts me every day and every night. My fear follows me everywhere. But I force myself to look beyond it. To see the good in humans and the good in the world. The good in *you*. Because that's life. Shit happens and you deal with it and you force yourself to believe that not everything and everybody is out to get you. I let myself love again because I saw how special you were. How special our connection was. But everything's different now.'

'You love me?' Frankie's voice quivered.

Sunny shook his head. 'What do you think, Frankie? I love everything about you,' Sunny said, his pain making him effusive. 'I love the little crease in your forehead you get when you read the sad parts in books. I love it when you reach for my hand in your sleep. I love how your voice changes when you talk on the phone when you're on the train. I love that you always say thank you twice when your food arrives. I love that you can't pick favourites. I love your smile, your eyelashes, the tiny freckle on your hip bone that's shaped like a heart. I love the way you cross your arms when you're thinking. I love how much you cherish Cat and Seb, and how, even when reading a book for the millionth time, you still gasp when you get to the twist. I *really* loved you, Frankie.'

Frankie let out a small whimper. *I am loved. I am loved by a man who really sees me for me. Who notices me and is endeared by me, warts and all. Have I ruined everything?*

'Please, Sunny! Please don't let this change things,' Frankie begged. 'I'll go home and delete the blog right now! Screw the publisher. Screw the book! You're more important than any of that. I just want to go back to the way things were. Let this be a little blip that we'll laugh about a few months down the track. Please, Sunny, this can't be it. Because,' Frankie mustered the courage to let herself admit, out loud, what she had been too afraid to tell him. She gave herself permission to be vulnerable. Sunny was worth the risk. 'Because I love you too.'

'You don't get it Frankie. You're too late,' Sunny breathed. 'You've lied to me throughout our entire relationship.' He turned his back to her. 'I want you to be happy. I truly do. I want you to succeed and realise your potential. But I won't be able to move past this.' The realisation hung precariously in the air between them. Plump tears tore down Frankie's cheeks. She felt her breath quicken.

'Sunny ...'

With his back still facing her, Sunny quietly said, 'I think you should go.' And before she could utter another word, he walked into his bedroom and closed the door behind him. Without even a glance in her direction, he left her teetering on the brink of the couch, calling out to him wordlessly.

A moment (or an eternity) later, Frankie heaved herself off the couch. She considered banging down Sunny's bedroom door in one last effort to make him see how sorry she was, how committed she was to him. *But what's the point? His mind is made up.* Frankie looked around, for what felt like the last time. She took in his beautiful graphics hanging from the walls and his creative words sliding off the kitchen table. *You don't know what you've got until it's gone. God, what a cliché.*

Frankie gathered her belongings and quietly padded out the front door, closing it behind her with a conclusive clunk. She allowed herself a moment to lean up against its firm wood, silently willing Sunny to come out, to catch her before she was gone. Before it was too late. She waited a moment, listening painfully for the familiar sound of his feet moving towards her. She pictured him wrapping her in his arms and kissing her furiously on the cheeks and neck, whispering to her that it was okay, that he forgave her, that they would make this work, that he loved her unconditionally. She waited. But he didn't come.

As she dragged herself downstairs and through the evening foot traffic, her grief felt physical. Her skin prickled and her heart twisted. *Is it really over? Just like that? Oh God, I've fucked it all up!*

Frankie picked up her pace as she neared her tram stop. She couldn't wait to get home and hide under the covers. In fact, she might never leave. She might just live there forever, surviving off chocolate bars and tins of corn and wine. Frankie pulled out her phone to check the departure timetable, welcoming the temporary distraction, and was so engrossed in her search she only looked up a split-second before she slammed headfirst into a passer-by, sending her phone skidding out of her palm and clattering to the ground, followed by loud expletives.

She looked up. 'Tom!' she gasped. Tom from the train date. Tom from the train date experiment that had just obliterated her relationship with the guy for whom she cared desperately. *Sunny.* Of course she was running into Tom now.

'Frankie.' Tom bent down to retrieve her phone. He kissed her on the cheek as he planted it in her palm. 'Fancy running into you. Literally! How have you been?'

Frankie attempted to casually cover her bloodshot eyes with a handful of stray hair. 'Ah, good, great,' she stuttered. 'You, how about you?'

'I'm well, thanks. Just on my way home from a night out. I was actually thinking about you the other day. I finally got around to reading *1984*, like you said I should. Now I totally get your exasperated "What are you waiting for?" That Orwell, hey? It's just crazy how accurate his predictions were. And that line about being so loved that you're understood, or something. It's been ringing in my mind since I put the book down!'

Frankie nodded politely. A day ago, a literary remark like that would have had her running for her laptop (and perhaps a cold shower). But now, everything sounded different. The strain of holding herself together made it impossible to conjure up a simple response. She nodded again.

'I better run, I have an early wake-up tomorrow morning.' Tom checked his watch with a flick of his wrist. 'But I'm so glad I bumped into you, Frankie. You know, reading that book made me think how much I wished we could have found another time to meet up.'

'I'm sorry I didn't get back to you. It was a hectic month at work.' Frankie trailed off, looking over his shoulder. *Where the hell is the tram?*

'These things happen. Don't sweat it.' Tom waved her off. 'Would you mind if I maybe tried again? Asking you out?'

Frankie's body tightened. *Do not say anything*, she told herself. *I repeat, do not say a word.* 'Um, ah,' was all she mustered.

'Sorry, I don't mean to put you on the spot. How about I give you a few days to think about it?' Tom gave her arm a light squeeze. 'Let's say I call you at the end of the week and see where you're at?'

Frankie stared mutely back at Tom, offering a weak smile.

'Have a great rest of your night,' Tom said, and off he jogged.

Frankie let out a long breath, wondering if she had taken in any air at all during that conversation. She instantly regretted her exchange with Perfectly Lovely But Still No Spark Tom. *He was probably just being polite, asking me out again,* Frankie told herself as she stepped aboard the waiting tram.

—37—

Frankie was floating on a giant, watermelon-shaped lilo. Intermittent flashes of light shuddered over her closed eyelids. She draped her arm lazily across her forehead in a vain attempt to block out the sun's rays, while her other hand drifted along the cool surface of the water. A copy of *Sense and Sensibility* lay open on her bare stomach. The words 'know your own happiness' drifted rhythmically through her head. Apart from these four little words, she was free from thought or worry, her mind was almost entirely and peacefully vacant.

The breeze began to pick up, marking Frankie's skin with a light dusting of goosebumps. The water swelled beneath her, light waves tilting the lilo up and down. A flock of seagulls swooped overhead, squawking loudly. 'Frankie! Frankie! Frankie!' they called. Without warning, the waves grew in their intensity, splashing and thrashing her around. 'Frankie! Frankie! Frankie!' the gulls jeered. The movement was suddenly intoxicating, the sound jarring. All she wanted was to get out of the water and rest her feet on dry land. 'Frankie! Frankie! Frankie!' She twisted and turned. 'Frankie! Frankie!'

Frankie jerked her eyes open. And there, inches from her face, stood her mother, clutching her shoulders and shaking her furiously.

'Frankie! Frankie, darling! Wake up,' Putu hissed.

'Mum, what the hell are you doing here?' Frankie wiggled out of her mother's grasp, sloppily worming her way into a sitting position. 'What time is it?' she asked, rubbing her eyes.

Putu flicked on the bedside table lamp in one swift and cruel movement. 'Rise and shine, my dear little chestnut. I'm kidnapping you!'

Frankie grumbled and pulled a pillow over her face. *Dear Lord Austen above, why must you be so vengeful?* She felt the pillow being yanked away and, once again, Putu appeared uncomfortably close, peering down at her.

'Mum, it's the middle of the night. I was asleep. In the bed that resides in my locked apartment. What do you think you're doing here? You have to leave. Now.'

Putu pulled back Frankie's covers in one brisk blow. Frankie tried to hastily pull her singlet down over her bare legs. Her bleary eyes focused on Putu, who was wearing a multicoloured silk top, sequined harem pants and a huge smile. *Tomorrow, I'm changing the locks.*

'Get dressed, Frankie,' Putu purred. 'You're coming with me.'

Ten excruciating minutes later, Frankie staggered into her living room wearing leggings and an oversized sweatshirt.

She flopped down on the couch, her head thrust back on the cushion. It was 6am and still dark outside. She could smell the faint stench of last night's too-oily pad thai wafting from the plastic container still sitting on her coffee table. Frankie pulled the hood of her jumper low over her head.

'Darling, it's been two weeks since you broke up with Sunny. It's time to get out of this house and try to move on,' Putu cooed, pressing a warm hand to Frankie's cheek. 'Come on, time to get a wriggle on, Frankston!'

Where did her mother get the energy? Frankie had never felt more clearly than in this moment, just how far the apple had fallen from the tree.

'Mum, can't I just go back to bed? Where are you taking me anyway?' Frankie curled over on her side, peering up at her mother. Putu smiled down at her and brushed away the piece of sleep that had saddled itself to Frankie's cheek.

'You can't hide away forever. You've got to get out of this apartment some time, Frankston. And the time is now!'

Frankie peered out the window of Putu's moving car. A lone walker trailed slowly after her enthusiastic poodle. A car pulled out of a driveway, its high beams blinding Frankie. Two possums scurried up a tree, relishing their last few moments of relatively undisturbed nocturnal activity. Putu chattered away, barely stopping for air, about how 'mindfulness was the poor man's meditation' and 'break-ups are balm for the soul'. Frankie tried desperately to block her out.

Putu parked the car and danced straight out, grabbing two rolled-up yoga mats as she went. Frankie followed reluctantly, pulling her jumper tight under her chin. She squinted after Putu and spotted the sign to Fairview Park hidden behind the trunk of a eucalyptus tree. Beyond, she could see the faint outline of the Yarra River in the distance.

Frankie trailed Putu down a gravel path that wound through stout bushes and prickly shrubs. They arrived at the base of the river and found a secluded spot to unfurl their mats. Putu ushered Frankie onto one and fell straight into a lotus pose with her feet tucked up into the creases of her knees. She nodded for Frankie to follow suit.

'Now Frankston, darling, I'm going to guide you through a basic yoga session.' She clasped her hands together in front of her chest as Frankie rolled her eyes. 'Don't try to resist it. By attacking the physical impurities in your mind and body and focusing on the upper abdomen area we can begin to heal your Solar Plexus Chakra.'

'Mum, please leave my chakra out of it. It doesn't need the "soft, healing touch" of yoga. It needs a strong skinny latte. And a chocolate croissant. Can't we cure my deprived chakra over breakfast?'

Ignoring Frankie, Putu demonstrated the first pose. 'This is known as the *Ananda Balasana* pose, or the Happy Baby Pose.' Putu lay back, clasping her heels and pulling her legs outward until she looked to Frankie like a frog that was stuck on its back. 'Ah, let the wind peel through you and hold for ten, nine, eight—'

'Jesus, Mum, you said this was going to be easy,' Frankie cried as she struggled to kick her legs back over her head, managing to grab one foot before immediately rocking to the side and grazing her nose on a stray twig.

Putu jumped into the next pose. The Knee-to-Ear. 'Your mind is closed to your ability to succeed,' she incanted serenely. 'Tell your body that it can, and it will. Remind yourself that once upon a time we were all as limber as chubby babies, living within our mother's womb in a tiny fetus position. Don't let yourself be distracted by that negative voice that exists only within your mind's eye.' Putu leapt up onto her right foot and pulled her left up behind her with her hands. The sun had begun to cast a warm glow across both of them, and the sounds of birds calling to each other flooded the park.

Frankie hoisted herself up, slowly pushing up off her knee. She had never been a smoker, but in this moment she craved the burn of nicotine; anything to scorch away the agony of this morning. She grabbed her ankle and attempted to stand on one leg, but only succeeded in hopping around.

'Breathe in through your nose and out through your mouth.'

Frankie closed her eyes and tried to force herself to relax, but felt the sudden squirt of a light, pungent mist across her face.

'What on earth, Mum!' Frankie jumped back, swatting away Putu's outstretched hand. 'What the hell is *that*?'

'Patchouli oil, sweetheart,' Putu hummed. 'It's the perfect antidote to a broken heart!'

Frankie nudged Putu away and jumped off the mat. 'That's enough! You are beyond selfish, Mum. You drag me out of bed to do yoga, which you know I can't stand, then spray me with hippie oil and meditate. You talk, talk, talk, all the time, but you never listen. You have no idea what I've been going through. Absolutely no idea! You couldn't pick out my problems in a line-up. Now, stop telling me to do the Downward Dog, stop breaking into my apartment and stop trying make everything better – it's not working!'

Putu grimaced before relaxing her face once more. 'Darling, your aura is a mess. You're holding so much tension in your shoulders. If you just lie down on your back, I can massage the tender spots to release some of the pressure.'

'You're still not listening to me.' Frankie was almost yelling. 'I don't want you to massage my aura. Why can't you just be normal for one, bloody second! Can't you see none of this is helping me? That I'm teetering on the edge of insanity and no amount of yoga is going to fix anything?'

'Now, darling—'

'Don't "now, darling" me! My life is in ruins. I'm a failed writer, and the man who loves me can't stand to look me in the eye! And why should I be so surprised my life's a mess? I've got a mother who constantly talks over the top of her practically mute husband and has never, for even a second, stopped to put herself in another person's shoes and consider their needs or their values. And newsflash, Mum: there's no changing me.

This is what you get. This is me.' Frankie ran her fingers through her hair as she paced back and forth. 'And the worst part is, you've never even tried to see me for who I am. You just force your Ashram principles and your vibrating bells on me, in the hope that I'll miraculously become the little Buddhist daughter you've always wanted.' Frankie finally stopped and took a proper breath. She looked up at her mother. Putu had crouched down over her yoga mat, as if she was winded.

'Frankie,' Putu started. 'I've only ever tried to love you the best way I know how.'

'All I've ever wanted was for you to be there for me, in a real way. Not just to read my horoscope or to check that I'm cleaning my teeth with organic floss. I just want you to ask me about my life. To want to know what makes me laugh and what keeps me up at night. You're constantly gallivanting about the place talking about all these lofty ideals, but you never ask the real questions. It's stifling!'

Putu walked towards Frankie and pulled her into her arms, squeezing and rocking her. 'I'm so sorry, Frankie. I love you so much. All I want is for you to be happy. I'm sorry I've let you down.'

Frankie pulled away. 'I know you love me, Mum. And I know you want to help me. But you have to know that dragging me out of bed at the crack of dawn won't solve anything.'

'I just wanted to do something to get you out of your funk. You barely leave home these days, except to go to work. I was just trying to help.' She hung her head.

'I know.' Frankie sighed.

'Things will work out, I know they will.' Putu rubbed Frankie's back in slow, rhythmic circles.

'How do you know? Sometimes things just stay shitty. Or get shittier!'

'Darling, you have your health, you have your friends, you have your family, even if it doesn't always seem that way. And you have your talent.'

Frankie rolled her eyes.

'The world is a beautiful place filled with inspiration and promise; you just have to know where to look.'

Putu gently turned Frankie around, facing her towards the horizon that peeked through the gum leaves. The sun had just started to rise and the sky was awash with vibrant pinks and oranges.

'You're going to be okay, my beautiful Frankie. I know you don't think it, but my mother's intuition tells me that you will be.'

They sat on their mats and peered out across the water, watching the colours dance through the trees. Frankie let herself relax into her mother's side, resting her head on her shoulder. Putu pulled her closer and ran her fingers through the loose plait that trailed down her spine.

'I know I'm not perfect, but I really love you, Frankie,' Putu said with a squeeze.

'I love you too, Mum.'

They leaned against each other in silence, watching the sky turn from orange, to yellow, to a dusty blue.

—38—

💬 Frankie:
Dear Sunny,
I understand why you haven't been answering my calls
or responding to my text messages. I know what I did
was terrible, unforgivable. I get it. But please, just hear
me out.

Sunny, they say that you only get one true love and
one big regret in life. I think I've used both of mine
on you.

There's not a day that goes by that I don't regret what
I did. That I don't wish I could take it all back. I want you
to know that I never meant to hurt you. All the dates I
went on, they meant nothing. I love you, Sunny. I love
you more than writing, more than books, more than
breathing, more than puppies, more than pizza – more
than anything. And I'm sorry it's taken me so long to
build up the courage to tell you. You mean everything
to me, and I don't know if I can move on without you.
If you could find it in your heart to forgive me, I promise
to spend the rest of my days making it up to you.

I miss you.
Frankie xo

💬 Frankie: Cat, he just deleted me off Facebook. ☹
Tragically yours,
Frankie

—39—

Break-ups and books

Break-ups are like finishing a good book.

I'll tell you exactly what I mean using Elisabeth Kübler-Ross's Five Stages of Grief, from her book *On Death and Dying*.

1) Denial

You've just finished the book of your dreams. It was all going so well. You had some ups and downs, but everything was finally working out. And just when you thought you might keep reading a bit more – BAM! The book's over. You can't quite believe it. You *won't* believe it. You dream up ways of reading more. 'Maybe I'll go back to Chapter One and read it from the start …' 'If I just drunk text the author, they might write another book, just for me.'

2) Anger

You've now accepted that the book of your dreams is over. You can never read it for the first time ever again. And you're MAD. Really, really mad. You throw things at the book, swear at the book, write abusive Facebook messages to the book and tell anyone who'll listen what a horribly mean book it is.

3) Bargaining
Being livid at the book didn't bring it back, so now you try making deals with it. You'll swear to be a better reader. 'I promise to appreciate your witty one-liners and perfect prose this time around!' You'll pledge to introduce the book to more of your friends. You'll do absolutely anything for just one more page of its literary goodness.

4) Depression
You can't go on without the book. There's no point reading anything else. You quit literature forever. Nothing will be as good as the book you just finished. You can't eat, sleep or talk without thinking about the book. You drown your sorrows in a bottle (or twelve) of red.

5) Acceptance
Little by little, you learn to forgive the book for finishing. You dabble in other books. Nothing serious at first, just a little light chick lit here and there. Then you start to get back in the game, reading a historical novel or two. Gradually, days go by without you ever thinking about the book. And when you do, you smile, and recall fond memories.

Until next time, my dears.
After all, tomorrow is another date.
Scarlett O' xx

Leave a comment (1005)

Miss Amanda Marple > My life.

No offence but ... > Books and break-ups are completely
different. Get your head out of the pages, Scarlett.

> **Stephen Prince** > @Nooffencebut ... Come on! This was
> funny!

> **No offence but ...** > @StephenPrince, about as funny as
> your terrible one-liners.

Cat in the Hat > I've got a tub of ice-cream waiting for you
at work xx

—40—

Frankie sat cross-legged on her bedroom floor, wearing nothing but her bra and undies.

'I am a strong, independent woman,' she repeated, inhaling deeply, eyes closed. She peeked one eye open to look at her laptop screen: the woman in the YouTube clip was massaging her temples. Frankie monkeyed the action, caressing her own face with her two index fingers. After trying all her usual anti-heartbreak techniques (gorging on ten bags of M&Ms, binge-watching *The Baby-Sitters Club* and reading her favourite parts from every Jane Austen novel), Frankie was just as depressed as ever. So, just like the last time her heart was broken, she sought help from her friend, the internet, typing 'how to heal heartbreak' into YouTube, and had been watching the clips that came up, on repeat. These sad, repetitive videos reminded her of the immutable heartache she felt when she lost Ads. *Yet this pain is so much worse.*

'I am beautiful …' Frankie repeated after the woman in the video, then she groaned, realising she was on the verge of reciting the lyrics from a Christina Aguilera song. She slammed her laptop shut and lay back, her hands covering her eyes. *How did I let this happen? How did I lose the one guy who I could have had everything with? What is wrong with me?* Cat, Seb, Putu and even Claud had been trying to get her to move on, to go out and face the world again, but Frankie couldn't get Sunny out of her head. And with his gorgeous face looming over her every thought, closure seemed impossible.

Her thoughts were interrupted by her phone ringing, and she shot up – *Sunny!* – and raced to the couch where it lay precariously.

One incoming call from Claud Cooper.

'Shit,' Frankie said. Since his meltdown a few weeks ago, Claud had been calling her every so often to tell her how things were going with Cat. 'She seems mad at me – do you know why?' 'She's looking more beautiful lately – have you noticed?' And then he would always ask: 'Has she mentioned if she still loves me?' Frankie had tried to tell him that she could not be an impartial jury or really tell Claud anything at all, because, well, Cat was her best friend, and she would relay all conversations to her immediately. But Claud didn't care, he just needed someone to talk to. And Frankie, now despairing and boyfriend-less, apparently had all the time in the world.

'Claud?' Frankie sighed into the phone.

'Frankie, is that you?' He sounded exasperated.

'Yes, Claud, it's me.' *Who else would it be, Claud?*

'Frankie!' Cat shouted into her ear. They were on speaker phone.

'Cat? Claud?'

'I'm in bloody labour!' Cat bellowed.

'What? Oh my God. Where are you?' Frankie rushed into her bedroom, switching her phone to speaker as she slid on a pair of jeans and a black sweater, and dug around for matching shoes.

'We're in the car on the way to the Royal Women's. We're about a minute away. Claud! Drive faster. I can feel it coming!' Cat shrieked.

'I'm on my way!' Frankie pulled on a pair of loafers and frantically ordered an Uber.

'Frank. You won't guess how it happened. Claud and I were *doing it* and then all of a sudden I thought I'd peed myself and then we looked down and my waters had broken. Achhh!' Cat called out in pain.

'Doing *it*? You mean ...' Frankie had made her way down to the street to wait for her driver.

'Yes, we were making love,' Claud called into the phone, cheerily.

'I thought ...' Frankie uttered.

'Yeah, Claud was too scared to "make love" to me for nine bloody months, in case he hurt the baby. Achhh! But then one of his knitting friends said that sex could induce the baby, and, well, desperate times call for desperate measures. Turns out he was right. One time with him and my waters break! Achhh!' Cat explained between screeches of pain.

'Okay, that's enough information. The Uber's pulling up now. I'm about twenty minutes away. Try to hold on for me!' Frankie said, hanging up the phone.

As Frankie sprinted through the front doors of the hospital, a strong clinical smell invaded her nostrils. People in wheelchairs crept slowly past her, while doctors wearing blue scrubs zipped in front. Butterflies filled her stomach. For the first time since she lost Sunny, Frankie felt something other than desperation. She was anxious for Cat, but she was also excited. She couldn't wait to meet the little bundle they had all been dreaming of for the last nine months.

'Excuse me, where's the maternity ward? My best friend is about to give birth!' Frankie animatedly asked a dour-looking woman sitting at the front desk. The woman pointed ahead, barely looking up, and Frankie turned around swiftly. She raced around the corner to the elevators – and then stopped dead in her tracks. There, standing in front of her, waiting for the lift, was Sunny. His stubble was scruffier than usual, his eyes a little bloodshot. He wore a grey knit and black jeans. Frankie yearned to run over and jump into his arms, but she stopped herself.

'Sunny,' she said, motionless. His head turned and, as he caught sight of her, he flinched. Frankie's heart twisted.

'Frankie,' he said, monotone.

'What are you doing here?' she asked.

'I'm working,' he said, nodding at the rolled-up drawings he carried.

'Of course. I'm here for Cat. She's in labour,' Frankie said, cracking her knuckles.

'Oh. Give her my best.' *His best? What was she, a work colleague?* The elevator doors creaked opened and Frankie and Sunny walked in together; a white-haired man in a wheelchair was already inside, smiling up at the two of them. Frankie took three deep breaths and put her hand lightly on his arm. 'Sunny, I'm so glad I ran into you. I've been trying to call you—'

'Stop,' Sunny interrupted, pushing Frankie's hand away. 'Frankie, just stop. Stop calling me, stop messaging me, stop emailing me. There's nothing you can do. You and me, we're over. It's time for you to move on,' he said coolly.

'Sunny, please, I love you,' Frankie whimpered pathetically.

He looked ahead, unmoved. As the elevator doors opened, he walked out. Unwelcome tears silently slid down her face as she watched the doors close, shutting out Sunny, along with all her hope.

'Don't worry, dear, I'll love you,' the old man said from the corner of the elevator.

🐢

'Catherine Cooper. Can you *please* tell me which room she's in?' Frankie said for the third time to the woman sitting at the nurses' station, who placed a piece of chewing gum in her mouth and glanced back at Frankie with no interest at all.

'Like I said before, I will help you as soon as I finish this paperwork,' the nurse said, smacking her gum. Frankie tried calling Claud for the tenth time, but it went straight to voicemail.

'Listen, lady. My best friend, Catherine Cooper, is somewhere in this building, giving birth. Right now. She's scared shitless and I have her Push Playlist. She needs to listen to *I'm Coming Out* now! So, if you don't tell me where she is, I'm going to go into each room and interrupt each woman in labour, until I find her,' Frankie snapped.

'Be my guest.' The nurse blew a bubble. Frankie stormed off, walking into door number one.

'Cat? Claud?' she called, peering around the door. A large, freckly, very pregnant woman was squatting in the centre of the room, butt naked. She squealed as a man rubbed her back.

'Sorry, wrong room,' Frankie apologised, dashing out and into the next one. *It's going to be a long day.*

'Cat, Claud?' Frankie said halfheartedly, poking her head around door number thirty-two.

'Frank?' Cat's croaky voice called. *Finally!*

Frankie skidded into the room and saw Cat propped up on a pillow, cheeks flushed, holding a tiny wrapped bundle. Claud stood gawkily next to her, stroking the blanketed mass.

'Oh my God, Cat! You've already had the baby?' Frankie said, tears welling again. 'You're a mum.'

'Yes, he was a quick one. Shot right out. What took you so long?' she replied huskily, not taking her eyes off the baby. Frankie was about to tell Cat about her run-in with Sunny, and the evil nurse, but then realised that this was Cat and Claud's moment. They were parents. Nothing else mattered.

'It's a he?' Frankie crept up beside Cat, who was uncharacteristically quiet. She kissed her best friend's sweaty forehead. Frankie delicately moved the blanket aside and stared into his cute, wrinkly red face.

Frankie froze, silently gasping.

'Isn't he gorgeous?' Claud cooed.

'So gorgeous.' Frankie's heart fluttered.

'His face is puffy because he got a little squished on the way out,' Claud said.

'Okay …' said Frankie uncertainly. 'Does he have a name yet?' she asked.

'Not yet, we're still undecided,' Cat purred.

Frankie looked from Cat, to the baby, to Claud. *This is not good*.

'Let me get us some coffees,' Claud said, dragging his eyes away from the baby. 'I promised Cat a coffee as soon as she gave birth. She's been holding out nine months for this! I'll be right back,' he chuckled as he left the room. Cat was still, eyes glued to the baby cradled in her arms.

'Cat, he's beautiful.' Frankie rubbed Cat's arm.

Cat smiled.

'He's also very Korean-looking.'

'I know.' Cat flinched, her face flushing with guilt.

'He's Jin Soo's, right?'

'Yeah.'

A silence filled the room, echoing with nothing but the baby's gurgles.

'Oh, Cat. How did this happen? Will you tell Claud? Surely he knows?'

'Let's not talk about that right now. Let's just focus on how incredible this little human is,' Cat said, kissing her baby's forehead.

Frankie gently stroked the baby's head. Cat looked up at her, and to Frankie she had never looked more beautiful.

'You did it, Cat.' Frankie smiled.

'*We* did it,' Cat replied. Frankie smiled again, unsure whether she was talking about Claud or herself.

'Want to hold him?' Cat asked. Frankie bit her lip. She had never held a baby, and he looked so small, so fragile.

Cat nodded at her encouragingly, delicately placing him into Frankie's outstretched arms. Frankie liked this new, maternal side of Cat. Her serenity was rubbing off on Frankie, and she felt instantly calm as she gently placed her hands under the baby and held him close to her chest. His warmth reverberated across her body and it felt like he really, truly fitted there, like he belonged. *Will I ever have this?* Frankie thought before quickly pushing any trace of Sunny from her mind. *Look how beautiful and perfect he is.*

'So, what do you say?' Cat asked, breaking into Frankie's daydream.

'About what?'

'Will you be his godmother?'

Frankie felt on the verge of tears once again. 'Really?'

'Of course, silly. Who else would it be?' Cat's eyes were unusually wet. 'You know you're my only family, Frank. I mean, I love my dad but he never talks to me unless it's to ask for money or a job reference. And who the hell knows where my mother is? Rose, you're like my sister, my mum and my best friend all rolled into one.'

Tears dripped down Frankie's face as she clutched the sleeping baby in her arms.

'I love you and I love this nameless, half-Korean baby,' Frankie cried.

'I love you too, you big sook.'

The two silently sobbed next to each other, not speaking a word, but saying everything.

The door opened and Claud, carrying three paper cups of coffee, entered. 'What have we got here?' Claud kissed Cat's forehead. 'I've been thinking of more names. What about Edward, after my father?' Claud suggested.

'No, that reminds me of Edward Ferrars,' Cat dismissed. The baby had started to wake and was wriggling in Frankie's arms. She passed him delicately to Cat, who collected him with eager arms.

'And that's a bad thing? I love Edward Ferrars.' Frankie laughed.

'Romeo?' Claud suggested.

'Are you kidding?' Cat and Frankie said in unison.

'You want our child to be named after a boy who rebels against his family and then kills himself?' Cat said.

Claud rolled his eyes. 'Well, I don't hear you coming up with any great ideas.'

'I need to get to know him. Work out what name suits him,' Cat cooed as she stroked her baby's hair and smiled, her eyes twinkling. She stared at her baby for what felt like forever and then said, 'I want to call him Jin Soo.'

'Jin Soo? What sort of name is that?' Claud asked. Frankie suddenly focused her attention on the hot cup of coffee in her hand.

'It's the Korean character's name on *Lost*. I like it.'

'Cat, you've officially gone insane,' Claud remarked.

—41—

Reading between the lines

You might have been wondering where I've been these last few weeks (or not, because you most definitely have a far more interesting life of your own to worry about). But if, for whatever reason, you are just a little bit curious, here's where I'm at.

I went on my final train date with the South American acrobat/poet (yep, you read that right) who found my copy of *The Alchemist*. He was tall, dreamy, could throw me in the air with one seamless swoop, and had a heady accent. You'd think I'd be all, 'Would you mind if I stroked your abs?' and, 'Can we run away to the circus?' But really, I was all, 'What am I *doing* here?' and, 'I should be lounging on my couch with the man I love.'

You heard it here first, folks: I'm in love. And this was just the start of my undoing.

Stopping the train-date experiment has been a long time coming. I could no longer deny my feelings for Edward Cullen, or my guilt for that matter. But before I had a chance to come clean, he discovered my treachery in the most undignified of circumstances; a run-in with said acrobat at a mutual friend's party. Justifiably shocked and beyond hurt by my deceit, there was no convincing him out of dropping me like a hot potato.

I've stopped sleeping. I've stopped eating (fresh produce; it's all canned food and over-processed snacks for me). And I've stopped being able to look at myself in the mirror. He has blocked every one of my attempts to reconcile and I have been left suffused with my own regret. After fighting falling for so long, I now know how ridiculous I've been. How this whole experiment has been one long exercise in procrastination.

And then there's Perfectly Lovely But Still No Spark Tom. I happened to run into him after the previously mentioned – and extremely traumatic – hot-potato-dropping incident. He deigned to ask me out again. And I deigned to shut down emotionally and pretend he didn't exist. But three unreturned text messages and a phone call later, while at a particularly low point ('I'll never love again and will die all alone!') and, against my better judgement (You really should not listen to friends who are high on post-labour pain meds), I dared to give him another go. Being rejected by the love of your life time after time, and the fear of becoming a cat lady (I really don't like cats) will do that to a girl.

So, we met for a coffee after work. We discussed the merits of sequels, the correct placement of the apostrophe in Mothers' Day ('The day doesn't celebrate just one mother! It's ludicrous!') and how books make us more empathetic beings. And as we all could have predicted, the date was perfectly lovely. He lured me in with his deep respect for the written word and wowed me with his literary insights and social commentary. Tom is smart, attentive, kind and classically good looking. He is like John Steinbeck: one size fits all. But he just isn't Edward Cullen; the man who's harder to crack than a freshly shucked coconut and who has worse taste in books than my second cousin's twelve-year-old daughter.

Suddenly, everything seemed so blatantly (and almost uncomfortably) clear. Ever read *Enduring Love* by Ian McEwan? I have been re-reading sections of it on my way to work. In it he writes about only discovering love is a gift once it's gone – and so we should always fight for it from the beginning. Don't you love it when a book just seems to get you?

This *can't* be the end to our star-crossed love story. I *will* find a way to win him back.

Until next time, my dears.

After all, as the *other* Scarlett O' once said: 'If he's forgotten me, I'll make him remember me. I'll make him want me again.'

Scarlett O' xx

Leave a comment (1271)

Martha Stewing In It > Grass is always greener on the other side, hey? I hope it's not too late for you two!

No offence but ... > That's what you get for lying to someone you love.

> **Stephen Prince** > @Nooffencebut ... Ah Stephanie, I knew I could count on you for a snarky comment. PS I'd never lie to you ;)

> **No offence but ...** > @StephenPrince, you're a creep. PS Is that even your real name? I can't find you on Facebook.

> **Stephen Prince** > @Nooffencebut ... Now who's the creep? Stalking me online! And yes it's my real name. I just don't have Facebook.

> **No offence but ...** > @StephenPrince, Pfft ... I couldn't care less. Just checking you weren't a complete weirdo.

Tully McGregor > Go get him, gurl! And be sure to keep us updated.

Cat in the Hat > Took you long enough. PS @StephenPrince & @Nooffencebut ... love watching you guys flirt! ;)

Frankie was drunk. Not charmingly tipsy, not accidentally-had-a-few-too-many. She was stupidly, pitifully sloshed. She swayed back and forth, burying thoughts that this was a terrible idea. After drinking a bottle of Barossa Valley shiraz (the one she was saving for a special occasion) alone, she picked up her phone and drunk-dialled Sunny. It rang out to voicemail, like it always did. With her head spinning and her heart aching even more than usual, Frankie tied her hair up in a topknot and drunkenly stormed out of her apartment. And here she was, one nauseating Uber ride later, standing at Sunny's front door. At two in the morning.

'Sunny!' She banged on his door, her knuckles reddening. 'Sunny!' She knew Sunny was probably asleep. He was undoubtedly resting casually on top of his blanket, his sketchpad and pen balanced on his bare torso. Frankie's chest fluttered at the thought.

'Damn it, Sunny! I know you're in there,' she slurred, sloppily thrashing her hands on the front door. She heard brash, thumping footsteps and inhaled. *He's coming to get me.*

'Frankie. What the hell are you doing?' Sunny swung the door open. His hair was tousled, his boxer shorts hung loosely around his hips and, just as she had imagined, his chest was irresistibly exposed.

'Sunnnnny,' Frankie gurgled, resting her hands on his chest. 'Just the beautiful man I wanted to see.' She leaned into his torso and kissed it, laughing.

'Jesus, Frankie. You're wasted.' Sunny's forehead creased in the centre, like it always did when he was frustrated. He pulled her away and looked her up and down. She was wearing nothing but her silk pyjama shorts and camisole, and tiny goosebumps covered her body.

'And you're handsome.' She giggled, then hiccupped indelicately.

'Fuck, Frankie. You're freezing. Come on, I'll call you an Uber home.' Sunny reached into his pocket to take out his phone, but Frankie grabbed his hand before he could.

'No, I want to come in. Invite me in, silly billy.' She laughed. *Everything is so funny tonight.*

'That's not a good idea, Frankie.'

'What? Why? Do you have someone else here? Another woman?' Frankie asked, lilting to the side. 'Hello! Other woman? Hello!' she called behind Sunny.

'You're being ridiculous, Frankie. I'm calling you an Uber,' Sunny said angrily.

'You *do* have another woman in here! I can't believe it!' Frankie pushed past Sunny's barricading body (she was particularly strong when she was intoxicated) and ran into his bedroom.

'Hello? Mrs Sunny! Come out, come out wherever you are.' She stopped at the side of his bed. Sitting on his bedside table, for the whole world to see, was a sketch of her. In it, her hair was tied up, just like it was now, and her head was thrown back in fits of laughter. He had drawn every detail of her perfectly, right down to the freckle above her eyebrow.

'What's this?' Frankie picked up the sketch, her hands shaking.

'Get out of my bedroom, Frankie,' he barked.

'What *is* this?' she asked again, standing on her tiptoes to press the sketch up to his face.

'It's nothing.' He snatched the paper out of her hands and ripped it in half. 'I was drawing you out of me, line by line.' He let the torn drawing float to the floor.

Frankie stepped back as she watched it fall.

'You didn't have to do that.' Frankie pouted, looking at the torn drawing at her feet.

'Frankie, please, you have to go. You can't be here.' Sunny's forehead crease was particularly prominent. He looked tired, exasperated even. She was about to leave when she noticed his eyes trail her body, from head to toe. They glazed over in … in desire? Frankie crept closer to him and placed a hand on his bicep.

'You don't really want me to leave, do you?' she purred.

'Frankie, stop it,' Sunny snapped, pulling his arm away.

Frankie smiled and brushed her hair away from her face. She was overcome with her newfound, alcohol-induced confidence. She edged towards Sunny, reached out to him and seductively whispered in his ear, 'Come on. It doesn't have to mean anything. Just a one-time thing.' She softly kissed his bicep.

'Frankie,' Sunny uttered, his voice faltering.

Frankie took his hesitation as a sign, and slowly leaned into him, kissing his bare chest. 'Come on, don't you miss this?' She kissed him again.

'Frankie,' he groaned.

'Shh …' She sighed, kissing him over and over. 'Do you miss this?' She gently nipped his skin. She heard him inhale, waver and then release.

'Fuck it,' he grated, and picked her up over his shoulder. He threw her hastily down on his bed, and almost fell on top of her before she had a second to breathe.

'Don't you miss this?' She sighed into his skin, letting his weight engulf her. He answered by kissing her with a fervent, angry passion, like he was livid and hungry with desire all at the same time. She kissed him with equal lust and rage, until they were both entangled in a mess of aching fury.

Ach, my head.

Frankie peeled open her eyes and was shocked to find herself in Sunny's bed. Naked. Light crept through the curtains, making her head throb. Then it all came back to her, like a startling, raw flash. The drunken confrontation, the sketch, the *kiss*. She groaned, pulling the sheets over her head. She breathed in deeply, the sweet scent of Sunny surrounding her. How she had missed being in this bed. Frankie rolled over lazily, wanting to drape her arm over him. But instead, her arm hit the exposed mattress.

'Sunny?' she called hesitantly.

No reply.

She staggered out of bed and threw on one of Sunny's T-shirts. *This is all too familiar. Heartbreakingly familiar.* She crept towards the bathroom, her bare feet grazing the cold tiles, and carefully opened the door. He wasn't there. She scoured the kitchen, the living room, the study. He was nowhere to be found.

'Sunny?' she called again, her head pounding, her eyes still half-open. She found her phone lying near the front door and clicked it on. One SMS from Sunny, sent an hour ago, awaited her.

💬 Sunny: Damn it, Frankie. You can't do that. You can't just come to my place in the middle of the night and pretend like nothing's happened. We're over, Frankie.

279

We are well and truly over, and I shouldn't have done anything last night to make you think otherwise. Please, stop calling me. I've left for the day. Lock the door after you.

Frankie breathed in and out, tears burning behind her eyes. She squeezed the phone, threw it to the other side of the room and let out an ear-piercing, thunderous scream.

—43—

Frankie moved on autopilot. It was only hours after she had ashamedly left Sunny's home, and she felt empty. She reached into her bag, pulled out her train pass and tapped onto the waiting tram. She shuffled towards an empty seat and slumped down onto it, barely registering her surroundings. A dark, ominous cloud had descended around her and she couldn't shake the immense feeling of loss. She was so buried in her thoughts, Frankie failed to notice the tattered copy of *Still Alice* sitting unaccompanied on the seat next to her. If she had, she might have picked it up, flipped through it and discovered her own handwriting scrawled on the seventh-last page. A few weeks ago this serendipitous train ride would have brought her immense excitement, but now, all she felt while riding public transport was the echo of her latest string of bad decisions.

Frankie was on her way to visit Cat and baby Jin Soo. Cat would be leaving hospital the next day and had insisted that Frankie take a break from being stand-in bookstore manager to be there for the final baby-bath demonstration with the midwife. 'As godmother, you need to know the basics of baby care,' Cat had told her over the phone. 'Lesson number one: when to know when Mamma needs some alone time.' Cat had been behaving even more erratically than usual these last few days; all sunshine and smiles one moment and then a ball of tears the next. Claud had been texting Frankie incessantly, asking her what he should be doing to support his turbulent wife. Ordinarily, Claud adored Cat's eccentric mood swings and latest obsessions, but now that there was another human in the picture, and one for whom he was responsible, he was desperate to cocoon his new family in knitted wool. But fatherhood, it seemed, had injected him not only with a new warmth but also, somewhat loveably, uncertainty. Feeling completely out of his depth, he was questioning even his most basic intuitions. Frankie had tried to console him by insisting that he was doing a great job and that it was just the post-labour hormonal rollercoaster. She advised that he make himself useful by ensuring an on-tap array of coffee and soft cheeses, and also to support Cat during each extremely confronting and painful postpartum bowel movement. Frankie hoped that Cat would, in turn, settle once back home, but she feared her friend's feelings ran much deeper than a hormonal imbalance.

The tram jolted to a stop and Frankie flew forward, knocking her head against the metal pole in front of her. *If that's not karma, I don't know what is.* Rubbing her head, she grabbed her bag, threw a half-hearted glare towards the conductor's seat and jumped off. Navigating her way towards the hospital, she obsessively refreshed each one of the apps on her phone: Mail, Facebook, Messages, WhatsApp, Snapchat, and even Calendar alerts, in the hope that Sunny had contacted her. Closing each empty app, one after the other, was like another nail in the coffin.

Frankie wound down the corridor of the maternity ward until she arrived outside Cat's room. The door was just slightly ajar and from it escaped the sound of muffled wails. Frankie smiled at this new noise, which pulled deeply at her heartstrings. She heard Cat's feet shuffling back and forth, and over the noise of the distressed baby, bits and pieces of one half of her friend's phone conversation wafted towards her.

'I can't keep this a secret anymore,' she hissed.

Pause.

'I know you're not ready for this, but guess what? We can hardly ask for a refund.'

Pause. Heavy breathing. Crying.

Frankie tentatively propped open the door and slid inside. She planted a kiss on Cat's cheek and took little Jin from her arms, breathing in his delicious baby smell.

'I better go. I'll call you later.' Cat hung up the phone and carefully lowered herself onto the armchair that sat next to the only window in the room. The bench alongside her was littered with an array of flowers, nappies, baby clothes, baby bottles and dummies; all the paraphernalia for Cat's new life.

Frankie smothered Jin Soo with kisses, managing to love his gurgling cries into submission until she was able to gaze down at his scrunched-up face and marvel at the touch of his silky skin.

'I just want to eat him,' she cooed.

'I'll tell you what *I* want to eat ...' Cat didn't need to finish her sentence; Frankie had already kicked her handbag over to her. Cat clapped her hands with delight, bent over with a small wince, and riffled through its contents. She pulled out a small paper bag containing fresh salmon sushi, holding it above her head like she'd just won the Australian Open. 'You are an absolute godsend. I've never loved you more!' she said, chowing down on one of the rolls. Between mouthfuls of rice she absentmindedly whipped out her left boob and began squeezing it absentmindedly. Frankie looked on in horror.

'What are you doing?' Frankie nodded towards her chest.

'Just your average colostrum massage. Got to get these boobs working,' Cat replied, beginning to massage her right boob.

'Does it hurt?'

'Well, it's no trip to the Caribbean, but it's okay.' Cat tore at the second roll of sushi.

'And you don't mind getting the girls out in front of people?' Frankie ran her index finger along Jin Soo's silky baby hair, entranced. She had never felt anything more velvety.

'Firstly, you're hardly *people*.' She chewed. 'And secondly, flying body parts is just a fact of birth and babies. I'm constantly naked these days.'

'So, nothing much's changed, then?'

Cat smirked.

Jin Soo stirred in Frankie's arms, stirring a deep longing in her. She leaned down and kissed his warm forehead. Without taking her eyes off him, she inquired casually, 'Who was on the phone just now?'

Cat slowly swallowed her last bite. 'Jin Soo.'

'He's very advanced, that Jin Soo. He already knows how to work an iPhone?'

'Well, he wasn't born yesterday,' Cat retorted, slowly easing back into the chair.

Frankie laughed. 'So, what's going on with you two?'

'Frank, I don't know what to do.' Cat sniffed.

Frankie looked up. She had never seen her friend look so terrified.

'I can't keep this lie up forever,' she said, sucking in her breath.

Frankie gazed down at the little baby cradled in her arms. How could something so innocent and sweet already be at the centre of a situation so complicated? 'It's a wonder Claud hasn't cottoned on yet. You know, in cavemen days, if the baby didn't look like the father, he'd just kill it. That's why newborns always look so much like their dad,' Frankie said. 'But right now, Claud's just seeing everything through rose-coloured glasses, he's so smitten. We have to come up with a game plan.'

'I'm not talking about Claud.' Cat resumed her rigid pose in the armchair, eyes averted.

'What *are* you talking about?' Frankie asked as she rose from the edge of the bed, bobbing up and down in soothing, rhythmic movements.

'I'm talking about *you*, Frankie,' Cat said quietly. 'I haven't been totally honest with you.'

'You shat during the birth, didn't you? I knew it. You won't get a single poo past me!' Frankie chuckled into Jin Soo's opening eyes, trying to elicit a smile from her suddenly solemn friend.

'I'm being serious, Frankie. I haven't been completely honest about Jin Soo and me.'

Frankie glanced at Cat, who was nervously rearranging packets of nappies as she pulled her top back on. Finally sorted, she walked over to Frankie and lovingly scooped the baby back into her arms.

'Armour,' she said, nodding down at Jin Soo. 'Now you can't get mad at me.'

Frankie's arms fell to her sides. She suddenly felt even emptier. 'What's going on, Cat?'

'Jin Soo and I weren't exactly a one-time thing,' she said almost inaudibly as she started to turn away.

'What was that?' Frankie gently took Cat's shoulders and turned her back so she could look her in the eye. 'Cat?'

'Jin Soo and I weren't a one-time thing!' Cat said, sniffing loudly. 'I lied. I lied about it being just once.'

Frankie felt her jaw drop. 'What are you talking about? So, what – you did the dirty, two, three times?' Frankie asked, her eyebrows raised at her mute friend. 'Five times?'

Cat's eyes dashed back and forth, looking for somewhere, anywhere other than Frankie's face to rest on.

'Oh my God, Cat, how many times did you two do it?'

'I couldn't tell you exactly.' Cat rocked the baby side to side, clearly regretting jumping down this rabbit hole.

'You better get out your calculator and tell me this instant, young lady.' Frankie was beginning to lose her patience.

'I can't tell you how many times, because it's too many to count!' Cat's voice rose a fraction. 'We've been on-again, off-again for months.'

Frankie sat down hard on the edge of the bed, unable to believe what she was hearing. *Months?* Her friend – her pregnant friend – had been unfaithful to her husband for *months?* And she had kept all of this from her? Cat and Frankie told each other everything. Everything. Frankie had been the first to know when Cat lost her virginity. Cat had texted her mere moments after finishing: 'Deed is done. Why doesn't anybody ever talk about how sticky it is?' And it had been Frankie who was first on the scene when Cat's mum abandoned her and she was insisting that she was 'seriously fine'. Frankie and Cat just didn't keep secrets from each other. And when it came to emotional breakdowns, they definitely did not miss a beat. *Have I been too caught up in my own love life and flailing career to notice that my best friend really needed me? God, I am a terrible person!*

'Jesus, Cat. I don't know what to say.'

'I've fucked up, Frankie. Big time.' Cat attempted to cover Jin Soo's ears at the mention of the 'f' word. 'And Jin Soo keeps calling, saying he wants to be in his son's life and that he loves me and wants to be with me. But he has no idea what I have at stake here! Or what it actually means to have a child. A child that is going to be around forever. Forever is a fucking long time, Frankie.' Tears began to stream down Cat's face, a couple ricocheting off Jin Soo's plump baby cheeks. Frankie rose from the bed and went to balance on the arm of Cat's chair, wrapping her arms tightly around her blubbering friend.

'I don't know what to do, Frankie. All I've ever known is Claud. And he may be far from perfect, but he's *my* Claud: the handsome man I fell in love with when I was barely old enough to know better and then vowed to be faithful to for the rest of my life.' Cat leaned her head against Frankie's shoulder. Frankie could feel her cries ripple through her. 'God, look at me, I'm a bigger baby than this little tot!'

'Cat, it's totally understandable for you to feel this way,' Frankie said as soothingly as she could. 'You've just had a baby. I mean, you've freaking pushed a real, live human being out of your vagina! And now you're faced with this awful dilemma.'

'Yeah, the awful dilemma that I got my stupid self into.'

'And look what came from it.' They both looked down wistfully at Jin Soo. 'It could be worse.'

They sat, leaning against each other, staring at the culmination of passion and longing and confusion. Jin Soo slept on peacefully, not yet aware of the turmoil that was unravelling around him.

'Look at him,' Cat finally said. 'He's just so beautiful. How could I be so cruel as to welcome him into a world filled with my problems? Hello daddy issues!'

Frankie simultaneously rubbed Cat's back and the bottom of Jin Soo's feet.

'I'm already the worst mum in the world,' Cat cried.

'That is so far from the truth. Just look at him! He's warm and happy and loved. I mean, so beyond loved! And he has not one, but two fathers who adore him and want to be in his life.'

'Extra dads don't generally mean that kids turn out extra well adjusted. What have I done?'

'You *will* make this work. You just need to come clean.'

'I can't. Claud will be devastated. He'll never forgive me!'

'I'm not talking about Claud, Cat. I'm talking about you. It's time you were honest with yourself. You need to decide what you want. *Who* you want. Make a decision and stick to it. Nurture your baby with love, stability and attention, and you'll have yourself a winner.'

Cat smiled for the first time. 'When did you get so wise, Rose?'

Frankie smiled at Cat. 'You're going to be okay, Catty. And so will Jin Soo.'

During Frankie's visit, the sky had cleared and now shone a bright blue. The air still nipped at her, but as Frankie headed home she felt healed by the presence of the sun. By the time she had left, Cat had regained her composure and was sitting happily in bed, nursing her new baby. Frankie had no idea whom Cat would choose, which life she intended to pursue. But she knew that she trusted her friend to make the right decision, not just for herself, but for her child. Out of habit, she pulled her phone from her back pocket and flashed the screen on, searching for any sign of contact from Sunny.

Head buried in her hunt, she didn't notice a man step out from the doorway of a cafe. As she raced past, Frankie tripped on his outstretched foot and toppled onto the footpath.

'Jesus Christ, man,' Frankie berated. Still flat on the ground, she turned over and squinted up.

'Are you all right? I am so sorry.' The man stepped into her line of sight, his face shadowed by the glare of the sun. He cradled two takeaway cups on top of each other and put out his hand, half-pulling, half-lifting Frankie up off the footpath.

Frankie brushed herself off, grumbling under her breath.

'Are you sure you're okay? Do you need ice? Are you bleeding?'

'No, thanks.' Frankie inspected her hands before shielding her eyes with them. 'Oh my God, Jin Soo?'

'Sorry, do I know you?' a slightly startled Jin Soo replied.

'I'm Frankie, Cat's Frankie. I've been to your class. I was just visiting your b— Ah, visiting Cat in hospital.'

Jin Soo shifted the coffee cups nervously in his hands.

'It's okay. I know everything.'

Jin Soo looked at her with a sudden intensity. 'You know, I really love her. It's been so much more than some casual fling,' he breathed. 'I can't live without her. Or him. Isn't he just gorgeous?'

Frankie blinked twice before staring him coolly in the eye. 'Yes, he is. I know his father, Claud, thinks so too.' And she stepped around him and made her way back along the street.

As Frankie waited for the pedestrian light to turn green she leaned forward, peering down Church Street. Just a couple of blocks away from her apartment, she was anxious to get home, to get lost in her copy of *The Gulf*. She watched a tram lumber down the street, ringing its bell to signal its approach. At the stop sat a man reading *The Dry* by Jane Harper. He was so engrossed that he didn't notice when the tram pulled up alongside him. Frankie yearned to escape to another world, to fall prey to the pages of somebody else's sorrow, jubilation, loss and redemption. *Redemption.* The word resounded in her mind.

She needed absolution. But how? She watched the man jump as the tram tolled its bell once again, the clang sounding loud and impatient. He stuffed his book under his arm and jumped on, and from where Frankie stood she could see him sit down and curl back into the pages of his book.

She half-smiled at the thought that just a couple of months ago she probably would have chased him down, egging on this travelling bookworm to find one of her books. *A reader of high-quality Australian fiction? Sign me up!* She scolded herself under her breath for being so deluded, so superficial, so immature. Now, she was absorbed by thoughts of only one (Young Adult) bookworm. What she would give for him to discover her trail of stories and be compelled to call her. Or text her. Or email her. Even if it were just to accuse her of breaking his heart all over again. She craved his contact like Amy March craved pickled limes.

How could she make him listen, forgive, forget? The tram whizzed past her, the force of it tossing her hair back.

—44—

By George (Orwell), I've got it!

Now that I know what I'm going to do to win back my man (*sassy clicking*), I can't quite believe it didn't occur to me earlier.

Once I finally realised that leaving voice message after voice message on the hour, every hour and staking out Edward Cullen's apartment just wasn't going to do the trick, I knew I had to get creative. And fast. There's a delicate timeframe in which a break-up turns quickly from hurt feelings, to devastation, to hatred, to a terrifying and rapid determination to move on. And that time is called Tinder.

So, I put my thinking cap on and got to work. Here's what I realised I had going for me.

1. Edward Cullen digs a romantic gesture. In fact, he once told me that there was no problem too big or situation too grave that a good old-fashioned, sweep-you-off-your-feet act of love couldn't fix.
2. I have access to books. Plenty of books! And thankfully, I at least understand books, and when a situation calls for a good one (it's my job, after all).
3. If I've learned anything from this derailed experiment, nothing brings people together quite like a brilliant paperback.

So, that's where I started: books and romance. It wasn't much, but it was something.

First, I thought, write the best Young Adult dystopian novel he has ever laid his beautiful, broad hands on! Then he'll have to take me back! I grabbed my laptop, clicked open a fresh document, and got as far as: *THINK OF A SCINTILLATING OPENING LINE FOR A YOUNG ADULT BOOK. HELP!*

Once I recovered from that two-and-a-half hours of torture, I moved on to my next grand idea. I grabbed a pile of books, some scissors and a piece of butcher's paper and made my own love quotes comprised of random words cut from the pages of some of the greatest love stories of all time. 'Let me be the words written on your heart.' *sigh*

I took a step back and surveyed my handiwork … and realised that it looked like a bad ransom note. I scratched that idea pretty quickly.

Then I started to get a little desperate. I googled, in order: 'top ten romantic gestures', 'how to win back your ex', 'what to do when you've fucked everything up', and 'how to glue your relationship (and books) back together'. But nothing!

And finally, it hit me: it all started and ended on a train. Our first electric kiss and the final blow, the disastrous discovery of my train date plot – all the secrets that I had been keeping from him. Maybe it was one last (or several final) ride(s) on the rails that we needed. I reassessed the books lying before me and realised I was looking at this from the wrong angle. I was only thinking about this from my point of view (#typical #turningintomymother). I was picking out of the works of fiction that had moved *me* and had failed to consider which books would actually get *his* heart racing. So, I went back to the drawing board (ahem, bookstore). I scoured it for some of his favourite books and piled them on top of each other.

The Hunger Games
Divergent
The Perks of Being a Wallflower
The Knife of Never Letting Go

Cringe. Cringe. Cringe.

Next, I pulled up the online train timetable and noted every train line I knew Edward Cullen took and every time of day he might travel. What I came up with was a neat little plan to book-ninja the hell out of Melbourne's public-transport system. Over the next few days I would release as many Young Adult books as I could muster on as many carriages as possible, in the hope that he would discover one such book with these words scribbled inside:

I'm sorry. I love you. Please call me – Frankie xo

After all, 'Longing hearts could only stand so much longing.'
Until next time, my dears.
Scarlett O' xx

Leave a comment (1232)

Love Affair with Books > Such great books. Damn, there are some superb writers out there. Fingers crossed he finds your book!

No offence but ... > I don't think a book or two is going to make up for your mistake.

Stephen Prince > @Nooffencebut ... There you are!

No offence but ... > @StephenPrince, you're actually obsessed with me.

Maddy Pretty Picky > Love your work, Scarlett. Praying for you xx

---

The Book Thief by Markus Zusak
Route 11 tram to Brunswick Street

An Abundance of Katherines by John Green
Glen Waverley train line to the city

Stargirl by Jerry Spinelli
Frankston train line to Flinders Street

Wonder by RJ Palacio
Alamein train line to Alamein

A Monster Calls by Patrick Ness
Route 11 tram to Brunswick Street

Frankie looked on either side of her and, when the coast was clear, discreetly placed her brand-new copy of *Looking for Alaska* on the seat beside her. She pressed her hand inside the book, feeling for the dog-eared page on which was written: 'I'm sorry. I love you. Please call me – Frankie xo'. She sighed, subconsciously crossing her fingers and toes. *Please, please find this book, Sunny*, she silently chanted. Since she had concocted her plan to win Sunny back, Frankie had gone crazy distributing Young Adult books on train, tram and bus lines. Copies of *Eleanor & Park*, *The Maze Runner*, *We Were Liars* and even *Are You There God? It's Me, Margaret* now travelled the Melbourne public-transport network. With Cat on maternity leave, Frankie and Seb had full rein of the The Little Brunswick Street Bookshop (including organising that event with Maxine Beneba Clarke which Claud had said was totally out of their budget), and one or fifty 'borrowed' Young Adult books. Usually she would be embarrassed to walk around carrying piles of these books in her bag, but now she didn't care. She cared only about winning Sunny back.

Frankie leaned back in her seat and watched the tram travellers, wondering where they were headed at the end of another week. A chubby man wearing large black headphones moved to the beat, holding the handrail. *Probably off to a poetry slam at a bar in Footscray.* Two schoolgirls crossed their legs identically on the seat in front of hers, chewing gum and twirling their hair. *On their way to a friend's house to watch the latest episode of* Jane the Virgin. Was anyone watching her? wondered Frankie. Were any of her fellow commuters curious about where she was off to this Friday evening? Would they guess that she was on her way to open up the bookstore for her seventeen-year-old second-best friend, who had accidentally left his school bag there earlier in the day? She hoped she gave off a slightly less pitiful vibe than that.

Frankie took out her phone and refreshed the screen, flicking on and off the 'silent' button. Just in case someone called. Just in case *he* called.

At the same exact moment that she pressed the screen, a call came through, and Frankie accidentally slid her finger across the glass, accepting the call. 'Hello?' she heard someone call from the other end of the phone.

'Uh, hello?' she asked hesitantly, her heart skipping a beat. It sank when she heard a female voice.

'Frankie! It's Marie from Simon & Schuster! Sorry for calling so late, love,' she hollered.

'Uh, that's okay. No problem. How are you?' Frankie played anxiously with a hole in her stockings.

'I'm great. I hope you are too. Anyway, down to business. I never received an email from you about turning your blog into a book. What are your thoughts? Shall we set up a meeting for Monday?' she said chirpily.

Frankie hesitated. 'Uh … I'm not sure I want to go ahead with it.'

'With what, dear?' Marie asked.

'With the book. I don't think I want to do anything with the blog. Due to, um, personal issues.'

'Nonsense! Personal issues? What do you mean? Frankie, you'd be crazy to turn down an opportunity like this. Did I tell you we're thinking international sales? Film options? The lot?'

'Yeah. It's just, there's this guy …' Frankie started.

'A *guy*? Don't tell me you're considering putting your dreams on hold for a guy? Let me be frank, Frankie. This kind of opportunity only comes around once in a lifetime. No man is worth sacrificing your dreams. Trust me,' she said, with a hint of bitterness in her voice.

'I know, it's just …'

Marie persisted, insisting on a 'no strings attached' meeting, just to meet the team and talk it all through. Backed into a corner, Frankie took a deep breath and, somewhat reluctantly, accepted.

'Lovely! Have a fab weekend and see you Monday at eleven,' Marie finished with a trill.

Somewhat overwhelmed and a little confused, Frankie tucked her phone back into her backpack, in between her copies of *Red Queen* and *If I Stay*, and slung her bag loosely over one shoulder as the tram pulled up at the Leicester Street stop. She walked swiftly towards the exit, dropping a copy of *Percy Jackson and the Lightning Thief* on a spare seat on her way out.

'Miss, you left your book!' the man with headphones called after her a little too loudly. She turned to him, smiled, and said, 'It's not mine,' as she stepped off. Huddling for a moment under the tram shelter, she took out a copy of *Holes* and placed it on the vacant seat. As she turned to leave, she stopped, frozen to the spot.

There it was, lit up in neon lights, even more beautiful than she had imagined. A striking watercolour painting of the gruesome scene from *Romeo and Juliet*, the words *KIDNEY-CROSSED LOVERS* emblazoned over the top. Sunny's painting. Sunny's ad. Even though she had seen him working on it for the last few months, it was startling to see it in public. It was so confronting, so arresting, so striking. Frankie felt her heart quicken.

Frankie took out her keys, fiddling with them as she walked down bustling Brunswick Street to the bookstore. She pulled down her beanie so it was covering her entire forehead, and wrapped her puffa coat tightly around her body, protecting herself from the chill. A woman in skyscraper heels and a barely-there black dress sashayed past her, blowing smoke in her face. As she approached the front door of the bookstore, she saw, with a touch of concern, that it was slightly ajar.

'Hello?' She called out hesitantly through the gap in the door. No response. Apart from her, only Cat and Claud had keys to the store. *And I did leave my spare set at Sunny's.* She took in a deep breath of fresh air, pressed her keys between the knuckles of her right hand, placed her left hand on the cool glass of the door and slowly edged it open.

'Hello? Is there anyone in here? I've got a weapon!' she called out. She smelled fire. *Shit. Arsonists?* She took out her phone to call the police, as she crept inside.

The bookstore lit up before her. Hundreds of tea-light candles lined the floor and benchtops, flickering wildly, and among them lay a trail of rose petals leading towards the Romantic Fiction aisle.

Sunny? Has he found one of my books? Is this his romantic reply? Her heart raced as she made her way along the floral path. She turned into the row of shelves and found a shadow kneeling in a bed of petals.

'Sunny!' she called.

The body before her stirred and looked up. It took a moment for Frankie to make sense of what she was seeing.

'Seb? What are you doing?' Frankie stuttered.

Seb wore a suit that looked two sizes too big, and his usually scruffy hair was combed back. 'Frankston Rose,' he said, then cleared his throat, still kneeling on the floor, the glimmer of the candlelight dancing wildly between them. 'You're weird and nerdy and ridiculously awkward.' Frankie stared, her mind racing as she tried to hear his words and understand what was actually happening. 'But so am I,' Seb continued. He was looking down at the floor, as if trying to remember lines for a school play, his hands shaking. 'The last two years have been the best of my life. And that's because I've been able to spend them coming into this bookstore with you. Seeing your face, listening to your stories and hearing your nonsensical reasons why romantic literature is better than sci-fi – well, they've been the highlights of my days. I know there's a lot of things pulling us apart, but, Frankie, there's so much that's holding us together.' Frankie looked wildly around for support, but neither Jane Austen nor any of the Brontës could help her now. 'I guess what I'm trying to say is: Frankie, I'm in love with you. Completely and utterly. And in the words of Jane, "I have loved none but you".' Seb slowly stood up, holding onto the bookcase to steady himself.

What the hell am I going to say? screamed Frankie's inner voice. *Why did he have to do this? Oh Sunny, why isn't this you? This is supposed to be you!* Seb was fidgeting with his oversized tie, staring at her in anticipation.

'Seb,' she said finally, in a voice she hoped sounded neither unpleasant nor eager. She edged back towards the front counter, giving herself a moment to compose her thoughts. Seb slowly followed, pressing his back against the firm wooden bench

'I love you too, you know I do,' Frankie finally said, taking a deep breath. 'You add sparkle to my days, you really do. But I'm eleven years older than you. You're like the brother I never had. And ... you know I'm in love with Sunny.'

'Ouch.' Seb jolted back like he had been slapped.

'I'm sorry, Seb.' Frankie looked down.

'Hey.' Seb paused. 'You asked for a romantic gesture. At least I tried.' He shrugged, but Frankie heard the tremor in his voice. 'Looks like it's a life of fake girlfriends for me!'

'You made Celeste up?' Frankie gawked at Seb, who was turning pinker by the minute.

'Thought it might send you wild with jealousy! Nothing like a love triangle to get the juices flowing, eh?' Seb said, faking nonchalance. Then he paused, and said sheepishly, 'I'm going to get out of here, if you don't mind. You right to clean up this mess, Frankston?' He gestured to the candles and petals.

'Sure, Seb. Anything for you.'

Seb slung a backpack over his shoulder and headed to the front door. 'Hey,' he said, turning around, 'when I'm twenty-nine and you're forty, call me.' He winked, jingling the bell as he left.

🐢

'So, that's why he asked for my key.' Cat laughed. Jin Soo (the baby, not the man) was wrapped in a light blue blanket and attached firmly to her right breast, greedily guzzling milk. Cat sat on her bed, wearing an entirely unbuttoned floral fleecy pyjama shirt, casually revealing both her breasts.

Frankie reclined beside her, staring in awe at the baby affixed to her best friend's boob. 'Oh, Cat. It was terrible. Poor Seb. I just don't see how he could've thought—'

'That you were remotely interested in him? He's a completely deluded seventeen year old. You know, like we used to be?' Cat stroked Jin Soo's soft, black hair.

'You know, I always thought he was gay.'

'Me too. You never know, Frankie, maybe you just turned him.' Cat laughed. Frankie swatted her lightly.

'So, how are you feeling, you know, about everything?' Frankie asked hesitantly.

'Oh, you mean when am I going to tell my husband about my baby daddy? I'm not feeling too great about it, surprisingly!' Frankie rubbed Cat's arm to show her support. 'Tell me about you. Any word from Sunny?' Cat carefully switched Jin Soo to her other breast.

'Nope.' Frankie sighed. 'I must've put out about a hundred books by now. All around his area. But no word. Surely he's spotted one.'

Cat rubbed Frankie's back with her spare hand. 'Give him time, Frank. Embrace your scars and give him time and space.'

'That sounds like a quote from a Cormac McCarthy book,' Frankie said as she rolled her eyes.

'It's not, but I thought it would make me sound smart.' Cat grinned.

Frankie jumped at the sound of the front door slamming.

'Claud's home,' Cat said anxiously.

'You haven't told him yet, right?' Frankie murmured.

'No, but I feel like he might be finally catching on.'

'How's my little James?' Claud waltzed into their bedroom, cheeks flushed, and patted Jin Soo's hair. A pair of knitting needles poked out of his bag.

'His name is Jin Soo.'

'I'm not calling my son Jin Soo,' Claud bit back, the tension in the air as warm as ice.

'How are you, Frankie?' Claud turned to her, as if just noticing she was there. 'I heard you might be getting published again. That's great!' He feigned a smile.

'Oh well, I'm still sceptical. I have a meeting with my publisher Monday morning, so we'll see.' Frankie shrugged.

'You do?' Cat asked. 'That's so exciting, Frank!'

Frankie nodded nervously.

'Baby James, you're a hungry little one, aren't you?' Claud gushed over his son.

'If you call him James one more time, I swear to God ...' Cat sighed.

Frankie picked up her handbag awkwardly, the weight of the books inside pulling heavily at her arm.

'I better go,' Frankie said, backing towards the door. Cat and Claud were mid-argument, now shouting about everything from circumcision to public versus private schools. They didn't even notice her sneak out.

🐢

Frankie was standing on the Mind the Gap floor sign on the platform of Brunswick station reading aloud from Jandy Nelson's *I'll Give You the Sun*. She found herself mulling over a beautiful passage about slipping out of people's lives and not being able to find a way back to them. It was one of the Young Adult books she had taken to plant on the train for Sunny to find, but having left her copy of *Tin Man* at home, she had started to read it as a last resort. She had skimmed the first few pages and instantly become addicted. Consumed by the flawless writing and underlying themes of first love, family and loss, she couldn't deny that she was thoroughly enjoying this book. *Damn you, Sunny.*

The train pulled up at the platform, its engine slowing down in beat with the pace of her heart. As the doors opened she stepped forward, head still buried in the book. Her foot fell inelegantly through the gap in front of her, and she braced herself, ready to tumble forward. Just then, she felt strong hands catch her from behind, steadying her onto the train carriage. She turned around, butterflies rioting in her stomach. *Sunny?*

'Mind the gap,' the man, who was definitely not Sunny, said. He was handsome in a refined sort of way. Big black glasses framed his green eyes, his hair was combed neatly to the side and he was so tall he almost had to crouch to fit inside the train carriage. He was the sort of man Frankie would have swooned over. BS (Before Sunny), that is.

Frankie offered her thanks breathlessly, and went to sit down. The man followed, sitting opposite her. She returned to her copy of *I'll Give You the Sun*, inhaling the words like the scent of freshly baked cookies.

'Any good?' the man inquired, nodding towards her book. She looked up, and saw that he was reading *My Dear Cassandra*. Frankie bit her lip. *Of course he's reading one of my favourites.*

'Yeah, it's great actually. It's a Young Adult book,' she said.

'Oh, that's nice. I haven't been able to get into any yet, but I've heard good things. I'm loving my book.' He nodded towards *My Dear Cassandra*. He seemed to be itching to discuss it.

'Never heard of it.' Frankie shrugged, turning back to her novel.

'Tickets please!' She heard the shrill voice of a train inspector entering her carriage. She casually reached inside her bag for her train ticket. *Shit.*

'Everything okay?' the man asked.

'My ticket, it's in my other bag. I always do this!' Frankie said, frazzled.

'Oh dear,' the man said unhelpfully.

Frankie looked around anxiously, thinking about the last time she was stuck on a train without a ticket. *If only Sunny were here.* She glanced at the man busily reading his book. *I could do it right now. Just kiss him. Why not?* she considered, and then buried the thought.

'Tickets please,' the inspector instructed, standing in front of her and the man. The officer's dark brown hair, speckled with grey flecks, was tied in a tight bun on top of her head. She scowled at them both, as if challenging them to fail her.

The man took his ticket unhurriedly from his wallet, and handed it over to the woman. As she returned it, he thanked her and then looked down, avoiding all eye contact with Frankie. *Well, thanks for nothing.*

The inspector turned to Frankie with one hand outstretched expectantly and the other resting on her hip. Frankie searched through her bag, pretending to look for the ticket she knew wasn't there. The man coughed, embarrassed, and looked out the window. *Goody two shoes.* 'Uh, look. I'm really sorry. I must've left my ticket at home—' Frankie began.

'Stop right there!' The inspector held up her hand, making Frankie flinch. 'I know you,' the woman said animatedly. 'You're Period Girl! My daughter and her friends were obsessed with your video. Forget about the ticket. Can I get a selfie?'

—46—

From: Benjamin Norwood
To: Scarlett O'
Subject: I'm glad this book has an owner

Dear Scarlett,

First, I must say thank you. Thank you for giving me the gift of a finely crafted story. My sister discovered your copy of *The Shadow of the Wind* during her morning commute and, since she passed it on to me a few weeks ago, I haven't been able to tear myself away. I was deeply moved by the words of Carlos Ruiz Zafón. In fact, I devoured his book with a highlighter at the ready, underlining quote after quote. This story is not only a dark and intoxicating tale of loss, murder and love, but also manages to dream up a world in which books are personified and a love of literature is sacred. If you remove the themes of death and destruction, I think I'd quite like to live in this kind of book utopia!

Now, I hope you don't find me presumptuous when I say, I think you too may wish to inhabit one such world.

Since discovering your note near the back of the book (I actually stumbled across it halfway through reading it after the book, fatefully some would say, fell open to the page after I knocked it off my nightstand), I haven't been able to stop thinking about who the woman behind the scribble might be. I tried to create an image of you as I read, picturing the kind of person who would carefully select this text for what I feel is such a daring plan. I fear I may already be quite besotted with you.

I hope you'll do me the kindness of allowing me to take you out for a drink. Because, if Zafón is correct about books being like mirrors and reflecting what's already inside you, I have a feeling we have more than just good taste in books in common.

In anticipation,

Ben

From: Scarlett O'
To: Benjamin Norwood
Subject: RE: I'm glad this book has an owner

Dear Ben,

Thank you so much for your email. So, much. I can't believe you found my book! And I can't believe how much you sound like a royal prince of England. Are you sure you aren't actually Prince Harry?

While you are obviously an incredibly smart, refined and wonderful gentleman of well-read proportions, unfortunately I cannot accept your generous offer to take me out. You see, when I put all those books out there on trains (there must be over a hundred out there by now!), I didn't realise that there was actually no point to any of it. Because I had already found the man of my dreams. I just couldn't see it because I was too much of a scared little book snob. Do you know what it's like to find the man of your dreams and then mess it all up?

I am just so scared that he'll never forgive me. I wake up in the middle of the night terrified that I'll never see him again and that he will always hate me. Always!

No, Frankie, NO! You can't think like that. You are meant to be with Sunny. (That's his name. Isn't it the sweetest name?)

He *will* find one of those damned Young Adult books and he *will* see how much you love him and he *will* forgive you! But then, I've put so many books out there, and still, nothing. That's why I'm drowning my sorrows in a bottle of red. I can't bear the thought of him never knowing how much I care about him.

But seriously, can you even believe he reads YA books? I mean, Jane Austen would be rolling over in her grave if she knew that *Twilight* is ranked number twelve in the top 100 best-selling books of all time. TWELVE! And the sequel is sixteen on the list! That's a whole forty-two (or is that forty-nine?) levels higher than *To Kill a Mockingbird*. I mean, *really* …

Anyway, I digress. All I really wanted to say was, thank you for your offer, but I am determined to win back my man if it's the last thing I do!

In anticipation (for Sunny to love me again),

Frankie

PS If you actually are Prince Harry, please ignore everything I just said. And yes, be a jolly good fellow and take me out on a date! Drinks and some nosh at Buckingham Palace will do just fine. Cheerio!

— 47 —

An Old Adult reading Young Adult

So, I have a confession to make.

I've been reading Young Adult books.

Lots of them.

I know, right? Who is this juvenile amateur and what have you done with Scarlett?

Well, as you might remember, I've been dropping Young Adult books all over Melbourne's trains, trams and buses in an effort to win back the love of my life, Edward Cullen. Now, usually I would never (and I mean *never*) be caught dead reading a YA book. Heck, I'd rather read a sport autobiography. And that's saying something. But desperate times call for desperate measures. I was recently stuck on a train with no choice but to either stare at a woman clipping her toenails (yep, people do this in public) or to hopelessly try to lose myself in the copy of *I'll Give You the Sun* that sat waiting in my backpack. I wasn't expecting much more than a few eye rolls and pretentious sniggers, but, from the first page, I was seriously hooked.

Since then, I've not only dropped tens of Young Adult books on public transport, I've also … read them. (Don't judge me, Cat!) Now, I wouldn't call myself a YA addict, but I've certainly come to appreciate the genre. I think what I love most about them is that they're about shaping who we become as adults, which I can relate to because I haven't quite figured that part out about myself yet (#almost30goingon13). Plus, I've realised that many of them are made into movies starring a Hemsworth – which scores serious points with me.

So, I guess what I'm trying to say is, I'm glad I can add a whole new genre to my 'To Be Read' pile. Because, as Christopher Paolini writes of the character Jeod in *Eragon*, books are his friends and companions, which help him find meaning. And I am in desperate need of some companions right now. One in particular, who refuses to acknowledge my existence due to the fact that I royally fucked everything up. As you all know, I've been dwelling over this fuck-up for quite some time, until I read *It's Kind of a Funny Story*, which showed me that it's only people who have failed who use regret as an excuse.

So now, instead of regretting what I've done, I'm just trying to make it better. To win Edward Cullen back once and for all. The problem is, my plan doesn't seem to be working. I haven't heard a single word from him. I'm trying to stop feeling so utterly heartbroken about the whole thing but, as John Green so aptly wrote in *The Fault in Our Stars*, 'That's the thing about pain. It demands to be felt.'

The funny thing is, I'm no longer afraid of fully committing myself to him. Of opening up to this one single human, and giving him my all. Not long ago this would have terrified me, but now my only true fear is that I've lost him for good. In fact, I just read *Divergent* (and am streaming the movie as we speak – hello there, Theo James) and in the book, this hunk of a man called Four (I know, ridiculous name, but hear me out) says it's not about being fearless, because that's impossible – what we have to do is find out how to manage our fear, and be free of it. What did I tell you? YA is on message. (And yes, I'm a teenager at heart.)

So, Edward Cullen, if you're reading this, I'm not giving up. I'm not losing you, and I'm not losing faith. Like Laini Taylor beautifully wrote about in *Daughter of Smoke and Bone*, hope is such a powerful thing – you can make things happen with it, like magic.

Here's to hoping I can make us happen again. In the words of Colleen Hoover, 'My heart made its choice, and it chose you.'

Until next time, my dears.

Scarlett O' xx

Leave a comment (2321)

Cat in the Hat > YA books? Tut-tut. I'm disowning you as my best friend.

Pawfully cute > I LOVE YA BOOKS! Happy to send you some recommendations.

Cat in the Hat > @Pawfullycute, sorry to say, but you have pawful taste in books.

Pawfully cute > @CatintheHat – FUCK YOU, BITCH!

Cat in the Hat > @Pawfullyycute, great comeback. I can tell you read high-quality literature.

Stephen Prince > @Nooffencebut ... No snarky comment this time?

No offence but ... > @StephenPrince ... I've been working. Miss me?

Stephen Prince > @Nooffencebut maybe just a little ... By
the way I have a creepy confession to make. I know what
you look like (Facebook stalked) and swear I saw you
working in my favourite cafe the other day.

No offence but ... > @StephenPrince YOU CREEP! But yep,
new job. Next time say hi ...

—48—

📱 DO NOT UNDER ANY CIRCUMSTANCE ANSWER
THIS NUMBER: Found your book. I'll be your Sunny.

—49—

Jane knows best

You know what?

SCREW THIS.

I take back everything I just said.

I just placed a copy of Marissa Meyer's *Cinder* on the train, in the hope of rekindling with Edward Cullen. I was all, 'This might be the book that reunites us and then we'll get married and have several children and buy a pizza store together. All because of this novel loosely based on the Cinderella fairytale.'

Anyway, as I was saying, I dropped the book on the train and as I was about to hop off an inspector pulled me back by the cashmere sleeve. He fined me for littering. Can you believe it? For littering! I tried to explain my quest for love, but he wasn't having a bar of it. He called me ridiculous.

That's when I started to wonder. *Am* I being ridiculous?

I'm spreading paperbacks all over the city like a disease, justifying myself with false hope and Young Adult quotes, in a vain attempt to make Edward Cullen fall in love with me all over again. But who's to say that he will? I'm sick of throwing myself at a man who doesn't even give me the time of day.

Obviously no longer able to trust my own judgement, I turned to my oldest and wisest best friend, Jane Austen, for guidance.

She said, and I quote, 'A lady's imagination is very rapid; it jumps from admiration to love, from love to matrimony in a moment.' And yes, that's me. Me in a nutshell. I'm putting all my books in one basket, so to speak, because I think Edward Cullen is my one true love. But who's to say there aren't other heartthrobs just around the corner, waiting for me to throw myself at them?

You know what else my bestie said? I believe it was in *Pride and Prejudice* that she wrote, 'Angry people are not always wise.' WISER WORDS HAVE NEVER BEEN SPOKEN, JANEY! I'm mad. Like, super mad. I'm mad at myself for letting my love go, and I'm mad at him for not taking me back. And as a result, my decisions of late have been, well, reckless, to say the least. It's time to cut the cord and start being smarter. For in the words of Jane, 'I may have lost my heart, but not my self-control.'

And you know what, Edward Cullen? If there's no room for Jane Austen in your heart, maybe there isn't any room for you in mine.

Until next time, my dears.

After all, tomorrow is another date.

Scarlett O' xx

Leave a comment (3567)

Cat in the Hat > I thought I was your best friend?

No offence but ... > You sound like you have split-personality disorder. By the way, I say give him one more chance.

Stephen Prince > @Nooffencebut ... Oh Stephanie. I love your unqualified diagnoses. PS May pop into your work soon ;)

No offence but ... > @StephenPrince, I'm far more qualified than you! See you soon, Mister ;)

—5o—

The Complete Poems of Winnie-the-Pooh by AA Milne

Frankston train line to Melbourne Central

'So, today's my last day.'

Frankie was carefully applying mascara while talking on the phone to Cat. She wore her favourite green silk shirt that made her eyes pop, paired with her 'I'm a published author' pom-pom coat, black skinny jeans and heeled boots. Everything had to be perfect for her meeting with Marie.

'Last day of what? Bad choices? Regret? Abstinence?' Cat joked.

'All of the above, my dear friend. All of the above.' Frankie carefully drew a black stroke ending with a dramatic flick along her lash line. Today called for a fierce winged eye. 'It's going to be my last day of dropping books. Of trying to win Sunny back. It's been weeks. I have to move on.'

'And you're okay with giving up?' Cat asked.

'I'm not giving up. I'm letting go.' Frankie tied her hair into a ponytail and stepped back to look at herself in the mirror. 'Sunny obviously doesn't want anything to do with me. And that's … well, it's okay. Look at *Gone with the Wind*, *Doctor Zhivago*, *The Sun Also Rises*. Everyone has that one person that got away. Now it's time for me to look for my new person. And you know what? I think I'm going to give Tom another shot.' Frankie puckered her lips, layering them with a thick, plum-coloured tint.

'Boring Tom?' Cat said through mouthfuls of what Frankie imagined to be sashimi, soft cheese, or most likely both.

'He's not boring. He's just not Sunny. And that's probably a good thing. He's kind, smart and sensitive, not to mention well read.'

'Well, he sounds perfect.'

'Exactly. Plus, today's all about new beginnings. Cat, I have an okay feeling about life again. Is that weird?'

'Well, this all sounds fabulous, Frankie. You know I'm all for it. But it also slightly sounds like you're having a mental breakdown.' Cat panted now, as if she were running.

'I'm not.'

'Are you sure?'

'Yes.'

'Positive?'

'No.'

'So, you could be having a mental breakdown?'

'Yes.'

'Okay, well, I'm glad we have that sorted then,' Cat said.

'Cat? What was that?'

'What was what?' she said evasively.

'Was that a boarding call in the background? Are you at an *airport*?' Frankie asked.

'Ah, sorry Frank, I have to run! Love you. Good luck with the emotional meltdown!' Cat hung up. Frankie tried to call her back, but it went straight to voicemail. She would have to deal with Cat and her escapades later. Right now, she had to focus on the meeting with her publisher, which was in exactly one hour. She spritzed her wrists with her 'special occasion' perfume, grabbed her polka-dot handbag and let herself out of her apartment and into the big wide world.

It was another excessively cold Melbourne day, and as soon as Frankie left the warm embrace of her apartment, the harsh air gnawed at her skin even as she wrapped her coat tightly around her body. She checked her handbag again to make sure she had her train ticket, and then took out her phone, refreshing her emails. Out of the corner of her eye, she spotted somebody lurking in front of her.

'Dad?'

Rudolph smiled sheepishly at her. He was dressed in nothing but shorts and a T-shirt, even though it couldn't have been more than 8 degrees outside. *Typical.*

'What are you doing here? I can't be long. I have a really important meeting to get to,' Frankie said, a little too tersely.

Rudolph handed her a small parcel wrapped in brown butcher's paper, with a plain blue card stuck haphazardly to the front.

'For me?' Frankie asked, taking it from her father's rough hands. Rudolph nodded. She carefully removed the card and read it out loud.

Dear Frankie,
I know that Mum and I sometimes drive you nuts. All right, all the time. But know that we love you more than anything and are so proud of you and all that you have achieved. Here's a little something we found when we were moving house. It reminded us of how many of your dreams you've already made come true.
Love always,
Mum and Dad

'Oh, Dad.' Frankie wiped a runaway tear from her eye. 'This is so unexpected.'

Rudolph nodded his head towards the present in Frankie's hand. She pulled at the twine holding the parcel together, and the brown paper unfolded gracefully as if it were a magic trick, revealing a piece of thick blue cardboard. On the cardboard, stuck messily to the right-hand corner, was a photo of Rudolph, Putu and Frankie, who looked about six years old. Scribbled next to the photo, in her own childlike scrawl, it read:

> *My dream in life is …*
> *To be a writer and a good human like my mum and dad. They are the best humans in the world. Also to own a chocolate farm and eat chocolate every day for the rest of my life. Also I love hamsters.*

Frankie looked closely at the photo. Her eyes were closed, mid laugh. Her head was resting on her father's shoulder, and Putu was looking at her with that same look she had seen so many times before. A look she had naively come to believe was filled with judgement. But now she knew it wasn't that at all. It was adoration.

'Oh, Dad. This is too much. Thank you for this. You'll tell mum how much I loved it?' Frankie smiled. Rudolph kissed her cheek before bringing her into his arms for a full embrace.

After a few long moments she reluctantly pulled away with a smile. She carefully deposited the gift in her bag, gave her dad a final warm kiss on the cheek and raced down the street, as Rudolph soulfully waved goodbye.

Frankie halfheartedly dropped a copy of *To All The Boys I've Loved Before* on the station bench beside her. A woman wearing a beautifully embroidered dress and heels sat next to her, reading a clothbound copy of *Pride and Prejudice*. Frankie analysed her face, trying to imagine which part of the book she was up to. From the slight frown and the white of her knuckles, she guessed it was Chapter Eighteen – Oh, how Frankie loved that chapter! – the Netherfield Ball, when Elizabeth finally wins the chance to exact revenge on Darcy. She wondered if this was the first or, like her, the eleventh time she had read the book.

She looked away and up at the information board: the next train would arrive in two minutes. That should give her plenty of time to make it to the Simon & Schuster office. She cracked her knuckles and tapped her feet; the nerves were settling in, rendering her unable to read. If this meeting was a success, it could herald her next big break, her foot back in the door of the exhilarating world of published writing. Her heart twisted at the thought of her dad's gift. Ever since she was young, she had wanted to be a writer. She had made it happen twice, and now she was (fingers crossed) about to make it happen again.

As the train arrived, the woman placed her copy of *Pride and Prejudice* in her bag and stood up abruptly. Frankie followed, scurrying towards the train. Frankie sat down, placing her handbag next to her, and silently recited the lines she had prepared for the meeting. *I believe my time off from writing has enabled me to experience more of the world, and thus become a more skilled and sensitive author. It is important to me that this book reflects my experiences both as a writer and as an ordinary twenty-something woman struggling through love and life. Please, please, please, sign me. Okay, maybe not that last one.*

Frankie continued to run through her lines when something caught her eye. A stray book sat on the seat in front of her. She stood up to get a closer look, and saw that the same book was scattered on even more seats throughout the carriage. She took a deep breath. *Is someone copycatting me? And if so, are they beating me at my own game? There must be at least fifteen books on this carriage alone!*

She crept up to one of the books and looked to either side of her. A man had fallen asleep with his headphones on, and a woman was bent over, looking intently at her mobile phone. Frankie swiftly picked up the book – and gasped. In her hands, she held AA Milne's *The Complete Poems of Winnie-the-Pooh*. She slowly opened to the first page, her hands suddenly trembling. And gulped as she saw handwriting that had become as familiar as her own:

In the spirit of AA Milne, I care too much – I think it's love. Meet me at Sunbury station at eleven this morning. – Sunny

'Oh my God,' Frankie exhaled, to no-one in particular. She pressed the book to her chest, butterflies pounding within her. She took the book in her right hand and picked up another, which sat idly on a seat nearby. She opened the book to the first page. The same note. She ran to the next book, sitting on the seat in front, and then to the next. The same note was written in every single one of them. She opened the door at the end of the carriage and passed through, rushing down the aisle, picking up book after book. A copy of *The Complete Poems of Winnie-the-Pooh* had been strategically placed on every single aisle seat of the train. *He must have left hundreds.* Frankie edged to the train door, ready to hop off at the next stop and head full throttle to Sunbury station – but then she remembered her appointment with Marie.

She took out her phone and dialled the number she had promised herself she would never call again.

'Hi, you've called Sunny. Leave a message.' *Shit.* 'Sunny, it's me. I'm just on the train. I found your books. I can't believe it. Talk about a romantic gesture! But I only found them now, and it's already ten-thirty. You probably thought I'd find them on my way to work, but I didn't go to work this morning because I have a really big meeting with my publisher at eleven,' she rambled. 'It's sort of make-or-break. I'm not sure I'm going to make it to Sunbury on time. It's over forty minutes away and—' The voicemail cut out. *Shit. Shit. Shit.*

Frankie peered out the window, watching the buildings glide past as she cradled five copies of *The Complete Poems of Winnie-the-Pooh* in her arms.

> 💬 Frankie: Sunny, I'm not sure I'll make it to Sunbury
> station on time. I'm coming up to Flinders Street for
> an important meeting with my publisher. Please
> call me.

She paced the carriage, weighing her options as the train pulled up at Flinders Street station: she could jump off now and try to make it to Sunbury, or she could stay on board and get off at Melbourne Central, and make it in time for her meeting. The train came to a halt. Commuters pushed past her haphazardly, grunting at her to move. A little girl dressed in a floral puffy jacket clutched a copy of *The Complete Poems of Winnie-the-Pooh* in one hand, while her other was wrapped firmly around her dad's leg. But Frankie was frozen. She stared at the open doors of the train, her heart racing.

'Please mind the gap, this train is ready to depart.' The announcement echoed throughout the station, ringing in Frankie's ears.

Fuck it! She jumped out of the closing doors and onto the platform.

—51—

'Fifty minutes?' Frankie looked at the neon timetable that hung above her head. 'The train to Sunbury takes *fifty minutes?*' *Why did he have to pick a station so far away?* She groaned in exasperation and tried calling Sunny again. She was expecting to get the voicemail she had heard the twenty other times she had called, and she was right. She left a quick message, saying she was running late, and not to leave. *Sunny, please wait for me.*

What was she thinking when she told Cat she was ready to let Sunny go? Her heart hadn't stopped racing since she found the books. Now, the chance to see him was so close, she could almost touch it. Images of his big blue eyes, his tall, shielding body, flooded her mind. But remembering him made her feel skittish, so she forced herself to stop. She picked up her phone, but this time dialled a different number.

'Frankie! So good to hear from you. We'll be seeing you in about ten minutes or so, right?' Marie chirped into the phone.

Frankie bit down on her lip, hard. 'I'm so sorry. I'm not going to be able to make it. An emergency has, uh, come up. Can we please reschedule?'

'An emergency? Frankie, I've called the entire publishing team to this meeting. And it's in ten minutes,' Marie snapped, her tone changing instantly.

'I know, I'm so sorry. You know I wouldn't miss this if it wasn't super important.'

'Is there any way you can attend to this *emergency* at a later date?' Marie asked. Frankie could almost hear her eyes roll through the phone.

'No, I'm sorry. I can't. I'll call you later today. Sorry again!' Frankie hung up quickly to avoid Marie's wrath, and in case Sunny was trying to get through. *Why can't we just meet in the city? Why all the way out in Sunbury?*

Finally, the train sluggishly pulled up to the station, making loud, ostentatious noises. Frankie hopped over the gap and swiftly into the train, ready to depart. She stood in the centre of the carriage, even though there were plenty of seats free on this 11am Monday express to Sunbury. As the train took off and the subtle movements of the carriage rocked her into tranquility, Frankie closed her eyes. It had been approximately twenty days and seven hours since she had last seen him, and in that time, she had experienced a rollercoaster of emotions: mostly gut-wrenching, horrifying heartbreak. She inhaled, remembering his musky, masculine scent. She recalled the way he would gently tuck her hair behind her ear when it drifted into her eyes; the back of her ear tingled at the thought. She reminisced about the way his eyes lit up when he was reading a Young Adult book or talking about his family holidays to rural Victoria. She remembered the last time she saw him: that gutted, inconsolable look splashed all over his usually carefree face. That look, she hoped never to see it again. She tried to count the reasons she loved him. *One: his stupid fear of bananas. Two: how, because of him, my kitchen will always be stocked with at least enough ingredients to make French toast. Three: the way he makes me feel safe. Four: everything about him.* Frankie rolled her eyes at her own cliché. One of AA Milne's best pieces of writing floated to mind: Piglet asks how to spell love – and Pooh says it's a feeling, not a word. That was how she felt about Sunny.

Frankie looked at her phone, ignoring the seven missed calls from Marie. She felt sick to her stomach. *Am I missing my one chance at a new book deal for a guy?* But then she thought, *Not for a guy. For Sunny.* She dialled Cat's number but it too went straight to voicemail. *Why is nobody answering their phone?* She rolled her head in a full circle, stretching her shoulders. She tapped her knees, stomped her feet. *Only forty-five minutes to go.* She stared at the people around her, trying to distract herself by guessing which book they might be reading if their heads weren't buried in their phones. *The blonde girl with the lip ring and cool earrings?* Walk of Fame *by Sharon Krum. The old man with the iPad?* When Breath Becomes Air *by Paul Kalanithi.* She groaned. Her mind still swam with thoughts of Sunny. So, she did the only thing she knew would always take her somewhere else entirely. She picked up her copy of *The Complete Poems of Winnie-the-Pooh*, opened to the first page, and read.

🐢

As the train slowly approached Sunbury station, Frankie jolted to attention. She was so consumed by the words on the page, she had momentarily forgotten where she was. She looked up at the remaining people on board. The lip-ring girl was still there, absently twirling a piece of blonde hair around her finger. A tall woman wearing a skin-tight sparkly dress and high heels swayed in the corner. The man with the iPad was now asleep. As the train came to a halt and the doors opened with a leisurely hiss, the passengers piled out. But Frankie remained standing, suddenly afraid of what awaited her at the station.

After everyone had evacuated the train, Frankie crept out like a hermit crab seeing sunlight for the first time. She took a deep breath. A good forty kilometres out of Melbourne, the air was crisper and fresher. She looked to her left and then to her right. And there, she saw him, sitting on a train bench, wearing a dark green coat. His legs were crossed and he was casually reading *Eleanor & Park*. Her copy of *Eleanor & Park* with the torn cover. As soon as she saw him, she forgot about Marie, about Cat, about all the dates and all the heartbreak. Her whole body yearned for Sunny, and she ran towards him, stopping right in front of him so that her knees were almost grazing his.

'Hey,' she managed to say.

Sunny glanced up from his book. 'Hey.' He looked her square in the eye. 'Thanks for the book.'

'My pleasure.' Frankie fidgeted. 'How are you?' *Is that the best you can do?*

'Good. You?' Sunny replied. He looked nervous as he ran his fingers through his perfect hair. *What I would do to touch that hair.*

'Good.' Frankie gazed at him and he stared back, his bright blue eyes burning holes right through her.

'So …' Frankie said when she couldn't take it anymore. She cautiously sat down next to him. 'Why am I here?'

Sunny half-smiled and went back to reading his book, as if he were casually waiting for a train and not sitting next to his ex-girlfriend. The ex-girlfriend he had just lured here using a cherished childhood story. Frankie watched him as he slowly turned a page, grinning to himself.

'Sunny,' she said, more firmly this time.

'Mmm?' He didn't look up.

'Sunny, you can't just tell me to meet you at Sunbury station with this huge, elaborate, romantic gesture, with our favourite book for God's sake, and then not even speak to me. I'm sorry, okay? I'm sorry about the dates, about the blog, about the lies. It was cruel and thoughtless. I'm sorry I resisted you and pushed you away. You were right. You were right about everything.

I used the other dates as a crutch, as a way of keeping myself at a safe distance from truly feeling. I was trying to protect myself, but I was selfish. So very selfish. No matter how hard I tried and how much I doubted, I couldn't help but fall for you, Sunny. And oh, how I've fallen. You're all I think about. You're all I want. Now I finally know what Jane Austen was talking about when she wrote, "When I fall in love, it will be forever". I love you, Sunny. My heart, my body, my soul, it's all fallen, head over heels, in love with you.' Frankie breathed for the first time since she started speaking, bracing herself for his response.

'I forgive you.'

'And another thing, you just, you make me—' Frankie paused. 'What did you say?'

'I forgive you.'

Frankie couldn't believe what she was hearing. *He forgives me? Just like that?* After weeks of unreturned phone calls and after the anger and resentment that she knew had brewed deep within him, he forgave her? Frankie's whole body relaxed, the tension of her grief suddenly melting away.

'You forgive me? What changed?' She didn't know if she was pushing her luck, she was suddenly terrified he would change his mind, that this was some twisted joke of revenge.

Sunny gazed down at the floor. 'When I found the first book you put out for me I was just so mad. I thought, how could you think that the same thing that tore us apart could bring us back together? I needed you to be out of my life. But then when I found the second book, and the third …' He looked up, his eyes beginning to crinkle. How Frankie had missed seeing his face slowly erupt into a smile. 'I couldn't keep ignoring you. Ignoring how I feel about you and all the good that you brought into my life. Finding each book was like this strange cathartic release of all the pent-up rage consuming me. But still,

I couldn't let go. Let go of what you did.' He looked at Frankie with such intensity, it made her flinch. 'Then, when Cat turned up at my door ...'

'Cat turned up at your door?' Frankie asked, shocked.

'She didn't tell you? YA book in one hand and baby in the other, she got on her hands and knees and begged me to take you back. She said she's never seen you so heartbroken before. That you were like a shell of a person without me. And well, I guess I was also a shell of a person without you.'

She couldn't help but smile then, and he smiled more broadly too as he continued. 'Something clicked. I wondered why we were both walking around so hopeless and heart-broken, when we could do something about it.' Sunny brushed his fingertips lightly over Frankie's hand, and she inhaled. 'So, I had to find a way to forgive you, Frankie. And I hope you'll forgive me too, for not always being open and for walking away and for not trying to understand you better.' He put his arms around her waist, pulling her just an inch closer. 'And Frankie, I can't deny my feelings any longer. I love you. "Most ardently."' Austen's words rolled off his tongue like they were chocolate.

'Oh,' Frankie gasped, suddenly lost for words.

'Can I kiss you now?'

'Yes.'

At this, Sunny grabbed her face hungrily and brought it towards his. He gently pushed her hair behind her ears and, before she had time to think, he kissed her, tenderly at first, and then with a rapid passion that made her hang on to him as if he were the only concrete thing in this unsteady, dizzy world. And finally she knew what Margaret Mitchell meant when she wrote, 'before a swimming giddiness spun her round and round, she knew that she was kissing him back'.

Sunny pulled back, a cheeky grin plastered on his face. 'I've wanted to do that for a while,' he confessed.

'So, why didn't you?' Frankie replied huskily.

Sunny pressed his thumb to her lower lip, his eyes fixed on her. 'I had to forgive you first, and I didn't know whether I could. Frank, I was so scared of getting hurt again. Of losing someone I loved. So, when what happened, happened, I shut down.' Sunny didn't take his eyes off Frankie, and she was terrified to look away. 'But then I lost you anyway. And then I lost myself.' He sighed. 'And that was just stupid. Even more ridiculous than buying someone a pet turtle on the second date.'

Frankie laughed, tears pooling in her eyes. 'Winnie was the second-best thing to ever happen to me these last few months,' she said.

'What was the first thing?' he asked with a glint in his eye.

'This incredible chocolate croissant I had this morning.'

He laughed softly. 'I love you, Frankston Line Rose. More than pizza.'

'Whoa. I never said I loved you more than *pizza*.'

'You did so. In your Facebook message.'

'You read my messages?'

'Yep. All hundred-and-twenty-three of them.' He grinned.

'Oh, God.' Frankie put her head in her hands. Sunny chuckled and slowly pulled her hands away. He held them in his own and kissed her once more.

'Sunny Day?' she said when she finally pulled back.

'Yes, Frankston Rose?'

Frankie looked around, taking in her surroundings. She sat on a bench at a train station in the middle of nowhere. There was not another person in sight. Lush green hills hovered in the distance and a fine air of chilly mist escaped their mouths when they spoke.

'Why on earth are we at Sunbury station?'

Sunny laughed. A big hearty laugh, like this was the funniest thing he had ever been asked. Then he leaned in close to her, as if he were letting her in on a secret. 'Sunny – it's short for Sunbury Station.'

Frankston Rose
8/12 Bell Street
Richmond
Victoria, Australia 3121

Dear Franks,
Hope you like the postcard. I have three things to tell you.

1) I intervened with Sunny. I know, I know. You've told me a million times not to butt into your love life, but I couldn't help myself. I hated seeing you so sad and heartbroken, day after day – and, well, no-one does that to my girl! So, I had a little word with my good friend Sunny Day, and it sounds like everything's worked itself out perfectly. YOU'RE WELCOME!

2) As you can see from the idyllic postcard snap, I'm in Sweden. With Claud. And Jin Soo (the baby, not the man). After talking to Sunny, seeing the love in his eyes, I realised that Claud has that love for me, Franks. And I have that love for him. I think I was looking for something exciting, something home-wrecking (Heck, I must get it from my mum), but Claud, he's the love of my life. Always has been, always will be. I came clean about the affair, and he's pretty upset. Well, very upset. But we're working on it. So, we've shut down the bookstore for a few weeks (Your paychecks will keep coming – don't worry!) and fled to Sweden. We're spending the next

few weeks at a knitting retreat. (I know. But it was the only way he would agree to go anywhere with me.) We're trying to reconnect, and Frank, I really feel like I'm falling back in love with him.

3) I love you so much.

I hope everything is going well with Sunny and the book.

Cat xo

—53—

How to fall in love

Emma and Mr Knightley.
Claire and Jamie.
Westley and Buttercup.
Ennis and Jack.
Fermina and Florentino.
Frankie and Sunny.

Yes, I did it. I, Scarlett O' – or as I am more commonly known, Frankie – and Edward Cullen – ahem, Sunny – can officially go down in history as one of the greatest love stories ever told. Who would've thought?

My advice for falling head-over-heels, completely and romantically in love? Well, it's fairly simple. No book drops, folk-dancing classes, grand romantic gestures or anxious analysis of every single glance, sentence, text message or Instagram post.

In fact, I'll save you the trouble. Here's all you need to know about falling in love with the love of your life. Are you ready? Four simple words:

JUST FALL IN LOVE.

Peace out,

Frankie xx

PS Liked my blog? Look out for my book *The Book Ninja* (published by Simon & Schuster) coming out on June 1st.

Leave a comment (562)

Sunny All Day Long > What about Hermione and Ron? Come on! P.s. I'm so proud of you, babe.

Cat in the Hat > YES! You two are my favourite love story of all. Well, besides Elizabeth and Mr Darcy; no-one can beat those two. Can't wait for your book, my darling author!

Stephen Prince > @Nooffencebut ... No comment again? You're off your A-game, Stephanie. PS Nice finally meeting you yesterday. You're a great kisser ;)

> **No offence but ...** > @StephenPrince ... Can you not publicise my kissing habits online for all the world to see? PS You're not too bad yourself.

The Book Ninja
book list

Northanger Abbey, Jane Austen

Emma, Jane Austen

Jasper Jones, Craig Silvey

The Crossroad, Mark Donaldson

Twilight, Stephanie Meyer

The State of Affairs, Esther Perel

High Fidelity, Nick Hornby

Wuthering Heights, Emily Brontë

Rosemary's Baby, Ira Levin

Fifty Shades of Grey, E. L. James

Fifty Shades Darker, E. L. James

New Moon, Stephenie Meyer

Persuasion, Jane Austen

The Goldfinch, Donna Tartt

Catch-22, Joseph Heller

Gone with the Wind,
    Margaret Mitchell

Lost and Found, Brooke Davis

Othello, William Shakespeare

The Hunger Games,
    Suzanne Collins

Mansfield Park, Jane Austen

Pygmalion, George Bernard Shaw

War and Peace, Leo Tolstoy

Vinegar Girl, Ann Tyler

Mila 18, Leon Uris

Lily and the Octopus, Steven
    Rowley

The Scarlet Letter,
    Nathaniel Hawthorne

Eat, Pray, Love, Elizabeth Gilbert

City of Bones, Cassandra Clare

Divergent, Veronica Roth

Northanger Abbey, Jane Austen

Sense and Sensibility, Jane Austen

Moby Dick, Herman Melville

The Rosie Project, Graeme Simsion

Animal Farm, George Orwell

The Thing about Jane Spring,
    Sharon Krum

And the Mountains Echoed,
    Khaled Hosseini

*The Complete Poems of Winnie-the-
    Pooh*, AA Milne

Chocolat, Joanne Harris

Ulysses, James Joyce

The Princess Bride,
    William Goldman

A Tale of Two Cities,
    Charles Dickens

*We are All Completely Beside
    Ourselves*, Karen Joy Fowler

The Jane Austen Book Club,
    Karen Joy Fowler

Sarah Canary, Karen Joy Fowler

Sister Noon, Karen Joy Fowler

1984, George Orwell

A Little Life, Hanya Yanagihara

Big Little Lies, Liane Moriarty

Never Let Me Go, Kazuo Ishiguro

The Great Gatsby,
 F. Scott Fitzgerald

The Art of Racing in the Rain,
 Garth Stein

A Series of Unfortunate Events,
 Lemony Snicket

To Kill a Mockingbird,
 Harper Lee

Go Set a Watchman, Harper Lee

Gone Girl, Gillian Flynn

The Girl on the Train,
 Paula Hawkins

My Brilliant Friend, Elena
 Ferrante

Something Borrowed, Emily Giffin

Wuthering Heights, Emily Brontë

The Secret Seven, Enid Blyton

The Secret History, Donna Tartt

The Time Traveller's Wife,
 Audrey Niffenegger

One Day, David Nicholls

My Sister's Keeper, Jodi Picoult

Middlesex, Jeffrey Eugenides

Lady Susan, Jane Austen

Death in the Afternoon,
 Ernest Hemingway

The Wind-Up Bird Chronicle,
 Haruki Murakami

The Hate U Give, Angie Thomas

The Giver, Lois Lowry

Finding Nevo, Nevo Zisin

Dear Martin, Nic Stone

Man's Search for Meaning,
 Viktor Frankl

Birdsong, Sebastian Faulks

The Course of Love,
 Alain de Botton

Station Eleven,
 Emily St John Mandel

Little Fires Everywhere, Celeste Ng

Alice in Wonderland, Lewis Carroll

Five Go Gluten-Free,
 Bruno Vincent

Eleanor Oliphant is Completely Fine,
 Gail Honeyman

Pride and Prejudice, Jane Austen

Little Women, Louisa May Alcott

The Alchemist, Paul Coelho

The Bronze Horseman,
 Paullina Simons

Belly Laughs, Jenny McCarthy

Catcher in the Rye, JD Salinger

I Feel Bad About my Neck,
 Nora Ephron

Indignation, Philip Roth

*What to Expect When You're
 Expecting*, Heidi Murkoff &
 Sharon Mazel

The Exorcist, William Peter Blatty

The Anatomy of Melancholy,
 Robert Burton

*The Unlikely Pilgrimage of Harold
 Fry*, Rachel Joyce

Dead Famous, Ben Elton

Brida, Paulo Coelho

Eleven Minutes, Paulo Coelho

Aleph, Paulo Coelho

The Pilgrimage, Paulo Coelho

Marley and Me, John Grogan

Koala Lou, Mem Fox

Loni and the Moon, Esther Takac

Under the Love Umbrella,
　Davina Bell

No One Likes a Fart,
　Zoë Foster Blake

Snow White, Grimm Brothers

The Kite Runner, Khaled Hosseini

Love and Friendship, Jane Austen

The Handmaid's Tale,
　Margaret Atwood

On Death and Dying,
　Elisabeth Kübler-Ross

Enduring Love, Ian McEwan

Still Alice, Lisa Genova

The Gulf, Anna Spargo Ryan

The Dry, Jane Harper

The Perks of Being Wallflower,
　Stephen Chbosky

The Knife of Never Letting Go,
　Patrick Ness

The Book Thief, Markus Zusak

An Abundance of Katherines,
　John Green

Stargirl, Jerry Spinelli

Wonder, RJ Palacio

A Monster Calls, Patrick Ness

Looking for Alaska, John Green

Eleanor & Park, Rainbow Rowell

The Maze Runner, James Dashner

We Were Liars, Emily Jenkins

*Are You There God? It's Me
　Margaret*, Judy Blume

Red Queen, Victoria Aveyard

If I Stay, Gayle Forman

*Percy Jackson and the Lightning
　Thief*, Rick Riordan

Holes, Louis Sachar

Romeo and Juliet,
　William Shakespeare

I'll Give You the Sun, Jandy Nelson

Tin Man, Sarah Winman

My Dear Cassandra, Jane Austen

The Shadow of the Wind,
　Carlos Ruiz Zafón

Eragon, Christopher Paolini

It's Kind of a Funny Story,
　Ned Vizzini

The Fault in our Stars, John Green

Daughter of Smoke and Bone,
　Laini Taylor

Cinder, Marissa Meyer

Doctor Zhivago, Boris Pasternak

The Sun Also Rises,
　Ernest Hemingway

To All the Boys I've Loved Before,
　Jenny Han

Walk of Fame, Sharon Krum

When Breath Becomes Air,
　Paul Kalanithi

Book club questions

1. The authors, Ali Berg and Michelle Kalus, use myriad social media communication devices to tell the story – text messaging, Instagram, Facebook, memes, online blogs. How does the use of social media enrich the story?

2. Frankie is scared to commit to anything important for fear of failure. What changes Frankie's mind to take real risks and go after what she wants?

3. Who is the stronger character – Frankie or Cat? Is there one character who dominates the friendship?

4. Sunny suffered a terrible loss as a young adult and carries heavy guilt because of it. How does Sunny try to overcome this, and is he successful in his attempts?

5. Berg and Kalus have brought to life not only the main characters of the story but also a variety of delightful supporting players – Seb, Claud, Jin Soo, Putu, Rudy, Winnie, and Ads. What roles do these characters play in *The Book Ninja*?

6. The authors' love of books is present from the first sentence of *The Book Ninja* – they weave the joy of reading throughout the story. How do the authors use books to reflect parallel ideas in their characters' lives?

7. 'Frankie has never judged a book by its title. Nor by its cover.' However, she does unashamedly judge others by their book choices. What does Frankie finally discover about the rules of judgement?

8. Frankie is torn between conflicting feelings – her brain says 'No' to YA readers and her heart says 'Yes' to spontaneity and passion. To make matters worse, she is presented with the reversed dichotomy in Tom – he's a sophisticated reader but he sparks no passion. What wins in the end – the brain or the heart? Or is it a matter of not winning, but rather the heart changing the brain's perception?

9. Will contemporary Young Adult literature provide as enduring a social commentary as the 'classics' of the eighteenth and nineteenth century?

10. Do you think social media, with its constant information sharing, is counter romantic?

Acknowledgements

A little over a year ago, Ali had a coffee with the incredibly vivacious and driven Anna O'Grady, Marketing Director at Simon & Schuster Australia, who dared to believe in two rogue Book Ninjas. From this chance encounter, we began dreaming about how to take the romance of Books on the Rail and turn it into a quirky love letter to literature, friendship and soul mates. Thank you, Anna, for planting this seed and for your subsequent support and passion for our story.

Our gratitude also goes out to the rest of the team at Simon & Schuster Australia. We will never forget the day we arrived at your office in Sydney, bleary-eyed from an early morning flight (and twelve months of manuscript writing). Having almost forgotten that anyone had actually read our little novel, we were so touched by your generous hospitality, hard work and the kind words you had to share about Frankie and Sunny's story.

A particularly special thanks to Bert Ivers, Managing Editor, Fiona Henderson, Publishing Director, and Dan Ruffino, Managing Director. Bert, thank you for your care and eternal love for *The Book Ninja*. Without your meticulous guidance, our book would not be what it is today. Fiona, thank you for all the excited calls and emails bearing news of each new country that you helped to fall in love with our book. We are overwhelmingly grateful for your championing.

A huge thank you to Hollie Fraser, for introducing Ali to Books on the Underground and inspiring her to start Books on the Rail in Australia with Michelle. And thank you to our Book Ninjas – without your passion and dedication, none of this would have been possible!

Thank you to all the people who helped get *The Book Ninja* off the rails and onto paper. A very special shout out to Henry Kalus, Doris Brett and the Australian Society of Authors, in particular Olivia Lanchester. Our deepest gratitude to our first readers and author role-models, the incredible Sharon Krum and Davina Bell – your generous counsel, wise insights and encouragement kept us writing. And of course, we would be lost without the support and good humour of our very dear Super Best Friends; you really are the super best.

Even though, after a year of co-authoring, we have slowly morphed into one person, you might be surprised to discover that we still have our own families for whom we care very much. So here are a few of our own, personal thank-yous.

Ali's acknowledgements

Ever since I could hold a pen, I declared to everyone I knew that I wanted to be an author. This has been met with a deluge of support and encouragement from those closest to me – and without your belief in me there is no way this dream book could have existed.

To my mum Cindy, you are my editor, my psychologist (when deadlines were looming at the same time as my wedding and my business starting up), and my cheerleader. I loved every minute of this journey with you – thank you for inspiring me since day one.

To my dad John, growing up in a house filled with your books of every genre, by authors from all around the world, taught me from a young age that a life without books is a life not worth living. Thank you for turning me into the bookworm I am today.

To my brother Josh, for not only being the most encouraging sibling, but the most understanding business partner, and for wholeheartedly supporting my days off for last minute deadlines and trips to Sydney.

To my beautiful sister Emma for your perpetual support and brilliance – your encouraging words and down-to-earth attitude kept me grounded throughout all the craziness – and I love you ever so much.

To my Lulu for all the licks and cuddles.

To my wonderful husband Alex, my rock. Thank you for planning our wedding while I was elbow-deep in edits, for sleeping next to me without complaint while I typed loudly into the wee hours of the morning, and for being so proud of me. As soon as I signed my contract you told everyone we met that 'my fiancée's a published author', even though I was very much still in the midst of manuscript Round One. I love you more than Frankie loves Sunny.

To my Nana Jacqueline, Zaida Harry, Oma Cilla and Opa Paul, thank you for being such proud and supportive grandparents – I am so lucky to have you all.

To my Hedgehog family, for all the Facebook posts, chocolatey support and name inspiration.

And finally, to my co-author, business partner, soul sister and best friend, Michelle. What a wild journey we have been on together. Thank you for offering up your copy of *The Bronze Horseman* to place on a train, which would become the first Books on the Rail book of thousands. Thank you for agreeing so enthusiastically to my insane suggestions like 'I think we should write a book together', and thank you for being you – because if you were anyone else this wouldn't have been possible!

Michelle's acknowledgements

To my family, my Kali clan, my source of joy, support, love and unlimited supply of fresh produce:

Mum and Dad, Susie and Allan, my loudest and proudest fans! Thank you for instilling in us a true love of learning, of giving, of striving for goodness and of appreciating the written word. You created a home which was warm and full of life (and animals! Shout out to Ruby!) and an environment in which we all felt safe to take risks. You have provided us with every opportunity to thrive, and for this, I will always be eternally grateful.

My little Lici Lou, my friend, roommate and sister-extraordinaire, how indebted I am to you. Thank you for making me laugh, making me lunch and making me feel whole with your contagious sparkle. I adore sharing my life with you.

Sarah and Iwan, for showing me what a happy ending truly looks like! Even while oceans divide us, you still manage to provide a steady stream of strength, encouragement and joy (not to mention, European envy). P.S. please move back to Melbourne already.

Dave, thank you for your endless cheerleading, charm and for providing plenty of inspiration for the romantic bits. How glad I am to get to love you.

And, of course, there's my Ormiston family! To the staff, for your friendship, cheer and baked goods. To the students, for your curiosity and for making me feel like a celebrity during each and every yard duty.

Last, but certainly not least, to Ali, my oldest, dearest friend and mighty muse. Thank you for being such a motivated, innovative, kooky and creative spirit who has sprinkled our book (and my life) with such magic. To spend time with you is to forget the world (but not our deadlines!) and laugh wholeheartedly. I am so beyond lucky to be able to share this crazy, literary ride with you!

About the authors

Ali Berg and Michelle Kalus have been best friends for life and share a burning passion for books and writing. Together they began Books on the Rail in Melbourne and their network is now Australia-wide. Ali is Creative Director and Co-founder of Hedgehog Agency, Melbourne, and Michelle is a primary school teacher.

See www.aliandmichelle.com and
www.booksontherail.com

booksandthecity.co.uk
the home of female fiction

BOOKS | NEWS & EVENTS | FEATURES | AUTHOR PODCASTS | COMPETITIONS

Follow us online to be the first to hear from
your favourite authors

bc

booksandthecity.co.uk   books and the city   @TeamBATC

Join our mailing list for the latest news, events and
exclusive competitions

Sign up at
booksandthecity.co.uk